Booktalk! 5

More Selections from *The Booktalker*
for All Ages and Audiences

Edited by Joni Richards Bodart

P9-CRJ-188

THE H. W. WILSON COMPANY
NEW YORK
1993

Front Cover: Students in Mr. J.B. Doze's Advanced Placement Sophomore English class, International Baccalaureate Program, Smoky Hill High School, Cherry Creek School District, Aurora, CO, May 1992. Cover photos © 1993 by Jerry Walters of Monty Nuss Photography, Littleton, CO. Cover design by Ron Schick, New York

Library of Congress Cataloging-in-Publication Data

Bodart, Joni Richards
    Booktalk! 5: more selections from The Booktalker for all ages and audiences / edited by Joni Richards Bodart.
       p.   cm.

Includes bibliographical references and index.
    ISBN 0-8242-0836-6
    1. Book talks.   2. Public relations—Libraries.
3. Libraries and readers.   4. Books and reading.
I. Booktalker. II. Title.
III. Title: Booktalk! five.
Z716.3.B638   1993
    021.7—dc28

                                 92-14017
                                     CIP

Printed in the United States of America

CONTENTS

DEDICATION

To all the booktalkers
who go out of their way
to infect as many people as possible
with the incurable addiction
called reading—

Without you, lives and imaginations
would be much less rich and full.

And to every student who has come up
after a booktalking program to say
"Thanks!" or "Cool!"
or "I'm gonna read . . . "
or "When are you coming back?"

Thank you.

I hope the answer will always be "Soon!"

ACKNOWLEDGMENTS

This book was not written in a vacuum—no book ever is. But since I had such an extensive list of people to thank in *Booktalk! 4*, and since that book and this are meant to be used together, I will merely list here the names of those people without whom neither of these volumes would have seen the light of day, and refer you to *Booktalk! 4* for more details.

Many, many thanks to: all the contributors to *The Booktalker*; all the fans of *The Booktalker*, who encouraged me with letters, calls, and personal conversations; to Patty Campbell, Cathi MacRae, Robin Dunn, Martha Franklin, Mary Jo Godwin, Norris Smith, Bruce Carrick, Joan and Chuck Lamb, and Patty Comer, friends and family members *extraordinaire*! Once again, I *never* could have done it without you!

—J. R. B.

INTRODUCTION

Welcome to the second collection of booktalks and articles that appeared in *The Booktalker*, a *Wilson Library Bulletin* supplement, between 1989 and 1992. The first collection—*Booktalk! 4* (1992)—included about half the contents of three years of *The Booktalker*, focusing on the earlier issues. This volume takes up where that one left off and completes the coverage with more recently published material. So if you are one of the people who wanted *everything* that was ever published in *The Booktalker*, now you can have it, contained within these two companion volumes.

Between them, these collections offer more tfYn 600 talks on titles published between 1988 and 1992, written for a variety of audiences ranging from elementary-school children to adults. I hope there is something here for everybody—and to locate it, there are indexes and listings by book title and author, by grade level, and by theme and genre (which should be helpful when you are trying to pull together a program for a specific group). The articles, all by booktalkers in the field, offer new ideas for projects as well as some reassuring answers to that perennial question, is it worth battling the butterflies and the bureaucracy just to talk about books? Again and again, people who have tried booktalking say it is definitely worth it—introducing people to books can be an exciting and rewarding experience.

I do want to point out, however, that these *Booktalker* volumes are basically collections of talks and articles; they aren't intended to instruct, except by example. If you want to learn more about booktalking techniques, and about how to prepare and present talks effectively, you can find that information in the basic text of *Booktalk! 2*, also published by H. W. Wilson. And if you want even more talks (MORE TALKS!), they can be found in *Booktalk! 2* and *Booktalk! 3*.

I hope that you will find much here to pique your interest and support your booktalking efforts. Please don't hesitate to write me at the address below, or care of the Wilson Company—I'm always interested in readers' reactions, and particularly want to know how these books can be made more useful to you. At the moment, I'm collecting new talks for a series on award-winning titles, the first volume of which has been scheduled by Wilson for the end of this year. If you are interested in participating in this project or writing for *The Booktalker*, just send at least two representative talks and a letter outlining your experience to the address below. I will look at your talks and get back to you. And don't be shy, or assume, if you're a beginner, that your work won't be good enough—take a look in *Booktalk! 2* at what a booktalk is and how to write one and give it a try. You may surprise yourself!

So dive right in, and have a good time. We enjoyed putting this book together, and I hope you'll enjoy using it.

Happy reading, and Happy Booktalking!

—Joni Richards Bodart
The Booktalker, Box 370688
Denver, CO 80237-0688
July 1993

CONTRIBUTORS OF BOOKTALKS

Bette DeBruyne Ammon
  Missoula Public Library
  Missoula, MT

Mark Anderson
  Fairfax County Public Library
  Fairfax, VA

Barbara Bahm
  Tonganoxie High School
  Tonganoxie, KS

Kathleen Beck
  Koelbel Public Library
  Littleton, CO

Jeff Blair
  Olathe South High School
  Olathe, KS

Marvia Boettcher
  Bismarck Public Library
  Bismarck, ND

Julie Bray
  Jasper County Public Library
  Rensselaer, IN

Lisa Broadhead
  Bartow Pubic Library
  Bartow, FL

Suzanne Bruney
  Lancaster OH

Margaret Butzler
  Bethel Park Public Library
  Bethel, PA

Mary Ann Capan
  Western Illinois University
  Macomb, IL

Maggie Carey
  The Barstow School
  Kansas City, MO

Monica Carollo
  Cumberland School
  Whitefish Bay, WI

Sandra Carpenter
  Hamilton Elementary School
  Hamilton, KS

Nancy L. Chu
  Western Illinois University
  Macomb, IL

Cynthia Cordes
  Onondaga County Public Library
  Syracuse, NY

Mary Cosper
  Terrebonne Parish Library
  Houma, LA

Bernice D. Crouse
  Fulton County Library
  McConnellsburg, PA

Cathy Crowell
  Oswego High School
  Oswego, KS

Dorothy Davidson
  Jackson Elementary School
  Abilene, TX

Diane L. Deuel
  Central Rappanhannock Regional
    Library
  Fredericksburg, VA

Barbara Diment
  Santa Fe Elementary School
  Kansas City, MO

Judy Druse
  Washburn University
  Topeka, KS

Marijo Duncan
  Phoenix Public Library
  Phoenix, AZ

Susan Dunn
  Salem Public Library
  Salem, OR

Paula Eads
  Booklegger Project
  Fremont Main Library
  Fremont, CA

Marilyn Eanes
  Grisham Middle School
  Austin, TX

Kathleen B. Ellis
  Berkeley Carroll School
  Brooklyn, NY

Sister M. Anna Falbo, CSSF
  Villa Maria College
  Buffalo, NY

Susan R. Farber
  Ossining Public Library
  Ossining, NY

Lesley S. J. Farmer
  San Domenico School
  San Anselmo, CA

Willa Jean Harner
  Tiffin-Seneca Public Library
  Tiffin, OH

Anna Biagioni Hart
  Sherwood Regional Library
  Fairfax County Public Library
  Alexandria, VA

Barbara Hawkins
  West Potomac High School
  Alexandria, VA

Mary Hedge
  La Porte County Public Library
  La Porte, IN

Di Herald
  Mesa County Public Library
  Mesa County, AZ

Betty A. Holtzen
  Abilene Public Library
  Abilene, TX

Olivia D. Jacobs
  Wichita Heights High School
  Wichita, KS

Rebecca E. Jenkins
  Tempe Public Library
  Tempe, AZ

Carolyn M. Johnson
  Ridgewood, NY

Patrick Jones
  Tecumseh Branch
  Fort Wayne Public Library
  Fort Wayne, IN

Susan A. Jones
  Pleasanton Branch
  Alameda County Library
  Pleasanton, CA

Carol Kappelmann
  Dover Grade School
  Dover, KS

Eldean Kechely
  Mickle Junior High School
  Lincoln, NE

Deb Kelly
  Park County Library System
  Meeteetse Branch
  Meeteetse, NY

Patsy Launspach
  Indian Ridge Middle School
  El Paso, TX

Frances W. Levin
  Bentonville, AR

Elizabeth Sue Lewis
  Beverly Manor Junior High School
  Normal, IL

Anne Liebst
  Baker University
  Baldwin City, KS

Mary Harn Liu
  Thomas Cooper Library, USC
  Columbia, SC

Cynthia L. Lopuszynski
  Tippecanoe Public Library
  Lafayette, IN

Mary MacNeil
  Shimek Elementary School
  Iowa City, IA

Cathi MacRae
  Boulder Public Library
  Boulder, CO

Rene Mandel
  Framington, MA

Cecelia May
  Lawrence Public Library
  Lawrence, KS

Wanda McAdams
  Booklegger Project
  Fremont Main Library
  Fremont, CA

Diantha McCauley
  Augusta County Library
  Fisherville, VA

Jan McConnell
  Kansas City Public Library
  Kansas City, MO

Mary McCurry
Brampton Public Library
Brampton, Ontario, Canada

Kaite Mediatore
Emporia Public Library
Emporia, KS

Kathy Ann Miller
Student, School of Library
and Information Science
Emporia State University
Emporia, KS

Rosemary Moran
Martin East Regional Library
Tulsa City-County Library System
Tulsa, OK

Paulette Nelson
Minot Public Library
Minot, ND

C. Allen Nichols
Rocky River Public Library
Rocky River, OH

Sharon O'Connell
Skaneateles Middle School Library
Skaneateles, NY

Linda Olson
Superior Public Library
Superior, WI

Sue Padilla
Ida Long Goodman
Memorial Library
St. Johns, KS

Paula Paolucci
Hamilton Public Library
Hamilton, Ontario, Canada

Kristina Peters
North Carroll Branch
Carroll County Public Library
Greenmount, MD

Robbi Povenmire
Veneta, OR

Faye A. Powell
Spauldings Branch
Prince George's County Memorial
Library System
District Heights, MD

Marianne Tait Pridemore
San Jose Public Library
San Jose, CA

Terrie Ratcliffe
Irving Public Library
Irving, TX

Blair Reid
Carroll County Public Library
Westminster, MD

Margie Reitsma
St. Mary's-St. Catherine's School
Remsen, IA

Tracy Chesonis Revel
Sussex Central Junior High School
Millsboro, DE

Karol Schmitt Rockwin
Longwood Middle School District
Middle Island, NY

Susan Rosenkoetter
Rochester Public Library
Rochester, NY

Kim Carter Sands
Rindge Memorial School
Rindge, NH

Donna L. Scanlon
Lancaster County Library
Lancaster, PA

Helen Schlicting
Sac Community School
Sac City, IA

Glenna Hoskins Seeley
Lakelanier Regional Library
Duluth System, GA

Nadeane Silbernagel
Bismarck Veterans Memorial Public
Library
Bismarck, ND

Colleen Smith
Caledonia Public Library
Caledonia, Ontario, Canada

Suzi Smith
Maxwell Park Library
Tulsa City-County Library System
Tulsa, OK

Terri Summey
Emporia State University
Emporia, KS

Anne Sushko
Jefferson Junior High
Dubuque, IA

Judy Thomas
  Dyess Elementary School
  Abilene, TX

Sharon Thomas
  Goddard Junior High School
  Goddard, KS

Sarah M. Thrash
  Seaford District Library
  Seaford, DE

Pamela A. Todd
  John A. Logan College
  Carterville, IL

Susan Trimby
  Fossil Ridge Public Library District
  Wilmington, IL

Diane P. Tuccillo
  Mesa Public Library
  Mesa, AZ

Cara A. Waits
  Tempe Public Library
  Tempe, AZ

Melinda D. Waugh
  Topeka Public Library
  Topeka, KS

Stacey M. Weaver
  Kent State University Library
  East Liverpool, OH

Susan Weaver
  Kent State University Library
  East Liverpool, OH

Nancy A. Weitendorf
  Oxford Lane Public Library
  Oxford, OH

Maureen Whalen
  Rochester Public Library
  Rochester, NY

Patricia Willingham
  Kent Library
  Southeast Missouri State University
  Cape Girardeau, MO

James Witham
  Lexington Public Library
  Lexington, KY

Melanie L. Witulski
  Holland Branch
  Toledo-Lucas County Public
  Library
  Toledo, OH

Susan Wolfe
  Central Dauphin School District
  Harrisburg, PA

Sue Young
  Ysleta Independent School District
  El Paso, TX

ARTICLES

How I Turned into a Booktalker—Overnight!
By Kaite Mediatore
Emporia Public Library, Emporia, KS

On June 18, 1991, I ceased to be a booktalking virgin. I made my debut in Gridley, Kansas, at a program in honor of their new library. I had had a taste of public booktalking in the nearby town of Leroy a year or so before; Joni Bodart had been asked to do a presentation for their local library and had invited me to come along, observe, and then booktalk a few titles too. I went, and after spending a good part of the evening making sure that none of Joni's books fell over in the middle of the performance, I tried several talks of my own. But I didn't consider myself a member of the booktalking set—not yet. I knew that I'd have to do a complete presentation on my own to be a *real* booktalker.

To be honest, when I accepted the Gridley invitation I had no idea what I was going to do. All I knew for sure was that I didn't want to copy everything Joni had done—to use her talks and her favorite titles and imitate her style. I wanted the audience to see me as a person, not a Joni-clone, so in planning my program I tried to keep my own tastes and booktalking strengths in mind.

I started with back issues of the *Booktalker*. I read every one of them over and over and marked the booktalks I would *like* to do. Then I went back and marked the talks I knew I *could* do. Out of that batch I chose the titles that the library had or that I had at home. Then I narrowed the field down again by tossing out any talks that seemed a little too specialized in their appeal. My audience would consist of men, women, children, and adolescents; anybody and everybody, aged 5 to 75, from all over the educational map. It would be a mixed bag of people, and I had to have a mixed bag of booktalks. This drove me crazy. I spent my evenings saying things like, "I can't do that booktalk, it'll put the kids to sleep," and "What can I say to make picture books appealing

1

to adults?" and "How can I present two Jude Deveraux titles and convince everybody that these aren't just trashy romance novels? And the men—I know they won't read Deveraux, but the talks have got to hold their attention," and of course, "This booktalk is too *long*—no one could possibly learn it!"

After I had selected all the titles I wanted to try, I began staging impromptu performances for my fiancé. He was not exactly enthusiastic about this, and appreciated it even less when I invited him to sit down in the living room, thrust a watch at him, and stood in front of the television announcing that *I* was the evening's entertainment. But in addition to needing a timer, I needed feedback—my cat, though clearly fascinated by booktalks, can't criticize worth a darn. So that left Pat with the less-than-enviable job of evaluating my performances (it's in *The Fiancé's Handbook of Rules and Regulations*, under "Other Duties as Necessary"!). And much to his surprise, he ended up getting interested in some of the books, including a few that he never would have picked up on his own. I realized then that booktalking had to be fun for the audience as well as informative—that entertainment was a key part of a successful presentation.

The other revelation of my practice sessions was that I regularly ran out of material before I had run out of time. I had forty minutes to fill and I was talking much too fast; but even when I slowed down my speech I still had ten long, silent minutes left over. I searched frantically for additional booktalks that I could learn quickly or had already learned in the past. Finally I came up with two I had once done in a class and submitted to the *Booktalker*. These two extra talks and a slower, more relaxed delivery brought me up to the required forty minutes.

On the day of the presentation I made photocopies of all the talks I was using from the *Booktalker* and glued them to large index cards. Booktalks that I'd written recently or collected from other sources I copied out on additional cards in a sort of pidgin shorthand. I placed all the index cards in the books as disaster insurance—if I forgot a character's name or suddenly went blank in the middle of a talk, I'd be able to grab the card and recover, however lamely, instead of dying of embarrassment.

When I reached the Gridley Community Center, I was about an hour and a half early. That was fine—I wanted to warm up in the room with no one present so that I would be comfortable with my surroundings by the time the people began to arrive. This turned out to be the best thing I could have done. After an hour of booktalking to 75 folding chairs, I felt at ease in the room; it had become my territory. I knew that I didn't want to stand behind the podium (which was too tall for me) but realized that I could stand to one side and use it as a holder for my note cards—they'd be there for me to glance at but invisible to the audience; I knew how loudly I'd have to speak to be heard in the room and how much space I would need on the table. I cleared an area on a small table for my books and put them in two stacks in proper order; then I arranged the cards in the same order and placed them on the podium. By the time the audience arrived, everything was set up.

I started off a little too fast (nerves) and was trying to slow down, relax, and look as though I were having a good time when suddenly I realized that I *was* having a good time! The crowd was small but interested, and they laughed at almost everything, including the picture books. I knew I had them when everybody, even the men, laughed during my Jude Deveraux talk.

All too soon (actually, eight minutes too soon) the presentation was over. I'd been speaking too quickly again, really racing through the introductory remarks and closing thank-you's. But no one seemed to mind, and I consoled myself by thinking, "Better too short than too long." Several people remembered me from the presentation in Leroy the year before, and one person asked how on earth I could remember all those talks. Another woman said, "You even made the YA novels sound interesting! I'm going to go look for them first." When several titles were checked out right after the program, I knew that I'd been a success.

On the way home I thought about what I'd do differently next time. I'd try hard to slow myself down, of course, but just in case I couldn't, I'd have some back-up books along to fill out the program. And variety was obviously important for the audience—perhaps next time I'd make the talks shorter so that I could include more different books. Suddenly I noticed that I was already planning my next program—*I* was a book-talker!

The Books I Used:

Lizzie, by Frank Spiering
Why Do Dogs Have Wet Noses? by David Feldman
The Real Story of the Three Little Pigs, by John Scieszka
A Knight in Shining Armor and *Wishes*, by Jude Deveraux
Everyone Else's Parents Said Yes, by Paula Danziger
Where Time Ends, by Thomas Baird
The Last Cattle Drive, by Robert Day
Don't Look Behind You, by Lois Duncan
Forward Pass, by Thomas J. Dygard
How Many Spots Does a Leopard Have? by Julius Lester
Frank & Ernest and *Frank & Ernest Play Ball*, by Alexandra Day
Growing Up Western, by Clarus Backes and Dee Brown

LiFE iN

BOOKTALK FROM H★LL		CHAPTER 22 How to BOOKTALK*
CLASSROOMS by grade	personal DEMOGRAPHICS	BOOKTALKER'S RANDOM THOUGHTS, SNAPPY COMEBACKS, IDLE CHATTER
GRADE 1	SWEET AND INNOCENT	AREN'T THEY CUTE!
GRADE 2	DICK AND JANE	WHAT DO you MEAN you SAW the VIDEO?
GRADE 3	MAGGIE AND BART	HEY! DOES your MOTHER LET you DO THAT!
GRADE 4	CAIN AND ABEL	NAAH - NAAH NAAH BOO - BOO !!
GRADE 5	DUDE AND DUDETTE	CENSORED
GRADE 6	WILD AND WOOLY	there MUST BE OPENINGS IN Adult services...
GRADES 7-8	PUZZLED AND PASSIONATE	the WONDER YEARS
GRADES 9-12	MADONNA AND WARREN	all of the above
three cuts to the heart... ☐ WE START AT 7³⁰ A.M. ☐ OUR AIR conditioning BROKE ☐ I thought you were coming Tomorrow!	Booktalk Hotline 1-800-YACK TRAINED READERS ARE STANDING BY to tAKE your CALLS	6 REACTIONS to BOOK tALKS UGH! So? YUCKY SWELL GROSS! Got ANY good books?

the library

© 1991 By
ANNA
HART

WATCH This SPACE (APOLOGIES TO MAtt GROENING)		
FAVORITE Books to SHARE	RooM TEMPErATUrE	BooK BAG WEIGH-IN
TURTLE AND SPOT (AN "I CAN SAY IT FOR MOMMY" book)	VERY WARM	to 10 Lbs. DAINTY
WHERE the WiLD TURTLES ArE	Hot	11-20 Lbs. proFessionAL
WHErE'S TUrtLE? FiNd TurtLe NoW	STEAMY	21-30 lbs. HeALTH CLUB
Loathsome Fighting TUrtle Stories to TeLL IN the DArK	CASABlANCA	31-40 lbs SHOW OFF!
FiERcE comBATiVE TURTLE TWiNS (series)	MENOPAUSAL	41-50 lbs INCredible HULK!
Repulsive MArtiAL Arts Reptiles iN Love	KiLLER heatwAVE	50+ lbs BeLUGA
TurtLes iN The AttiC IF there BE Turtles	DESERT STORM	1,000 lbs MAJOR homework
Turtle Lust CliFF notes Turtle Lust VHS	Hot And Bothered	N/A
BookTAlK contraindicAtions: prolonged bookTAlKiNG has been KNoWN to cause hives, coughing, Fever, hallucinATionS, rAsh, pimples, low self-esteem, iLLiterAcy, heArtbreAk, morbid FEAr oF best Sellers, cArTOONiNG And other SIGNS oF mALAdjustment iN otherwise healthy Adults. Extreme cAUTiON is Advised	76867 2	✗ CAUTiON: DO NOT AttEMpt To rEproduce BookTAlks iN your OWN home without the ASSISTANcE oF trAiNed LibrAry professioNALS

Give Them What They Want, Before They Know They Want It
By Faye A. Powell
Prince George's County Memorial Library System, Maryland

"His house was set afire with the whole family inside, because his father was the head of the local Marcus Garvey movement. After they got out, he watched it burn as he waited in the yard with his family, while the white fire-fighters and policemen stood around smoking and laughing, as though they were at some friendly get-together. This was not the Deep South, but his home town in Nebraska. Memories like this pushed Malcolm X, at sixteen, onto the streets of Chicago's criminal underworld, to escape the white man's power over his life. . . . "

"After receiving several beatings from her jealous classmates, Phyllisia Cathy sat stunned as this skinny, wiry girl named Edith Jackson (a girl she did *not* want as a friend) stood up in front of the whole class, ignoring the teacher, and announced: 'Phyllisia Cathy is my friend. And if anyone lays a hand on her again, they'll have to deal with me!' And no one said a word! Not even the biggest, toughest kids! But now Phyllisia is stuck with this poor ragamuffin. . . . Phyllisia has a lot to learn about herself, Edith Jackson, and being friends."

[The above are quotes from two booktalks, the first on *The Autobiography of Malcolm X*, as told to Alex Haley, and the second on *The Friends*, a novel by Rosa Guy.]

One February, about seven years ago, Jacqeline Brown Woody, a Young Adult Specialist in the Prince George's County Memorial Library System, asked me to do a special booktalk presentation with her. She told me that we were going to present "Black Booktalks" at a local high school, focusing on books by and about African Americans. I was excited about the idea and eager to try, but I wondered about student interest—would the black children think this was ancient history? Or the non-black feel completely uninvolved?

However, the reponse of the students was an eye-opener. These young people, from various cultures and backgrounds (black, white, Asian, hispanic), listened engrossed to what we had to say. I saw an aspect of modern teenagers that I hadn't seen before: they are fascinated by the puzzle of identity, and they have a true thirst to hear and learn about their own roots and a real curiosity about other people's. Then and there, I promised myself that I would find a way to meet their need for knowledge. Oh, sure, they already knew that there were books out there one could read for facts, and other books that offered pure entertainment. But I wanted them to see how books could be enjoyable *and* thought-provoking, and how the library could help. All they had to do was ask, and the Prince George's System would practically bring the material to their doors, by holding items *just for them* at their neighborhood branch. And all for free! What could be better than that?

I took the first steps toward my goal when I became head of programming at the new Spauldings Branch Library in Prince George's County, Maryland, in 1987. The branch is centrally located and serves a large portion of the county's schools. I discussed my idea with the three Associate Librarians and our Branch Manager before we began our regular booktalk scheduling, and they were as excited as I was. We decided to suspend regular talks during February (Black History Month) and instead present Black Booktalks exclusively.

We sent out the customary booktalk letters to the principals and media specialists in our community schools—with one addition: " . . . regular booktalks will be suspended during Black History Month in order to offer Black Booktalks." The replies came in immediately by telephone, requesting these special talks (" . . . and by the way, we would like to set up dates for the regular talks, too"!). It was very encouraging. We had begun with the middle schools and high schools in the area, but then the elementary schools heard about the program and asked for visits as well. This was more than we had hoped for in our first year.

We felt that we had made the right decision in beginning the special talks that first February, shortly after the branch opened. Obviously the community was interested in what we had to say; there *was* a need—deeply felt, though not yet expressed—for the sort of program we were offering. We could spread the word about the history and accomplishments of African Americans and encourage young people to use the new library to explore their heritage; at the same time we were showing the entire community that the library was concerned about their needs and wants—right from the start we were reaching out to them, even before they turned to us. Soon everyone working in or attending schools in the neighborhood was aware that the new branch was open (just in case they had missed the news) and that it was *their* library, close by and ready for their use.

When we spoke to middle and high school classes, we selected titles from *Black People, Black Life*, our system's annotated list of YA books by and about African Americans—a resource we've continued to use. The list contains about fifty titles, grouped into four sections: "I Am Somebody" (biographies), "Living Black" (fiction), "Our Yesterdays" (historical fiction and nonfiction), and "Black Voices" (poetry, plays, and rap). It is updated every year, so we have a wide choice of books for teenagers. We vary our selections from year to year, but there are three titles I always make sure to include: *Black Hollywood*, by Cary Null; *Brown Sugar*, by Donald Bogle, and *The Black Book*, by M. A. Harris. They sort of complement each other, and always furnish me with something interesting and new to offer. When we talk at the elementary schools, we make our own selection of books appropriate for grades k–3 and 4–6.

Of course, the trick is to pick titles that will stimulate the students' imaginations—to present fictional titles in a manner that grabs their interest right away; and to choose nonfiction titles that may shake them up and make them say, "I didn't know that!", or make them laugh; and most of all, to find titles that will make them think—and read!

Today, Black Booktalks are so popular in the Spauldings community that media specialists don't wait until the letters are mailed out; they come by or call the branch to reserve February dates as soon as school is in session. In fact, in order to accomodate all the requests we receive, we've begun scheduling the talks from the fourth week in January through the first week of March. The rewards are numerous, not only in increased circulation but in the questions we are asked, the interest we observe, and the desire the young people exhibit in their search to know more.

Now that I am able to offer these presentations, I have one final goal: to spread the word to my colleagues. Special booktalks about different cultures are a valid, effective means of persuading children that reading is fun; at the same time these talks can help children understand more about the different people they see around them every day, about their classmates, and about themselves. In our multicultural society, booktalkers can promote mutual respect and understanding, just by giving our children what they want, before they know they want it.

I would like to thank the people who joined with me to start the program at the Spauldings Branch in 1987: Cynthia Prine, the Branch Manager, and Associate Librarians Bertina Tyler, Jean Massey, and Marsha Quarles. Their support and encouragement were invaluable. Librarians who would like copies of the *Black People, Black Life* booklist can obtain them by writing to the Development Department of the Prince George's County Memorial Library System, 6532 Adelphi Road, Hyattsville, MD 20782. Please enclose a stamped, self-addressed envelope.

Successful Student Booktalking
By Marilyn Eanes
Librarian, Grisham Middle School, Austin, TX

"Booktalk"—the dreaded word that often strikes terror into the hearts of adults can have an even more alarming effect on seventh graders. That's what Hilda Ollmann, a language arts teacher, and I, a middle school librarian, discovered when we decided to team up and assign booktalks, rather than book reports, to a class of thirteen-year-olds.

We undertook this joint effort with several objectives in mind. Our number-one goal was to give the students a truly great reading experience, so that they would know the joy of a good story and the pleasure of sharing it with other people. Additional benefits—"icing on the cake"—would include:

• understanding the difference between an oral book report and a booktalk.
• practice in speaking before a group (preparation and delivery of talk).
• learning to listen (evaluating other students' presentations).
• discovering more books to read, through hearing other students' booktalks.

The teacher and I decided that a three-week period would be realistic for this assignment. To start off, I modeled a booktalk for the students (I used William Sleator's *The Boy Who Reversed Himself*). After the demonstration, the class discussed how a booktalk differs from an oral book report. We elicited some important points: that the end of the story is not given; that the booktalker needs to grab the audience's attention right away and maintain a high level of interest; and that a good talk leaves the audience wanting to snatch up the book and finish the story themselves. Then I went over the guidelines for writing a booktalk and gave the students copies of the Preparation Sheet. (Reproduced below. They had to have the sheet before they began reading so that they could fill it out as they read.) Our students were still skeptical about their ability to do this assignment, but we encouraged them to follow the step-by-step approach outlined on the Preparation Sheet—to take notes as they read and look for interesting characters, dramatic dialogue, unusual settings, and other special features.

We moved on to book selection. I had pulled some books that I felt would be good material for the students to look at. It is essential to pick high-interest titles for an assignment like this, and if possible match the book to the student. We had decided to stick with fiction, but we had stories with various themes—mystery, adventure, survival, and sports. Authors included William Sleator, Lois Duncan, Joan Lowery Nixon, Richard Peck, Paula Danziger, and Ellen Conford. The students were not limited to the pulled books—these were simply suggested titles. I stressed that they must each find a book they really liked, and if their first choice didn't work out, exchange it for another one. Reading time was provided every day, during the first ten minutes of class (DEAR— Drop Everything And Read), but the students also had to read at home to complete the assignment within the time-frame.When the students finished reading their books, they returned to the library to get instructions on composing their talks (we wanted them to write out their talks before giving the oral presentation). The three parts of a booktalk were explained:

- The first sentence must grab the attention of the audience.
- The middle must be filled with action.
- The ending should come at the climax of the story and leave the audience guessing, eager to find out what happens next.

We also discussed ways of approaching the material—whether to use first- or third-person narrative, for example.

Once the students had written out their talks, they used their manuscripts as the basis for notes on three-by-five index cards. They would need these for the actual presentation. We emphasized that the booktalks were not to be read but delivered, with the help of notes, and talked about the importance of speaking in a pleasant, audible voice and making eye contact with the audience. Practice sessions at home in front of a mirror (or even a pet—they're rarely critical) were encouraged. We were able to relieve some of the anxieties the students had about public speaking by reminding them that they booktalk unconsciously all the time—whenever they recommend a book to a friend, they are doing an informal booktalk. (As I know from my work in the library, networks exist in every school of students who share favorite books, and recommendations from peers matter a lot more to kids than recommendations from adults.)

In these days of the expanded curriculum, class time has become a critical issue, so the teacher and I devised a method whereby all the presentations could be completed within one class period. On presentation day, the teacher brought each class to the library. The students were seated four to a table. As one gave a talk, the other three filled out an evaluation form, rating both preparation and delivery. We used the evaluation form reproduced below, which appeared in the May 1987 issue of *School Library Media Activities Monthly*—it was perfect for our needs.

Bringing the students to the library and presenting the talks to small groups proved to have several advantages:

- The project, which had begun in the library, was concluded there, giving a sense of continuity.
- Even shy students were not intimidated, since their audience was composed of only three people.
- Because the students had to evaluate each other's talks, everyone was attentive and polite.
- Students became excited about each other's books and often ended up by exchanging books.

We knew how successful the assignment had been when some groups finished early. Instead of getting noisy and disruptive, they went to listen to the groups that were still presenting. There was tremendous interest in other students' books. We had to make up waiting lists for some titles because so many students wanted to check them out. Despite their initial fears about booktalking, the students actually seemed disappointed when the bell rang.

Would we do it again? Absolutely! There was real excitement in the sharing of the books, and several students said they wished they could have heard all the talks. With planning and cooperation, we had accomplished our number-one objective: to give our students a truly great reading experience!

Bibliography

Bodart, Joni. "Booktalking: Helping Create the Reading Junkie", *School Library Media Activities Monthly*, Volume II, number 8, April 1986.

Reeder, Geneva. "Booktalks and Literature", *School Library Media* Activities Monthly, Volume III, Number 9, May 1987.

[Forms to distribute to students appear on the next two pages. Although booktalks are normally 5 to 7 minutes long, the library media specialist and the teacher should establish time limits appropriate to the group.]

Name_____

BOOKTALK PREPARATION SHEET

**Author of
Book**_____

Title of book_____

Main characters_____

Plot outline (1–2 sentences)_____

_____

_____

_____

_____

Booktalk Hints

Preparation

Read a book of interest—one that you will enjoy.

Jot down notes.

Decide on your approach to the material—1st or 3rd person

Writing

First sentence—grab the attention of the audience

Body of talk—action-filled. **Do not assume** that the audience knows something about the book; present all the important background information. Summarize the plot up to the climax.

Last sentence—lead the audience to believe something is going to happen, but **do not tell the end of the story**.

Presentation

Practice the booktalk before presenting it to the class.

Before beginning, be sure to have everyone's attention.

Keep the attention of the audience. **Do not read** directly from note-cards; **do not ramble** on pointlessly.

Maintain good eye contact.

Sound excited about your book. Try to convince someone else to read it.

Have the book present when giving the booktalk.

Reminder: Booktalks should be between _____ and _____ minutes long.

BOOKTALK EVALUATION FORM

Presenter's name_____

Evaluator's name_____

Starting time_____**Ending time**_____

[Rate on a scale of 1 (poor) to 5 (excellent).]

A. Preparation

   1. Was the talk well prepared?   1 2 3 4 5

   2. Did the introduction grab your attention?   1 2 3 4 5

   3. Was the plot summarized well?   1 2 3 4 5

   4. Did the conclusion leave you wondering
    what happened next?   1 2 3 4 5

   5. Was the book a good choice for a booktalk?   1 2 3 4 5

B. Delivery

   1. Did the presenter have good eye contact?   1 2 3 4 5

   2. Did the talk flow smoothly?   1 2 3 4 5

   3. Did the presenter seem at ease?   1 2 3 4 5

   4. Was the presenter enthusiastic?   1 2 3 4 5

   5. Did the presentation hold the
    audience's attention?   1 2 3 4 5

I would give this talk a grade of _____.

Total points:_____ **Actual grade:**_____

[Forms from Geneva Reeder's article "Booktalks and Literature" in *School Library Media Activities Monthly*, May 1987.]

Books, Kids, and Videotape
By Bette D. Ammon
Missoula Public Library, Missoula, MT

Reading and TV—natural enemies? Not here in the Pacific Northwest! We're using videotape to "sell" books to kids. Specifically, we're selling the titles nominated for the Young Readers' Choice Awards.

This children's-choice award program is the oldest of its kind in the United States and the only one to have achieved international status. It was started by a Seattle bookseller over fifty years ago. The rules are simple: Each year, kids in grades four through eight and nine through twelve read all the books nominated for the award in their age group. Then they vote for their favorites, and the most popular title wins.

The Pacific Northwest Library Association, which sponsors the program in our area, allocates funds each year for the production of a videotape introducing the nominated titles. The videotape is used by schools and libraries throughout the Northwest to promote the contest and get young people involved. In the past we taped brief annotations of all the nominated titles, but last year we added a new twist: short booktalks presented by kids. As most librarians and teachers know (and many studies confirm), peer recommendation is a powerful way to attract readers to books.

One spring Sunday, eleven Missoula students, ranging in age from nine to seventeen, gathered at the public library to make the videotape. We had recruited our booktalkers through family (four of them were library staff offspring), friends, and our young adult program. A local producer and I videotaped each student presenting two or three booktalks. We used talks I had written for the basic format, but the students modified the language and content to make the talks their own. By the end of the day we had shot a good deal of tape. Thanks to our local community-access television station, we were able to edit and polish the footage at minimal cost.

The results have been great! Librarians love the new look, and the Missoula kids have become local celebrities. Some teachers and librarians are planning to show the video twice: once at the beginning of the school year and then again just before the students vote.

And a bonus: Recently I learned of a sixth-grade class in Columbia Falls, MT, who are producing a videotape of their own, featuring talks on the five picture books nominated for our new Treasure State Award, a children's-choice contest for primary grades. With their video, the sixth graders are hoping to persuade the younger children in their school to participate in the program. I love it!

BOOKTALKS

Acacia Terrace
By Barbara Ker Wilson

Grade 3–Adult

Have you ever thought of your house as a storyteller? A storyteller whose voice echoes the passage of time; a storyteller who reveals the memories of another era; a storyteller who has seen generations of characters?

In 1855, in the gold fields of Australia, young Michael Flynn makes a promise to Rose Robson—he will build her the "best house she has ever seen." In 1872, that promise becomes a reality when Michael builds his wife, Rose, and their four daughters a group of three connected houses, which they name Acacia Terrace. And Acacia Terrace becomes the storyteller who traces the history of this Australian family from the 1870s to 1945.

Acacia Terrace hears the cries of a newborn son, Albert; it sees the sheep pasture become a park, and it watches as other houses are built within its shadow. It recalls the bad times of 1891 when no one could afford paint or repairs. It reminisces about the gala celebrations for the newly federated Australian commonwealth.

Sorrowfully, it remembers war and influenza and the deaths that leave Rose Flynn alone within its walls. Acacia Terrace listens as Rose asks her daughter Kate to join her. It watches as they decide to take in boarders to make ends meet. And as 1918 draws to a close, the footsteps of lodgers cross its threshhold.

Once again Acacia Terrace experiences unhappiness. Rose dies. Her daughter Kate becomes the caretaker of the family home. Soon sister Alice marries, and she and her husband are invited to Acacia Terrace.

The years pass, and Acacia Terrace experiences the Great Depression, the Second World War, the sights and sounds of television, and the Age of Aquarius. It feels the damage of fire and the emptiness of abandonment. Will Acacia Terrace end as the target of vandals? Will the saga close with its demolition, or is there a chance for it to be re-

stored? Listen to an old house's memories—a story waiting to be heard.
　　　　　　　　　　　　　　　　　　　　　　　　—*Susan Wolfe*

The Adventures of Boone Barnaby　　　Grades 5-7
By Joe Cottonwood

Boone Barnaby lives in a little town called San Puerco in the Santa Cruz Mountains of California. It really is a little town—just a few people and a lot of redwood trees. It's usually so quiet that ducks sleep in the street. Hardly the place for adventures, you might think, but don't be too sure—things are starting to liven up in San Puerco.

First, Boone and his two best friends find their soccer team headed for the league championship, and then possibly a trip to the play-offs in Australia—*if* they can raise the airfare. They decide to earn the money by holding a Trashathon, where people in town pledge a certain amount of money for each pound of trash the team can pick up off their property. Stingy, mean Miser Tate tries to wiggle out of his pledge (of one dollar per pound) by cleaning up all his trash ahead of time. Boone outwits him, though, by finding three abandoned cars on his street, cars that together weigh over nine thousand pounds! That's nine thousand dollars toward the trip, and now Boone is on top of the world. But when his soccer team is unjustly kicked out of the league, he begins to wonder just how much difference any kid—even a smart one—can make. And finally something really ugly happens in San Puerco, maybe the worst thing yet. Someone begins to set Miser Tate's buildings on fire, one by one, and Boone's father is falsely accused of arson. Boone begins to question the rules of the adult world. How can these totally unfair things be allowed to happen? Boone goes looking for answers, and before his adventures are over, he's found some that he never expected.
　　　　　　　　　　　　　　　　　　　　　　　　—*Diane P. Tuccillo*

After-Shock　　　　　　　Grade 9-Adult
By Chuck Scarborough

It began at 1:21 PM. At first, for perhaps ten seconds, the ground rocked gently—a swaying motion, not severe, but back and forth. It was very noticeable in the park, where a crowd of people had assembled for a civic ceremony. Then the ground began to surge underfoot in great undulating waves, shock after shock. . . . a roar arose, inhuman, unfamiliar, terrible. The very important people—those sitting on platforms rather than standing on the ground—were suddenly tossed into the air as the platforms crumpled, collapsing onto the heaving earth.

During the first moments, no one made a sound. Then the screams of fear and pain began. The mature trees at the edge of the meadow came crashing down. Flagpoles bent and broke, striking those nearby. A fissure, thirty feet wide, opened at one side of the park, gaped, and closed again. Another opened near the site of the ceremony; most of the people there fell in, going down, down, landing at the bottom of a V that kept opening wider. They began to scramble up the sides, trying to get back to the surface.

When it was over, those who could got to their feet. They stared in shock across the river toward Manhattan. It was as though a giant invisible wrecking ball was at work. Buildings were coming apart before their eyes, falling outward, collapsing in on themselves. The Empire State Building swayed but held, the World Trade Center was firm, the Chrysler Building remained, but there was little else left standing. Clouds of dust made it hard to see, but in fact most of Harlem, the East Side, the West Side along the Park and Riverside Drive, Greenwich Village, and Wall Street and the Financial District had been flattened. In the space of just a few short minutes, one of the liveliest, most brilliant and arrogant cities in the world had been reduced to rubble.

Could it be rebuilt? What could be salvaged from the wreckage? Would the rest of the country be willing to foot the bill to make New York City live again? These are some of the questions the President and his advisors face in the aftermath of the disaster.

Over the next few days, heroes will emerge from the rubble, but so will criminals of all kinds, seeking to turn the tragedy to their advantage, as the fate of the stricken city hangs in balance.

Follow the lives of New Yorkers—the heroes, the crooks, the well-known and the unknown, the ones who lived and struggled, and the ones who gave up and died—and see how those few critical moments changed all their lives forever.

—*Faye A. Powell and J. R. B.*

Against the Grain   Grades 7–12
By Jean Ferris

If your older sister is a Grade-A Flake, then *nothing* she does should surprise you. Will Griffin wasn't happy when Paige jerked him out of his senior year of high school. He wasn't thrilled to be taken from the surfing scene of Southern California. He wasn't delighted to go to the remote reaches of the desert, but at least he wasn't surprised. Ever since their mother's death two years before, Paige had been Will's legal guardian—a silly situation, since it was Will (at seventeen) who was the responsible one. He was the one who made sure that the bills were paid, the house cleaned, and the groceries bought. Paige was the free spirit, likely to switch jobs, boyfriends, or hair color at the least provocation. This latest switch was just another of her attempts to find herself. She had taken a job as a waitress at the Snakebite Cafe, smack-dab in the middle of nowhere, and, like it or not, she'd signed Will up as the short-order cook. This was her flakiest move yet.

The desert seemed like an alien place to Will, who was used to the ocean's noise and energy. Paige seemed to fit right in, but then she had the easier job and she also had Timothy, her new love interest. For Will things weren't so great. How would he become accustomed to the vast silences of the desert? How would he manage his job when he had no experience? What about the new school, and where would he find new friends?

It was Sam Webb, a middle-aged cafe regular, who became Will's first friend. Sam discovered Will's natural talent for carving and taught him the secret of making a pattern fit the wood's grain. It was a lesson Will could use in dealing with not only his sister but also his pushy classmate Linda, who wanted too much from him; the troublesome, fascinating Mike Macey, the girl he would come to care for; and even with Sam himself.

Can Will use Sam's lessons to shape his life, or will he always be going *Against the Grain*?

—Sue Young

Agnes Cecilia   Grades 5–8
By Maria Gripe; translated from the Swedish by Rika Lesser

It seemed to happen only when Nora was home alone. Strange phone calls that kept her from walking into danger. Books that fell off shelves and opened themselves to significant passages. Mysterious footsteps that paced through the house, only to stop at the open door of Nora's bedroom.

Then one day her cousin Dag was there when the phone rang, and this time he answered it. The mysterious voice on the other end gave him a message for Nora—"Go to the Old Town in Stockholm, and ask for Agnes Cecilia." Nora didn't know anyone by that name, and she was afraid to go into Stockholm. But Dag volunteered to go with her, and now the two of them are standing outside a toy shop in the Old Town, waiting to meet Agnes Cecilia, whoever—or whatever—she is.

—*Kaite Mediatore*

Almighty Me   Adult
By Robert Bausch

It is interesting to imagine what a person might do, given the power of Almighty God—create cures for cancer and AIDS, make it rain only at night and have the sun shine every day, put kindness in every heart, designate chocolate and ice cream as non-fattening health foods, eliminate "fat" altogether, and invent a way to freeze a tomato perfectly so that it could be thawed, sliced, and eaten. Oh, the possibilities are endless, and Charlie Wiggins was given the opportunity to explore those possibilities.

One morning, Charlie picked up his mail and found a very interesting-looking letter. It began, "Congratulations! You have been awarded God's power for one full year. That's right, Goodman Wiggins, God's great power is yours, at no obligation or cost to you. For one full year from the date printed at the top of this page, you will be allowed to exercise the deity's power free of charge."

Being a car salesman himself, Charlie immediately thought this was a new sales gimmick, but he soon found out it was true! He also found out that unlimited power can have unforeseen consequences. For example, to please one of the dealership's secretaries, he started out exercising his new omnipotence by making it snow. Then he decided that for her it should snow all night! The next morning he was tired of snow, so he raised the temperature by 50 degrees—causing floods, tornadoes, and general devastation.

A little more cautiously, he turned his energies to saving his own marriage. His wife Dorothy had returned to college and wanted "to be her own person." Being her own person did not include him or the kids. He tried everything he could think of to keep her. He tried impressing her by throwing forty-seven perfect bull's-eyes in a dart game and by decking the state arm-wrestling champ. He tried putting thoughts of love into her head. He gave her father a temporary but serious illness, so that she would turn to him for comfort. He even planned the perfect family outing in the park, with blue skies and the whole works. But no matter what he tried, she still wanted out.

Charlie exercised his powers in other ways as well. He became a top manager at the dealership and gave himself a big raise to boot. He cured his boss's speech impediment. He gave a vicious attack of diarrhea to an overbearing young salesman, inflicted gout on an obnoxious TV evangelist, and vanquished his mother-in-law's arthritis. Sometimes his efforts were successful; sometimes they backfired outrageously.

But the ways in which Charlie used his powers changed after he was granted a tour of heaven. He discovered that his notions of heaven and God were very different from the real thing. He returned to earth with new insights about how he should use his gift and how he should treat his estranged wife.

As you know, there have been no major changes here on earth recently. Hunger and sickness are still with us, and tomatoes still won't freeze (though I should tell you that Charlie *is* partially responsible for the collapse of Communism). Yet Charlie is still trying, and he needs help. He has written this narrative so that you will know the "record of his term" and perhaps offer an answer to the last question in the book: "What do *you* think I should do?"

—*Susan Weaver*

Amazing Gracie   Grades 7–12
By A. E. Cannon

How would *you* like to be the parent in your family? Gracie is in high school now, but she's been the only adult in her family since she was seven. Just the two of them—Gracie and her mom, and even though Gracie loves her mom, she's afraid she'll grow up to be just like her.

When Gracie looks at her mom's old high-school yearbook, her insides go dead-cold with fear. Her mom looked happy then—normal, just like a regular kid. A kid just like Gracie. But Gracie's mom isn't normal. When she gets depressed, she just gives up on life. Once, when Gracie was just seven, her mom got so bad that the doctors sent her away to the state mental hospital, and Gracie had to stay with the neighbors.

Now every time her mom sounds sad or doesn't eat, Gracie gets worried. And ever since her mom got married again things have gotten worse. They've moved to a new town where there aren't any neighbors to help out; her mom seems *really* depressed; her new stepfather is just a big kid himself, and now Gracie has a new six-year-old stepbrother to look after besides.

It's true that Gracie is pretty amazing, but even she may not be able to keep this new family together. Will she ever have time for herself—for a boyfriend or a life of her own? And what if she *does* grow up to be just like her mom?

—*Marianne Tait Pridemore*

Amazing True Stories   Grade 5–Adult
By Don L. Wulffson

If you like watching *Unsolved Mysteries* on TV, you'll love *Amazing Stories*. Don Wulffson has collected over fifty stories too strange to be true, but they are. Here's an example:

In August 1975 in Scotland, three unlucky men set out to rob a bank. It took them a while to get *into* the bank—they got stuck in the revolving door. After being rescued by a security guard, they made it into the main room, but when they announced "This is a stick-up!" everyone burst out laughing. (After all, these were the guys who had just gotten stuck in the door.) "What's wrong with ya? This is for real, and we want $10,000!" More laughter. So the gang leader lowered his demand to $1,000 . . . $100 . . . finally to $1 each. At this point everyone in the bank was howling with laughter. Angry, the leader pulled out his pistol, jumped up on the counter to get everyone's attention, stumbled, fell, and broke his leg. In their rush to escape, his two buddies pushed the wrong way on the revolving door—and got stuck.

Not all the stories are comedies, though. The chapter called "Accidents and Disasters" tells about nine-year-old Justin Bunker, who fell through the ice while skating. He'd been underwater for twenty minutes by the time the paramedics were able to fish him out and rush him to the hospital. Doctors wrapped him in a heating blanket and put an oxygen mask over his face. After eight hours, Justin sat up, took off the mask, and (struggling to free himself of the heating pad) said, "Let go of me!" Justin went home a few weeks later, normal and healthy. How could anyone survive after being submerged for twenty minutes in ice-cold water? Justin did because he was "quick-frozen" and in a state of suspended animation.

And those are only two of the *Amazing True Stories* you'll find in this book.

—*Diantha McCauley*

Among the Volcanoes   Grades 7–12
By Omar S. Castaneda

"Trouble." That's the first thing everyone said. They took one look at the young American who'd just arrived to do medical research and they labeled him "trouble!" You see, here in our Guatemalan village, people prefer to do things the old way, the way they've always been done, generation after generation. And what I say is, have the old familiar ways ever gotten us anywhere? No! We're as poor, uneducated, and helpless as ever! Take my mother, for example. She's terribly ill, but she won't take medicine, simply because that's not the way we do things here. So now, since I'm the oldest daughter, I have to stay home and take care of the family, even though I want to go to school and become a teacher. I want to change the way we live, to make it better for my family and my village. My father says, "The poor have no possibility of changing anything," but I intend to try. I want at least *some* of my dreams to come true.

—*Sister M. Anna Falbo, CSSF*

Anastasia at This Address   Grades 5–6
By Lois Lowry

Anastasia, Meredith, Daphne, and Sonya have decided to give up boys—chasing boys, that is. However, this may be a little difficult for Anastasia, because she has just started corresponding with an SWM.

Going through the personal ads of the *New York Review of Books*, Anastasia came across one that read, "SWM, 28, boyish charm, inherited wealth, looking for tall young woman, nonsmoker, to share Caribbean vacations, reruns of *Casablanca* and romance." She found out that SWM stands for Single White Male, and she just knew she'd fit all his requirements, never mind about that fifteen-year age difference. Fifteen years is no big deal—after all, her dad is ten years older than her mom. So, Anastasia took the plunge and wrote SWM the first of many interesting letters, and she signed it with her new nickname, SWIFTY— Single White Intelligent Female: Tall, Young!

But waiting for a reply from SWM is not the only thing on Anastasia's mind. There's a wedding in the works, and Anastasia and her best friends are going to be junior bridesmaids. The trials and tribulations of getting a dress, shoes, choosing flowers, getting her ears pierced, deciding on a hairstyle demand every bit of Anastasia's attention—that is, until SWM himself shows up on the scene. To find out what happens when these two meet, read *Anastasia at This Address*.

—*Mary McCurry*

Andra   Grades 9–12
By Louise Lawrence

Did you ever play "What If?" Louise Lawrence plays "What If" in her book *Andra*. It goes like this:

What if a teen-age girl had to have an organ transplant?

What if the transplanted organ was the brain?

What if it was only one part of the brain, the part that controls vision?

What if . . . she started "seeing" life as it was 2,000 years earlier—in the year 1987?

What if this girl lived in strictly-controlled, post-nuclear, underground world, but yearned for the freedoms found in the natural world destroyed 2,000 years before?

What if she decided to rebel against the rigid structure of her world and to embrace the world that was?

What if thousands of other young people decided to join her?

What if . . . you read *Andra*, by Louise Lawrence?

—*Tracy Revel*

Angela and the Broken Heart   Grades 5–8
By Nancy K. Robinson

Angela's only six and a half and just starting second grade, but already she has problems! For one thing, how can she tell Eddie Bishop that she'll marry him when he hasn't come back to school? Then there's the whole wedding to plan while she waits for him to return, and in the meantime there's a new boy, Luther, who acts as though he hates Angela worse than anything else in the world. Her new teacher, Ms. Blizzard, doesn't seem to like her much either—why else would she take *The Wizard of Oz* away from her?

But that's not all. Starting high school has made her wonderful older brother Nathaniel dress and talk very strangely. He's in love—with a girl who doesn't know he's alive; Angela can't understand *that* at all! She wishes he could meet her friend Mandy's older sister, who seems much nicer. So when it's time for her birthday party, Angela thinks up the perfect plan to bring them together.

As usual, Angela's plans don't work out quite the way she intended, and now she has Nathaniel's broken heart to deal with. Can Angela fix a broken heart?

—*Donna L. Scanlon*

Animal Amazing   Grade 5–Adult
By Judith Herbst

Redsy wouldn't go. No matter how much his owner, William Montgomery, coaxed him, Redsy wouldn't get on the fishing boat. William couldn't understand it. Redsy loved riding on the boat. But now he just kept barking, crouching at the end of the pier. Redsy's weird behavior made William feel uneasy. Well, if Redsy wouldn't go, he would skip fishing today. It was a shame, though . . . perfect day for fishing—dead calm.

It was early afternoon when the wind rose. Storm waves forty feet high tore into the shore. By the end of that 1938 hurricane, six hundred people had been killed. William Montgomery would always say afterwards that Redsy had saved both their lives with his "canine radar."

Can animals predict natural disasters like hurricanes and earthquakes? Scientists in China think so. In 1974, after watching animal behavior, the Chinese authorities had over a million people evacuated from their town—just hours before an earthquake hit. American scientists use cute little cockroaches to help predict earthquakes. How can a cockroach predict an earthquake? You'll find out in *Animal Amazing*.

Psychic animals aren't the only mind-boggling creatures you'll find in this book. Animals that grow their own spare parts, animals that can apparently read other animals' minds, animals that fall out of the sky—they're all here! Think about that last one, by the way. There you are, minding your own business, when a herring lands on your head! Frogs, fish, lizards and even snakes have been known to drop out of the sky. Where do they come from? Beats me. Know what else beats me? How did those live toads get into the middle of those pieces of coal? Coal takes hundreds of thousands of years to form. How did the toads survive? But I think the best brain-beater in this whole book is the story about the thing that came out of that big piece of limestone in 1856. What was it? Read *Animal Amazing* and be amazed.

—*Julie Bray*

April Upstairs   Grades 5–8

Darcy Downstairs
By Susan Beth Pfeffer

Darcy, who is a friendly, outgoing seventh-grader, lives downstairs in a two-family house, and now her cousin April, who's the same age, is living upstairs. April and her mother moved into the house to be close to their relatives after the divorce, and close is what the two girls have become—their lives are interwined, even though their personalities are very different.

April, who's a little shy, is nervous about making friends at her new school, an elite private girls' academy. But although she joins the newspaper staff reluctantly, she gains instant fame after she has a telephone interview with a famous rock star on a mercy mission, whose plane crashes the following day. However, instant fame can cause problems, as April soon discovers.

Darcy spends most of her free time with April now, which is making her own friends jealous. To change this, the two girls plan a party—they'll bring both sets of friends together. Planning takes up so much of Darcy's time that she ignores her schoolwork, fails a test, and ends up copying her cousin's book report. If the party's a success, will it be worth it? And what will April do if she finds out Darcy has stolen her book report?

Living in the same house with your favorite cousin can be lots of fun—but it can also be a lot of trouble!

—Eldean Kechely

Note: The dust jackets of these books show girls who look sixteen or seventeen years old, but the characters are actually about thirteen.

Author! Author!   Grades 5–6
By Susan Ferris

It would be nice if we could pick our parents, but we can't. We can only decide to choose our own lives—and that is just what Valerie is in the process of doing. She's twelve years old, and she's just had her first book published, with the help of Tekla, an old family friend who is also a well-known poet. But being a published author is not all it's cracked up to be. Valerie's friends tease her, and interviewers ask her questions she can't answer because she doesn't remember why she wrote what she did—after all, she was only seven when she wrote *The Magic Butter Churn!* In fact, being an author is sometimes just plain confusing.

Maybe what Valerie needs is a really serious subject to write about— like perhaps her lost twin. She's always felt as if she and some shadowy twin had been separated at birth, as if she were a changeling. She doesn't look like either of her parents—in fact, she looks more like Tekla than anybody else. Perhaps *that's* why Tekla and her parents aren't such good friends any more—maybe she is really Tekla's child, and her mother gave her away to her own best friends. Then it's not her *twin* she misses—it's her *mother!* That's why Tekla understands her so well, too, and why she made sure Valerie's book got published.

And now that Valerie knows the truth, what is she going to do? Should she tell Tekla, or the people she has always called her parents? Maybe, just maybe, she should write a story about it. Tekla has said she wants to see Valerie's new novel—if she's one of the main characters in it, surely she won't keep the truth about Valerie a secret any longer.

Valerie is an author, but to find out if she really writes the true story, you'll have to read *Author! Author!* for yourself.

—*J. R. B.*

B-Ball: **Grades 5–12**
The Team That Never Lost a Game
By Ron Jones

For nine years, Ron Jones coached basketball for the Special Olympics. They were years of humor, love, frustration, and understanding, and he shares them with you in this book. It's amazing, but reading the descriptions of some of the games, with the running and the shouting and the unbelievable plays, you may almost think that Jones is writing about the pro leagues. And even if he's not, in the minds of the physically disabled and mentally slow people who make up the team, every time the ball hits their hands, or rolls across the floor, or (miracle of miracles!) goes in the basket, it is the crowning achievement of their difficult lives. Jones' methods of teaching them basketball are amazing. He knows that the best he can hope for is for his team to be frantic *within* a pattern. He sets up signals (which may be ignored), then watches in wonder as his players give each other their own signals and encouragement beyond anything a coach could ever plan! There are other amazing stories: a kid who talks to the ball, a hidden-ball trick, a kid who won't stop running—and don't forget the Pizza Defense (when things get too frantic, Jones knows the team will calm down if they're assured of pizza after the game). They play all comers, including a Chinese team. And once an opposing team played too rough, and Jones pulled his team off the court, because the confused, hurt looks in his players' eyes meant more than finishing the game. I think you'll agree. You know how true-life stories can be—you get involved. I still find myself wondering about the players—are they still alive, does anyone care about them and play ball with them? Meet some amazing heroes, and a truly unforgettable team, in *B-Ball: The Team That Never Lost a Game.*

—Mark Anderson

Babyface   Grades 7–8
By Norma Fox Mazer

Toni and Julie were inseparable. They weren't just next-door neighbors, they were buddies from the time they were very young. Although their birthdays were a week apart in May, they almost always celebrated together, with their families. At their fourteenth party, they blew out the candles on the cake together and they each made a wish. Toni wished for nothing in her life to change, while Julie wished for "tons of changes." And it was Julie's wish that came true.

That summer everything changed. Julie and Toni were separated from each other, and Toni and her older sister, Martine, grew closer. Toni had always felt that Martine treated her coldly, and she had hated the harsh way Martine would speak to their father. By the end of that summer, though, Toni not only understood Martine's attitude toward their parents but herself began to see them in a different light, because of something Martine told her, something that had happened before Toni was born.

What happened that summer to change Toni's friendship with Julie? her relationship with her sister? and her admiration for her father and mother? Find out when you meet Toni Chessmore, formerly known as Babyface.

—Kathleen B. Ellis

Balloons and Other Poems   Grades 3–4
By Deborah Chandra

This poem is called "Burglar." Is it about a robber? A thief? Let's see
who or what the burglar is, as it

    creeps
    upon my rooftop
    like a burglar
    in the night,
    runs fingers
    round my window,
    finding everything
    shut tight.
    Startled
    when the morning dawns,
    it dangles from the eaves,
    drops d
          o
             w
                n
    sneaking away
    without a sound,
    leaving small
    footprints
    on
    the
    ground.

The burglar who creeps and sneaks in the night is . . . rain.

These poems are about ordinary things—balloons and fireworks, autumn leaves and Christmas presents. But the words let us see the everyday in new and wondrous ways. Listen to "The Purr":

    My cat churns
    a purple purr—
    A throatful
    of pebbles
    turning slowly
    underwater,

her old song bubbles.

Swirling easy
through the lazy current
swims a warm, mouse-flavored
Meow.

Listen to "the purple purr" and the "mouse-flavored meow" of your own cat as you linger over *Balloons and Other Poems*.

—*Diane L. Deuel*

Bartholomew Fair   Grades 5–8
By Mary Stolz

Among the thousands of people who opened their eyes to that morning in London Town—to the fog, to the summons of the bells—were six folk of varying stations in life, from the great Queen herself to a starving apprentice, who would that day go to the Bartholomew Fair. It was the twenty-fourth day of August in the year 1597, and all of those fairgoers would return home that night, save one.

And who were the six who went to the fair that day? First there was Queen Elizabeth, once a brilliant young woman, now old, ugly, grouchy, and (some said) losing her touch with the common people of her realm. She was going to the fair to be seen by her subjects, to walk among them and perhaps regain their favor, if indeed she'd ever lost it.

Merrycat lived at the royal palace too, but she had never seen the Queen—she was one of the kitchen slaveys, a scullerymaid in the root vegetable kitchen. She wanted to go to the fair, and she slipped out through an unlocked door without permission, knowing she might not have a place to sleep that night if the vegetable cook found out she was gone.

Jeremy was one of the Queen's Scholars at the Westminster School, and he had a daring plan to persuade the Undermaster to let him and his friend Jones go to the fair. He almost couldn't believe it when his plan worked—now he and Jones had three whole hours to spend at the fair, instead of studying Latin.

John Kempton was a cloth merchant, very wealthy and very large. He had a big voice and a way of persuading people to do what he wanted even when they didn't want to. And today he was going to the fair, where he would see all the sights: the freaks, the acrobats, the puppet shows and minstrels—and of course the pickpockets. Merchant Kempton loved watching a skillful pursesnatcher at work, but he kept a close eye on his own money!

Will Shaw was an orphan, apprenticed to a stonemason who worked him long hours, fed him almost nothing, and let him sleep on a pile of straw in the unheated workshop. That morning he had been kicked awake and ordered to fill the cart with bricks. Work was all that Will had ever known, that and the hunger that never left him. That morning, dodging a pail of garbage tossed out onto the street from a window above, Will found a carrot—a whole, fresh, entire, large, and beautifully orange carrot! He snatched it up, wiped it off, and promptly ate half, giving the other half to the old carthorse, who was as skinny as he was. Perhaps it was an omen, that carrot—no sooner had he eaten it than he met a puppetmaster on his way to the fair, and not long afterwards he himself was going the same way. Words like "holiday," "fun," and "play" were as foreign to Will as another language, but today perhaps he would learn their meaning.

Follow these six people as they join the thousands who go to Bartholomew Fair on its last day in the summer of 1597. Discover how their lives changed because of the events of that day, and which of the six never made it home that night.

—*J. R. B.*

Be My Baby: Grade 9–Adult
How I Survived Mascara, Miniskirts and Madness, or
My Life as a Fabulous Ronette
By Ronnie Spector, with Vince Waldron

In early January of 1964, snuggling with John Lennon in a hotel room with a view of nighttime London, Ronnie knew that if someone had told her a year before that this was where she'd be, she would have thought the speaker was nuts. John felt the same way. The success of their groups—the Ronettes and the Beatles—had left both their heads spinning, but neither of them would have changed their lives back to where they were before for anything in the world.

Maybe if Ronnie had had a crystal ball on that night, she might have felt differently. She would have known then that marriage to the eccentric producer Phil Spector would effectively stop her career, as he tried to mold her into his concept of the perfect wife. She would have known that she'd be a virtual prisoner in her house, behind barbed wire;

known of the cycle of alcohol abuse and sanitarium treatment she would face; known of the inflatable Phil dolls, the false pregnancies, and the emotional battering she would live with for years. But even if she had been able to foresee her life, it might not have made any difference in the long run, because above all Ronnie Spector was a survivor.

From the beehives and heavy mascara of the Ronette days through her strangling marriage and into her later solo efforts, this is Ronnie Spector's story.

—Jeff Blair

Beast   Grade 9–Adult
By Peter Benchley

The legendary dragon of ancient sea lore is feeding in the deep waters off the coast of Bermuda. But there's very little food to be found—the deep waters have been fished out. Hunger drives the great predator upward to shallower waters—hunger so strong it will attack anything moving in or on the sea.

Whip Darling, an expert Bermuda fisherman, is having his own troubles finding any deep sea fish in the waters around Bermuda. He is struggling to make a living from a nearly barren sea. When Whip discovers a drifting, empty life raft with strange scratch marks on it, he doesn't know what to think. Then a fishing boat explodes close to shore for no apparent reason, and a whale-watcher claims to have sighted a monster. As the monster strikes again and again, Whip realizes what's out there. He knows it's a beast so gigantic, so driven by ever-increasing hunger, that it will kill and continue killing until it is destroyed. But what—and who—can destroy the *Beast*?

—Sue Padilla

Beauty   Grade 9–Adult
By Sheri S. Tepper

Father Raymond gave me a book, to write down all the things I cannot say to anyone. And it's my intention to tell the story of my entire life, so that when I am aged I can remember everything. Old people often forget; I've asked them. If I had a mother I would ask her. I never knew my mother. When I asked about her, I was hushed, and then I was punished.

So I think about my father, who's come back from another Crusade. He seems to have forgotten all about me. He's brought this weasely widow home with him, and she's kicked me out of my quarters, but my father doesn't even realize it. When she threatened to get rid of my cat, I escaped and went to see my half-sister (Father does philander). She looks just like me, only she's poor and has a mother all to herself.

We share lots of secrets, but one I haven't shared with anyone is about my mother. I found a box in the far-most tower, with a note from Her. She says she's a Faery, and that on my sixteenth birthday I'll prick my finger on a spindle and fall asleep for a hundred years. I've got to figure out a way to avoid this catastrophe. Maybe my half-sister. . . .

Beauty does not sleep for a hundred years, but there are times she wishes she had—like when she is transported into the twenty-first century, where all loveliness is gone and horror reigns.

Disney was never like this. And fairy tales may never again be the innocent pastime you thought they were. But it's a beauty of a story!
—*Lesley S. J. Farmer*

Bedrock   Adult
By Lisa Alther

Clea was a successful mother and photographer. She had managed a very open marriage for over twenty-two years, accompanying her husband from continent to continent, leading a New York City social life. And then she fell in love with bedrock New England, and abandoned everything for a run-down home in Roches Ridges.

Everything about Roches Ridges was perfect, quaint—even when the bathtub fell through the ceiling. It was old-time America revisited: sparkling laundry on the line, weed-free lawn, friendly priest, no locks on the doors. She would find peace and purpose, Clea thought, to replace the restlessness and boredom that had plagued her. And she'd find time to create something—the perfect coffee-table book.

Instead, Clea found time to rummage through her own past and confront her lifelong obsessions. She had time to see through the veneer of Roches Ridge and discover the meanness of small-hearted people, the petty scandals of the beehived wives, the despair of those with condemned sexual preferences. She had time to burn all her glossy photographs of this backwater village.

But somehow, in the jumbled-up lives of Clea, her family and friends, and the community of Roches Ridge, a startling acceptance began to take root. "Ever stop to think this whole dang town might be a few logs short of a cord?"

Like Clea, you too will smile and answer, "Well, it's not what I expected when I first arrived here. But it'll do just fine."

—*Lesley S. J. Farmer*

The Bell Tolls at Mousehaven Manor Grades 3-4
By Mary DeBall Kwitz

Minabell Mouse can't imagine who sent her this mysterious package. But she senses something threatening inside, so she quickly hides the package beneath the stones of the old fireplace in the music room. What she doesn't realize is the extent of the danger that has entered Mousehaven Manor.

It isn't until Count Von Flittermouse, an evil vampire bat, drops in for a visit and a mysterious fire breaks out in the music room that Minabell knows she must open the package. What does she find inside, and what *is* the connection between the Count and the mysterious parcel? Read *The Bell Tolls at Mousehaven Manor* to find out!

—*Cara A. Waits*

Benny and the Crazy Contest Grades 3-4
By Cheryl Zach

Have you ever wanted something *really* bad but just didn't know how to go about getting it? That was Benny's problem. He wanted a bike. Not just any bike, but a shiny blue mountain bike. You see, his old one was scratched, almost all the paint was gone, the front tire was always flat, and it was much too *small*. Worst of all, the girl next door, Melissa, had a new red bike, and Murray down the street had a brand new bike even shinier than Melissa's. Benny's other problem was he had no money for a new bike, and neither did his parents.

Then one morning Benny saw the ad for the contest: "Big Prizes!" And in the middle of the page was a beautiful blue mountain bike with all the trimmings a bike should have. Benny didn't even bother to look at the other prizes; he only saw that bike.

All he had to do was write a forty-five word entry about why he liked Potter's Peanut Butter. This turned out to be slightly harder than he'd expected. After all, what could he say about peanut butter special enough to make him a winner? Somehow he had to figure it out—it was the only way to win his bike.

—*Cara A. Waits*

Bering Bridge: Grade 7–Adult
The Soviet-American Expedition from Siberia to Alaska
By Paul Schurke

Though we have all heard about *glasnost* and how it may allow
Soviet citizens to relate more openly to Americans, it still seems unreal
to most of us. The USSR, our most powerful global rival, is so far away
and so alien—how many of us have ever met a Russian? How many
of us believe that we as individuals could affect the touchy relations
between our two countries?

Young American explorer Paul Schurke believed that he could literally bring change from America to the Soviet Union. Paul was an Arctic
adventurer who had experienced the glory of a successful expedition to
the North Pole. But for him, something was missing: a sense of mission,
of meaning behind his achievement. He wanted to go on exploring the
Arctic, but he needed a purpose. Suddenly an outrageous idea occurred
to him.

From his knowledge of the north, Paul was aware that the border between Siberia and Alaska, once open to the native peoples on both sides
who share a common culture, had been closed by over forty years of
cold war. Eskimo families had been separated, isolated by an imaginary
line that runs between America's Little Diomede Island and Russia's
Big Diomede. Paul saw the International Date Line, "the global seam
that separates today from tomorrow, and the United States from the
Soviet Union," as the perfect spot to bring the two nations together.
And he planned to do it himself.

Just like you and me, Paul did not know any Russians personally.
He was not involved in politics or government. But propelled by his
own vision, in March 1989 this young man set off with a brave team
of six Soviets and six Americans, ordinary citizens like himself, to cross
1200 miles of treacherous icy terrain by dogsled, ski, and walrus-skin
boat. These dogsled diplomats visited remote native villages from Siberia to Alaska, reuniting native team members from both sides with
long-lost family members and sharing the tribal customs that had en-
dured despite two nations' estrangement. At the journey's triumphant
climax, with the approval of their nations' leaders Gorbachev and
Bush, the team straddled the ice-bound Soviet-American border on the
Date Line, opening it for visa-free travel among natives.

How did an ordinary young American achieve this remarkable feat,
despite defections, sub-zero weather, primitive transportation, and
tricky team communications among five cultures and languages? Why

did Gorbachev himself and the Soviet people greet Paul Schurke as a hero, issuing a postage stamp in honor of his achievement, when most Americans never heard of his trek? What can Schurke's experience mean to you and me if we also long to make a difference? Let Paul Schurke tell you in his own words about *Bering Bridge: The Soviet-American Expedition from Siberia to Alaska.*

—Cathi MacRae

Bernie and the Bessledorf Ghost　　　Grades 3-6
By Phyllis Reynolds Naylor

How do you communicate with a ghost? That is Bernie Magruder's problem when a ghostly creature materializes in his family's hotel. Since the ghost appears to be a boy about Bernie's age, the Magruders fear it has come to take their son to his grave. However, Bernie has other ideas. He's convinced the apparition has come to ask for help. But it seems to have no way to talk with people. So Bernie and his friends, Weasel and Georgene, set out to learn all they can about ghosts and hauntings.

The three learn some surprising things about the old Bessledorf Hotel, the tragedy that occurred there, and the original owner's mysterious burial ground. Bernie finally thinks he understands why the ghost has come back to the hotel, but he *still* doesn't know how to communicate with it.

If you've ever wondered how to talk with a real ghost, read this book and find out.

—Karol Schmitt Rockwin

Beyond the Door　　　Grades 7-8
By Gary L. Blackwood

Tully wasn't about to give up on Scott, the tall, thin boy who was so reserved and so intelligent; there was something about him that intrigued her and made her keep on trying. Even though he had refused an invitation to her birthday party, forgotten he was supposed to meet her after school, hadn't wanted to come to supper with her big, warm family, had been clearly reluctant to help her at the library (which seemed to be his favorite hangout), and now said that he couldn't go with her on the annual Cedar Point trip—no, in spite of everything, Tully wasn't going to write Scott off just yet.

But she *was* going to give him a piece of her mind. He'd said he couldn't come to Cedar Point because he had to meet somebody, and she'd just seen him go into the library—alone. The nerve of him!

Tully ran through the library after him as quietly as she could, arriving at the study room just in time to catch the door before it latched behind him. Angrily, she heaved the door open to confront him—but he wasn't there! She was staring into darkness. Confused, she reached for the light switch but couldn't find it. Somehow she felt suspended in thin air. What was happening? Where was Scott? What was that hazy green landscape outside the foggy window? Wait—there *weren't* any windows in the library study room! What was going on?

—*Kristina Peters*

The Big Book for Peace   Grade 3–Adult
Ann Durell and Marilyn Sachs, eds.

It's not easy to learn about peace in our world. So much surrounds us that is just the opposite. Friends quarrel, strangers fight, countries war with each other. It's no wonder we long for peace—we never seem to have it.

Seth Laughlin knows about peace. Seth, a Quaker, fights quietly against the evil of slavery in pre–Civil War Virginia, and later against the evil of war itself. Jimbo Kurasaki knows about peace too. A young Japanese-American, he writes from a concentration camp where he is to spend who knows how many years, because America is at war with Japan and Jimbo looks like the enemy. Even animals, though they sometimes fight savagely, instinctively seek peace. Kristy sees that as she watches the song sparrows nesting in the nearby meadow while she awaits her father's return from war.

Peace. What a beautiful word when it is spoken quietly. What a strong rallying-cry when it is shouted fearlessly. And what a magnificent goal toward which to strive.

—*Nancy L. Chu*

The Big Book of Hell   Grade 9–Adult
By Matt Groening

Before Bart and Homer Simpson, there were Binky and Bongo. Before Marge and Lisa, there were Akbar and Jeff. Before life in Springfield, there was Life in Hell.

In the foreword to this book, Matt Groening admits to being torn between the desire to amuse and the desire to annoy. There's enough of both to satisfy everyone here.

Learn how Childhood is Hell. How School is Hell. Could it be that Work is Hell? Learn What Alarms Kids (teenagers, the smell of Grandma, nightmares of being naked at school, etc.). Visit Akbar and Jeff's Liposuction Hut.

All in all, you'll have a Hell of a good time.

—Jeff Blair

Billy   Grade 9–Adult
By Whitley Streiber

He was gone. He had vanished in the middle of the night, his bike with him. When his parents went upstairs to wake him up and call him to breakfast, he was nowhere to be found.

He was young and gentle and loving. He was *just* the kind of boy that Barton had wanted, had been looking for, the kind who could fill the hole that was left now that all the other boys were gone. Barton would take good care of him; to be sure of that, he'd cased the kitchen before going upstairs to Billy's room. He wanted to make sure that Billy would have everything he could possibly want, so he would never want to leave, so he would never make Barton have to be cruel to him. Barton watched him for a moment before covering his face with the ether-soaked cloth, and then after Billy was unconscious, packed some of his clothes in an old knapsack and carried the boy down the stairs and out to his van. No one stirred. No one knew he had been there, not even when he had to raise the garage door to get Bill's bike out. He would abandon it later on, and hope they would think Billy had just run away.

He knew it was a horrible crime, the worst he could ever commit—but he needed someone too, didn't he? And Billy was so special, so perfect, so wonderful. It was a sin that little boys grew up to be men—but he'd do his best to keep Billy a little boy for a long, long time. After all, Billy was *his* little boy now. Barton's had lots of experience in eluding pursuers, making himself inconspicuous—will Billy's parents and the police be able to trace his steps before it's too late? Before Billy gets too difficult, too demanding, too hard to keep alive?

—J. R. B.

Bizarre Birds and Beasts: Grades 3-6
Animal Verses
By James Marsh

Imagine a world where humans would
Do their best for the planet's good:
Water pure and forests fair—
No pollution to kill the air.
Can we change our ways much faster
And avoid complete disaster?

With this gentle query, enter a world populated by extraordinary animals, birds, fish, and insects: the tiger moth who prowls the night forests like his predatory namesake; the sea turtle whose babies know just where to head upon hatching; the polar bear whose white fur is more than just a fashion statement.

Each poem reminds us of the beauty and wisdom of nature with just a touch of whimsy. As the wise owl says:

Knowledge isn't hard to earn—
The more you listen, the more you learn.

Bizarre Birds and Beasts. Listen, learn, and enjoy!

—*Nancy L. Chu*

Black and White   Grades 3-Adult
By David Macauley

What is this book about? How many stories does it contain? That's up to you to decide—there may be four stories, there may be only one, there may even be four parts of one story. All the events may take place at different times, or they may all take place at the same time. What does it all mean? See for yourself, and you decide!

There are cows in a meadow, commuters waiting at a train station, some strange parents, and a boy returning home—to parents who may or may not be strange at all. What happens when the cows get out of the field, the parents dress up in newspapers, the boy sees things he doesn't believe, and the commuters get a big surprise? Discover the answers for yourself, but beware—those answers may change every time you read this book!

—*J. R. B.*

Black Ice Grade 9–Adult
By Lorene Cary

Lorene Cary was fifteen when she applied to and was accepted by St. Paul's, a formerly all-white, all-male exclusive prep school in New Hampshire. For the first time, St. Paul's was recruiting those it had once ignored—African-American boys and girls, students who weren't necessarily rich, privileged, or part of "the Establishment." Lorene was ready.

Even though she knew that the administrators and teachers of St. Paul's didn't expect their new students to do much besides survive in this elite setting, she was there to let them know that she could do more than that—she would excel!

When she arrived on the posh campus, one of the first students she met was Jimmy Hill, an African-American from Brooklyn and probably the skinniest boy she'd ever seen. Like Lorene, he was ambitious, curious, and unafraid of this rich new world they'd entered. "Listen to me, darling," he said to her, "we are going to turn this mother out!"

And so they began. Overcoming teenage snafus, failures, prejudices, and even a little rule-breaking, Lorene went on to become a teacher and later a trustee of the school. Her secret, she says, is that she always slid forward, never backward, on the rarefied and impenetrable surface that was the St. Paul's campus—so glassy, cold, and treacherous that she remembers it as *Black Ice*.

—*Faye A. Powell*

Blindfold Grades 7–12
By Sandra McCuaig

The headlines read:
YOUNG BROTHERS JUMP TO DEATH: LOVED SAME GIRL!
Sally O'Leary is that girl.

How could this happen? Why doesn't anyone believe that Sally is not to blame? Certainly none of her friends consider her blameless, nor do Benji and Joel's parents. And what about Sally's mother? What does she really believe? Not even Sally herself can face the truth, or talk about the brothers and her friendship with them, or explain why blind Joel was obsessed with the world of the spirits. Who can unlock the mystery inside Sally, so that everyone will know the truth behind Benji and Joel's deaths?

—*Barbara Diment*

Bloodroot   Grades 5-8
By W. D. Hobbie

Bloodroot is Lizzie's favorite place in the world, and Grama Ax is
Lizzie's favorite person. So it's no wonder that Lizzie is more than
excited about spending the summer at Bloodroot with Grama Ax while
her parents travel in Egypt. Grama Ax's farm, which is in the *real*
country in New England, where wildflowers bloom wildly and bears
drink at the streams, is named after the bloodroot, a tiny white
woodland flower that has a blood-red liquid in its stem.

When Lizzie arrives at the farm, she's surprised to find that there are
many battles to be fought this special summer, but she's as plucky and
spirited as her elderly grandmother and she has no doubt that together
they can conquer any obstacle. First she must help Grama Ax organize
the farming community to keep out a developer who plans to pave the
land with condos, parking lots, and a shopping mall. Then she must figure out how to stop horrible Nobby Miller and his wicked slingshot.

The third battle, however, proves to be the most difficult. After
Grama Ax suffers a bad fall while exploring the woods with Lizzie, Lizzie must convince her parents that Grama isn't too old to go on living
alone in the country. Is Lizzie the only one who understands that selling
Bloodroot would mean the end of Grama Ax? Old age may be the
toughest foe that Lizzie and her grandmother have come up against yet,
but they are a winning team—or are they?

—Elizabeth Sue Lewis

The Bookmaker's Daughter: Adult
A Memory Unbound
By Shirley Abbott

Do you remember playing jacks? The onesies, twosies, threesies,
allsies—all with one bounce? Eggs in a basket—no bounce! Hens in the
henhouse, cows over the moon, shooting stars. How about the jump
rope song, "Teddy bear, Teddy bear, turn around, Teddy bear, Teddy
bear, touch the ground"? Do you remember ration stamps and putting
yellow food coloring in oleo so that it would look like butter? Or how
about the "dawn of plastic eating," when Jell-O, Spam, Velveeta, and
instant pudding were on the kitchen shelf of every modern housewife?
Shirley Abbott reminisces about all these things as she tells the story
of her Arkansas childhood during the Forties and Fifties.

Her father was a bookmaker in Hot Springs, Arkansas, the town that had once been a get-away retreat for Al Capone and was now home to Owney Madden, proprietor of the famous Cotton Club. In the home of "Hat" Abbott, the sun rose and set by post time for the first and eighth races. Each day, dressed like a "gentleman bandit" in his tailor-made three-piece suit, he would go to the Southern Club where gamblers would lay their money down on horses at all the big tracks— Hialeah, Pimlico, Churchill Downs, Santa Anita, and Gulf Stream. The Abbott family prospered. Shirley was pampered and wore her hair in ringlets. The Abbotts bought their rented home, painted and papered, hung curtains, and filled the rooms with new furniture.

And Shirley's life was happy, too. She played make-believe with her dog Buster. Her parents were always willing to read to her; her father, especially, was a great lover of language and stories. "If our lives had been a newsreel," Shirley says, "my father would have been the narrator—the soothsayer, the bard, the scop. I was born, he thought, to listen." He introduced her to Athena, Zeus, Ivanhoe, the Happy Prince, and the Lady of Shalott. If he wasn't reading her stories from books, he was telling her tales of his troubled and adventuresome youth. And Shirley would listen for hours when the politicians like Judge Witt came to visit on hot summer evenings. From them she heard sly, comical stories about the town's do-gooders and reformers, and she laughed right along with the grown-ups when they ridiculed the foolishness of narrow-minded preachers.

But Shirley saw another side of family life as well. She saw the handkerchief tied around her father's head. He wore it like a sign that said, "Beware, Father has a migraine, stay away!" She saw the fury in his face nearly every night at dinner, when he would verbally abuse his wife for her Southern style of cooking. And finally she witnessed the reformers' revenge, when they won the election and put an end to Hot Springs' wide-open gambling clubs. This not-so-pleasant turning point in the Abbott family saga brought many changes in their lifestyle. The new house was sold and a farm bought instead. There were no more frilly dresses, patent leather shoes, or C-notes in stacks on the kitchen table.

Shirley's story, however, is of the father who bequeathed her his bookcase and the treasured books that she carries with her everywhere she goes, "my legacy, my impedimenta, sometimes my dead weight." He left her something greater than the riches reaped from gambling— his love for language and storytelling.

—*Susan Weaver*

Boonsville Bombers   Grades 3–4
By Alison Cragin Herzig

If you love baseball as much as Emma does, you're probably a card collector too. Would you be willing to trade your most valuable rookie card (of Owen Zabriskie) just to be allowed to play ball with the boys? Doesn't seem like a fair trade, does it? Especially when the game is over after the first out! You see, one of the players, Joe, doesn't think girls can play baseball. In fact, Joe thinks girls have arms like chicken wings and scream when they see a fly ball coming. But when Emma makes a shoestring catch on his first hit of the day, he is humiliated and ends the game by taking his bat (the only bat) home.

Needless to say, Emma is disappointed, but she focuses her attention on the big game Saturday. She and her brother are going to their first major-league ballgame ever, and Owen Zabriskie is expected to get his 3000th career hit! But there's one little problem: her dad has only three tickets, the game is sold out, and at the last minute Joe unexpectedly appears. It seems that her brother has invited him along, sure that Emma will give up *her* ticket. What will Emma do? This is a big game . . . is a fair trade possible?

—Lisa Broadhead

Borderlands   Grade 7–Adult
By Peter Carter

When Ma died, me and my brother Bo ran into a raft o' troubles. We were Texas ranchers, and like most of the other small ranchers back then, right after the War Between the States, we ended up cold and hungry most of the time. But we did own our land, free and clear. That is, we thought we did, until the preacher showed up with a note that said our ma had borrowed money against the ranch.

Being a man of God, he did what he considered right—and threw us off of the land that our grandparents had claimed. He did, though, direct us north to a man named Clark in the town of Lookout so that we could get us some work on a cattle drive. When we got there, after a seven-day trek, Clark was long gone. We didn't take to Lookout, and it didn't take to us. In fact, we weren't welcome there at all! But as we left town, the marshall came after us, proving that he wasn't such a bad sort after all, and told us about a drover off a ways who could maybe use some help. Bo got hired for money and I was allowed to tag along, but I sure showed them I could pull my weight. Walking those long-horns up to Abilene was hard and dirty, but I did a good job and made some friends.

The first thing we did when we got to Abilene was buy some new duds, and then me and Bo looked in on the saloons and the gambling halls. Bo took a hand in a crooked poker game, and got shot down dead in the street. That's when I changed.

I may look like a successful storekeeper here in Dodge, but I'm really the man who's going to get my brother's killer and make him pay for what he done. If you want to hang around and see how I do it, read *Borderlands*.

—Di Herald

The Boss Dog   Adult
By M. F. K. Fisher

Mary named him Boss Dog the first time she saw him. That was in the Cafe Glacier in Aix-en-Provence, France. She and her sister Anne and their mother had just arrived from the States for a year's stay, and they were feeling like lost souls. They had decided to stop at the cafe for a snack because they were just too depressed and tired to wander around aimlessly any longer. While they were sitting there, he entered the cafe, and they were all struck with his air of absolute authority and control. Anne realized right away that he was something ultimate. Physically he was a large fellow with a rather fat rear, and it was obvious that he came from mixed genealogical background. Not your typical French physique, and not even very handsome. Except for his unquestionable authority.

Anne said that he looked like the sort of character that adventures would happen to, and after they got to know him, they shared his adventures vicariously. He became a sort of orientation point for them during that often lonely, exciting, and frustrating year in a foreign country.

He was, without question, the most unforgettable character any of them had ever met. And he was also, unquestionably, a dog.

—Margie Reitsma

The Boy in the Moon   Grades 7–12
By Ron Koertge

Nick and Kevin and Frieda. Ever since third grade, they've been best friends, and it seems they always will be—an inseparable trio in their Missouri hometown. Together no matter what. But in September of their senior year, Nick begins to realize that the "always" part of friendship doesn't necessarily mean "together forever."

Nick's first inkling of change comes one afternoon when he returns home from his summer job at the local Funland amusement park. He finds himself thinking about Frieda in a whole new way, and suddenly realizes that over the summer his relationship with her has moved past friendship and into romance. When he goes to meet Kevin, who has just returned from a three-month visit to Los Angeles, he finds himself wondering whether Kevin has changed too. He's waiting for Kevin at the ice cream shoppe where they've all hung out for years when he spots a guy he's never seen before. This guy's talking to *two* girls, and he's funny and sure of himself. Nick notices his bleached hair combed straight up, the suntan, and the hip clothes. He's different from the Missouri kids for sure, yet something about him is familiar. Suddenly, Nick hears the new guy call his name. Somehow, this is Kevin! A bigger, stronger, different Kevin. At that moment, Nick realizes that Kevin has changed indeed, from Mr. Insecurity to Mr. Confident. With Nick and Frieda's new romance and Kevin's new image, there's no telling how their senior year will turn out, or where their friendship is headed.

—*Diane P. Tuccillo*

The Bread Winner   Grades 5–8
By Arvella Whitmore

The year was 1932. Sarah and her parents cried as they drove away from the farm they had owned for so long and had now lost because of the Depression. When they finally parked in front of an unpainted three-room shack, Sarah couldn't believe her eyes. It was worse than their farm machinery shed!

Sarah's father assured her that this house was only temporary; soon he'd find a job and then they'd be able to move to a nicer place. But months passed, and Sarah's father still didn't have work. One day Sarah came home from school to find a note from him that said: "To my way of thinking, it doesn't make a bit of sense to stay here and do nothing while I eat up all your share of the food. So I'm taking the first freight train west. All the way out to California if I have to. . . . There ought to be a decent job somewhere out there in this big country, and if there is, I intend to find it. . . . Now you two keep on doing your best to stay alive, and don't worry about me."

Tears streamed down Sarah's face as she ran toward the freight yards, hoping to catch him. When she returned home, tired and dejected, she found her mother sitting in the dark. The power company had turned off their electricity because they couldn't pay the bill. Without electricity, Sarah's mother couldn't run the washing machine to clean all the clothes they took in—which was their only source of income. While Sarah's mother started talking about the poorhouse, Sarah's mind raced frantically. She had to save the family! But how could a twelve-year-old succeed when so many hard-working adults had failed?

—Susan R. Farber

Breaking Out   Grades 5–6
By Barthe DeClements

Jerry Johnson, Jr. and Grace Elliott are both PKs, and that's why they're worried about entering seventh grade at Riverside Junior High. For Jerry, PK stands for Prisoner's Kid. His father was sent to jail for stealing, and Jerry worries that his classmates from elementary school will blurt out this awful information to his new classmates and teachers. Then, even *more* people won't want to associate with him. Grace, Jerry's next door neighbor and loyal friend, is another kind of PK—a Preacher's Kid. Actually her dad, the Reverend Elliott, is pretty understanding, but her mother has rigid ideas about how a proper young lady should dress and act. On the first day of school, Grace's mother makes her wear a dorky-looking plaid skirt and a long-sleeved blue blouse. For a minute Jerry thinks these may actually be *Mrs.* Elliott's clothes—they sure don't look like anything a junior-high kid would wear! So Grace and Jerry both have reasons to be nervous about starting seventh grade.

And all their worst fears come true. Somehow, those odd clothes she's forced to wear take the spunk out of Grace, and soon the other kids have nicknamed her "Holy Grace." And just as Jerry dreads, there comes the awful day when his favorite new English teacher, Ms. Castle, learns that his father is a criminal. Jerry tells the story of how he and Grace survive their first semester in junior high—in *spite* of being PKs!

—Maureen Whalen

Brother Eagle, Sister Sky   Grade 3–12
By Susan Jeffers (adapted from a speech by Chief Seattle)

When did we discover the fragility of nature? It seems like such a new consciousness, one charged with urgency and a vague fear of what might happen in the future if our ways are not mended soon. But it wasn't always like that.

Not so long ago, people who loved the land, water, and sky cherished them because that was how life should be lived, not because wasteful mistakes needed to be corrected. They recycled, but not because someone paid them or shamed them into doing it. It was just the sensible and responsible path to take, for people who loved the earth and knew they depended upon her. What was borrowed from the land was used until it could be used no more. Little was discarded, because the earth yielded useful things for the people who recognized her goodness and who took only what they needed.

Chief Seattle knew this. As the great chief of the Suquamish and Duwamish tribes saw settlers pouring into his Pacific Northwest homeland, he sensed and feared the changes to come. During treaty negotiation, he delivered an eloquent speech that was intended as a warning. Now his words haunt us because we didn't listen.

In the 1850s no one knew what Chief Seattle was talking about. Now we know. Listen, before it's too late, to words of the past that have extraordinary meaning for the future, in *Brother Eagle, Sister Sky.*

—Nancy L. Chu

Brother Moose   Grades 5–6
By Betty Levin

As Nell sat huddled in the train with her "almost sister" Louisa, she tried to imagine what life would be like in her new foster home. This should have been an exciting time, but Nell was worried about Louisa. They would certainly be separated—what would happen to her friend? Each time the train slowed to a stop, Nell tried to prepare herself for the worst, and finally after what seemed like an eternity, Louisa was led off the train to her new family. Nell hoped and prayed that Louisa would be happy. Not long afterwards, the train stopped again, and now it was Nell's turn to be let off. But there was no one there to meet her; she was told to wait. The night was cold and dark, and Nell was beginning to wonder if she had misunderstood. Maybe she was waiting at the wrong place. No one was there, no one was coming. Suddenly a wagon came rattling up, and the stranger driving it stopped, ordered her inside and started off again. Nell buried herself under the warm blankets and was just drifting off to sleep when she heard angry voices, fighting, and then silence. Without warning the wagon lurched forward, and Nell realized that the stranger was no longer in the driver's seat. Robbers had seized the wagon, and now she was being taken away in a different direction. After traveling miles, the robbers finally stopped for the night. Nell didn't know what to do, but she had to do something quickly. While they slept, she escaped with the wagon and began the task of trying to find the foster family she had never met. Will she find them? and if she does, will they still want her? Join Nell in *Brother Moose*, as she travels across the wilderness to find her new family.

—Paulette Nelson

Bugs Bunny: **All ages**
Fifty Years and Only One Grey Hare
By Joe Adamson

Gangway, man! I want to introduce you to a guy who could trade shots with Bart Simpson, a guy who could run with the Ninja Turtles anytime! My champion? You guessed it: Bugs Bunny! Bugs has been up against some tough dudes in his long cartoon life—Daffy Duck, Elmer Fudd, Yosemite Sam, a giant or two, a mouse, a boxer, a bull, a hairy red monster—and he has outwitted them all.

But he never goes looking for trouble; it's just that he keeps meeting up with characters who want to spoil his fun. Then, watch out! Bugs will use every bit of his genius to get something over on them. He may have to change his shape, employ some special tool, chase and be chased, tunnel like a mole or fly like a bird, but he will always survive. He has been known to stop the flow of Niagara Falls, turn himself into a ballistic missile, and tune a piano with a stick of dynamite (well, he *had* to get rid of that mouse!). Or maybe this time he'll just have to dance for his life with Daffy Duck or lead a symphony orchestra—whatever the problem, he'll keep coming back for more!

This book, *Bugs Bunny: Fifty Years and Only One Grey Hare*, traces the history of Bugs, starting with his creation by a great team of artists in the Warner Brothers studios. The whole behind-the-scenes process of animation is illustrated—the book is loaded with the different types of drawings and sketches that go into making a cartoon. And there are quotes from Bugs' creators, so we learn a lot about where all those wacky ideas came from. Digging into this book is a great way to learn more about something we already know—everybody loves Bugs Bunny!

—*Mark Anderson*

Cabin Fever   Adult
By Elizabeth Jolley

The memories come flooding back in disjointed fragments. The hotel room is unbearably hot and I'm restless, but I can't seem to move except through my memories. I remember ration books after the war, and getting extra rations because I was pregnant. I remember wonderful afternoons and a glorious night with Dr. Metcalf. I remember the doctors, professors for whom I worked as an *au pair* while I waited for baby Helena. And Sister and Mr. Peters at the lying-in hospital, who let me stay on after Helena was born. All these memories are paralyzing me. I know I am here at the hotel for a conference, but I've forgotten the days. I don't think I can leave the room. All I can do is remember . . . .

—*Linda Olson*

A Candidate for Murder   Grades 7–12
By Joan Lowery Nixon

Cary Anderson is a typical sixteen-year-old who stops being typical when her father, the owner of an independent oil company in Texas, decides to run for governor. Her life changes completely. Many of these changes she understands and accepts, but others take her by surprise, and some of them make her *A Candidate for Murder.*

At first the signs are small and annoying. For example, there are the unkind jokes about her father on the radio and in the editorial cartoons of the local newspaper, and the weird crank phone calls she starts getting. But one night she realizes someone is following her car, and then her room is broken into. These are no longer just campaign harassments. Suddenly *she* seems to have become the target. What has she stumbled upon? What does she know? Why would somebody want to harm her?

It's never easy being a candidate's daughter, but in Cary's case it could be more than difficult—it could be deadly.

—*Cynthia Lopuszynski*

Canyons   Grade 7–Adult
By Gary Paulsen

Take me, spirit.
That's what Brennan heard when he found the old skull on a camp
out in the canyons.
Take me, spirit.
The skull was that of Coyote Runs, an Apache Indian boy just Bren-
nan's age. Coyote Runs had been killed by soldiers—bluebellies—while
on his very first raid with the men.
Take me, spirit.
All these years, Coyote Runs' spirit has been trapped in that place
in the canyon where he was killed. Since he had not been able to make
it to the medicine place before dying, his spirit had not been set free.
Take me, spirit.
Now, for the first time, someone knows what happened to Coyote
Run. Someone knows where he died. And now, after all these many
years, someone can do what must be done.
Take me, spirit.
Brennan knows what he has to do—for both of them. He has to free
Coyote Runs.

—Melinda D. Waugh

Castle in the Air   Grades 7–12
By Diana Wynne Jones

A hero named Abdullah, a flying carpet, a genie trapped in a bottle—
all the elements of a fairy tale are combined in this exciting story of love
found, lost, and found again. Abdullah is a young, not very prosperous
rug-merchant who fantasizes that he's really a prince, stolen from his
rightful place by the evil scoundrel Kabul Aqba. When Abdullah falls
asleep on his new carpet, he awakens to find himself in the palace
garden of his dreams, where he meets the beautiful princess Flower-in-
the-night. They fall in love immediately, but Fate is not kind to the
young lovers, and they are soon separated. How Abdullah and Princess
Flower-in-the-night overcome her father's opposition and a terrifying
djinn, how they deal with an obstinate genie who is supposed to grant
Abdullah one wish every day, and how they are led by enchantments
to a castle in the sky make this a wonderful sequel to *Howl's Moving
Castle*. Read *Castle in the Air* for a real trip on a magic carpet.

—Rosemary Moran

Celebrate You!   Grades 7–12
By Julie Tallard Johnson

Do you feel different? Alone? Ugly? Fat? Disliked? Unloved? Even
hated? Everyone does sometimes, but if you feel that way all the time,
it can make you think you're a failure, and convince you that you're just
no good. It may sound like a never-ending circle, but there *is* a way out,
and this book may be able to help you find it. It's called *Celebrate You!*,
and that's what it shows you how to do—how to enjoy being yourself,
discover your good points and emphasize them. And we all have
strengths that will be valuable someday, even if we don't think they are
now. Take a chance—try it. You may learn how to feel better about
yourself, even to celebrate yourself, and that's the key. If *you* don't
celebrate yourself, neither will anyone else! Try it—you may just like
it, and you may just succeed!

                                               —Carol Kappelmann and J. R. B.

The Chickenhouse House   Grades 3–4
By Ellen Howard

Father traced an arc in the air with his hand. "It's all ours as far as
the eye can see," he said. "Good, rich land of our own." Mother shaded
her eyes against the sun and looked. Then she nodded and smiled. "At
last," she said. Alena looked out over the gold prairie grass. Not a bush
or shrub could be seen on the land, not a house or a barn or a shed.
Only, some distance away, a few cottonwood trees along a creek.

That first winter Father, Mother, Alena, William, and baby Fritz all
lived in a very small house—a chickenhouse built just before the cold
weather set in. It was small and drafty and crowded, and Alena wasn't
sure she was going to like it. But as time went on, she got used to it, and
so when their new house was finished it seemd too big to Alena. That
first night in the new house Alena could not sleep. When she closed her
eyes, she thought she could see the shadow of the chickenhouse house,
lonely and silent in the meadow. . . . Alena climbed out of bed. She
pulled her quilt around her shoulders and crept to the door. . . . The
moon showed her the way. The door of the chickenhouse house stood
open, waiting for her. . . . Alena curled up in her quilt in a corner.
Sometime during the night her father came and carried her back to her
bed.

The next day Alena helped him build nesting boxes for the chicken-house. "Will the chicks like our chickenhouse?" she said. "What do you think?" said Father. "It is the right size for chickens," Alena said thoughtfully. "And our house is the right size for us."

—*Deb Kelly*

The Christmas Ark   Grades 3-4
By Robert D. San Souci

Christmas Eve is here, and Elizabeth Branscombe feels . . . well, awful. Worse than awful! The ache in her heart just won't go away. It's hard to celebrate when you feel so sad.

The weather isn't very Christmassy either, with fog swirling eerily around their ship. But it's not just the weather; no, it's the changes that have invaded Elizabeth's life, all too quickly. Papa selling their farm in Maine to join the goldseekers in California. His letter telling Eliza-beth and her mother to take a sailing ship to San Francisco and meet him in their new home. They were supposed to arrive before Christ-mas, but now they are just one day away, fogbound and drifting at sea. No Christmas celebration, no St. Nicholas—and, of course, no Papa.

Mother says that St. Nicholas will find them, that Christmas is a time for magic. Well, Elizabeth could use a little magic right now, be-cause that's what it will take to reunite the family in time for Christmas! Little does she know that magic is on its way on a most unusual ship with an extraordinary captain.

—*Nancy L. Chu*

Circles   Grades 5-8
By Marilyn Sachs

Beebe Clarke is upset—terribly upset. The school drama coach, Mrs. Kronberger, who really understands Shakespeare, has had a heart attack, and now Mrs. Drumm, her substitute, is turning *Romeo and Juliet* into a production of *Renaissance Grease*. And (unkindest cut of all), Beebe has just found out she is not meant to be an actress. She might as well just stay home—except that her mother has started dating, and who wants to be around for that?

Mark Driscoll's life is upset too. He can't enjoy his favorite hobby—astronomy—in the foggy city of San Francisco. He's living with his fa-ther, but all his dad seems to think about are football and women. May-be Mark shouldn't have moved to this new city and left his mother, sister, brother, and best friend behind.

Beebe and Mark would be great together, if they could ever *get* together—there always seem to be obstacles in the way. Will their worlds
ever meet, or will they just go on making circles around each other forever?

—*Mary Cosper*

Coaching Evelyn: Fast, Faster,   Grades 5–12
Fastest Woman in the World
By Pat Connolly

Evelyn Ashford once said to her track coach, "I guess I run so fast
to keep from falling down!" That's an amusing way of looking at what
a world-class sprinter does best, and it sets the tone for this book,
Coaching Evelyn.

The author, Pat Connolly, was Evelyn's coach and friend over the
twelve-year span of the runner's career. Pat saw something extraordinary in the young sprinter—more than her muscle tone, her long natural stride, or her ability to hit high gear and pull away at the end of a
race. Pat saw championship potential.

"No pain, no gain" took on new meaning for Evelyn and her team-
mates as Coach Connolly set up killer workouts, pushing the women
to overcome physical and emotional obstacles. Evelyn rose to that challenge, and at meet after meet she raced against and beat the best women
sprinters in the world, including highly-trained athletes from the country that back then was known as East Germany. And the record book
shows what Evelyn did—she set a new 100-meter world record, and she
ran the anchor leg of the world championship 400-meter relay race.

There was a price to pay, though—big-time athletic success brings
with it a lot of pressure. Everybody wanted a piece of Evelyn Ashford:
wear our brand of shoe, smile for our magazine, and worst of all, try
this drug. From cortisone for injured muscles, to party drugs, to body-
building steroids, the temptations are spelled out in this book. And
that's where the tone turns serious. And Evelyn stayed clean. She got
her shoe contract, but she resisted the drug temptation. That may have
been Evelyn's—or any athlete's—biggest triumph of all.

—*Mark Anderson*

The Colors of Snow   Adult
By Kate Fenton

When Frankie Cleverdon, a successful painter, decided that she needed solitude to recapture her waning inspiration, she escaped from London to the northern Yorkshire moors. She leased an isolated lodge for the winter, four miles from the nearest small village. Her friends agreed that she, a city girl, didn't know what she was in for: with nothing but hills, hedgerows, and a small stream for company, she'd freeze, go crazy, or be back home in two weeks.

After eight days and nothing to show for them but unfilled canvases, she was beginning to think her friends were right. Then she happened to look out her window to see a lone fisherman standing in the nearby stream, looking like a dressed-up bear. He seemed so comical and peculiar, yet so much a part of this strange place, that she knew she had to capture him with her brush. When he began to wade away, Frankie leaped up and ran outside to ask if she could take a few Polaroid snapshots of him to work from later.

In retrospect, she now knew, that was the day her life changed, and in about the same amount of time it took for those instant photos to develop. That night her inspiration returned—followed by a blizzard of such proportions that she was snowed in for four days! Along with the blizzard came love and enchantment, fear and murder. Were these really *The Colors of Snow*?

—Faye A. Powell

Come Next Spring   Grades 5-8
By Alana White

World War II is over. Most of the fathers and older brothers have come home, but Howard Gardner wears a black patch over one eye, and Scooter's father will never come back. Now there's a new veterinarian in town, Michael Burmeister. No one wants to hire him, though. He's a stranger, and he's German.

In the Tennessee Smoky Mountain town of Pine Valley where Selina has spent the first twelve years of her life, things are changing faster than she could have ever imagined. Her best friend Mayella seems interested only in her rich relatives in Sevierville. Big brother Paul spends all his time with his foal, Sugar-Boy. And Scooter . . . Scooter is always there, always appearing when Selina wants to be with Mayella, or playing her guitar when she hasn't been asked, or insinuating that Rhett Butler never really loved Scarlett O'Hara at all. Scooter seems to want changes to happen. She thinks the new superhighway through the beautiful countryside will be good, because more tourists will pass through and maybe buy some of her mother's quilts. Scooter doesn't seem to understand that their rural surroundings will be destroyed. It can never be the same!

Selina feels as if change is pulling her in every direction, and she can't seem to find a way to stop it.

—*Carol Kappelmann*

Contrary Imaginations   Grades 5–8
By Larry Callen

Alex, the twins Joel and Lily, and their mother were having a family discussion. They'd had plenty of them in the past, beginning when their father walked out a few years before. But this was a new kind of family meeting. The others had centered around the making of family rules, or where to go for vacation. This one involved Mom's new boyfriend, Big Al. Would they be willing to allow Big Al to become a part of their family? Everybody had something to say, but nothing was really decided.

A few days later, a phone call disrupted their usually tranquil life. Mom wouldn't explain anything about the call, or why they all had to make a sudden visit to Granny Victoria for the weekend. Granny Victoria was their father's mother and lived on the beach in Louisiana. It was a long ride, filled with unanswered questions for Alex; the twins spent the entire trip picking at each other, almost (but not quite) fighting.

When they got to Granny Victoria's, there was a brown cardboard box on a card table in the den. A box of their father's ashes. He'd died a week earlier in a Florida hospital and, according to his last wishes, had been cremated and his remains sent to his wife in care of Granny Victoria. Suddenly their father wasn't just gone away—he was gone forever.

But his ashes were still there. What should they do with them? They took the box and Granny Victoria back home and tried to figure it out. Dad hadn't been part of the family for years, and yet he *was* part of the family. What would he have wanted? What did they want? What would be the right thing to do?

—*Patsy Launspach*

Coping with Death and Grief   Grades 3–6
By Marge Eaton Heegaard

"Why do we have to move?" "How come Daddy left?" "Why did Grandma die?" Have you ever asked questions like these? They're scary ones, because they're about our lives changing in unexpected ways. No one can avoid change—and sometimes it's good, like winter turning into spring, or a new friend. But sometimes it's hard—it's hard when someone you love leaves or dies. Usually when something changes, you notice first what you've lost. You are very sad, you feel terrible and *scared*—you grieve. Julie is feeling scared about being in a new town with her mother and stepfather, and no friends. Ann's grandmother is dead—she can never bake cookies with her again—and Mike is angry because his little brother died and now everybody's sad all the time. If you have scary questions about changes in your life, *Coping with Death and Grief* will help you feel safer and understand that learning to accept change and deal with loss is part of growing up.

—Jan L. McConnell

Cricket and the Cracker Box Kid   Grades 3–6
By Alane Ferguson

Have you ever felt lonely and friendless? Eleven-year-old Kristin Winslow, better known as Cricket, is lonely. She has no brothers or sisters. Both her mother and father work long hours away from home.

During a fifth-grade field trip to the Animal Care and Control Facility, Cricket spots Treasure, the springer spaniel she rescued and befriended the week before. The dog had run off before Cricket could approach her parents about keeping him. Now that she's found Treasure again, she uses all her persuasive powers and convinces her parents that she needs him.

Treasure changes Cricket's life. She's never lonely or sad now—she has Treasure to talk to, play with, and comfort her.

Shortly after Treasure enters her life, Cricket makes a friend at school. Dominic Falcone and his family have just moved from Florida. The two of them work together on a school project and end up being best friends. Cricket's life is perfect until she invites Dominic home to meet her dog, Treasure. That's when Big Trouble starts.

Cricket calls *her* dog Treasure. Dominic calls *his* dog Coty. And the dog responds to both names. Cricket got her dog from the animal shelter. Dominic bought his from a kennel. She loves Treasure. He loves Coty. They both love and want the same dog!

Whose dog it is? How will they decide who gets to keep it? And what will happen to their friendship?

—*Cynthia L. Lopuszynski*

Crow and Weasel   Grade 3–Adult
By Barry Lopez

Long, long ago, when people and animals spoke the same language, Crow and Weasel, two young members of a tribe that lived in the southern part of the land, decided that they wanted to travel far to the north and explore the lands of other peoples. At first their fathers forbade them to go, but after Mountain Lion, one of the elders of the tribe, had a dream about Crow and Weasel and their trip, they were allowed to set forth. Their journey would be a long one. They had no way of knowing, when they started out, that they would be different men when they returned—the strangers they would meet on their journey would change them forever. Together Crow and Weasel would visit lands that their people of the southern prairies had never even heard of; together they would learn lessons that all people must learn to survive in the world, whether it is the world of long ago or the world of today. They would learn how to be true friends; they would come to understand the importance of giving thanks; and at last they would see how learning about others, and sharing their lives and customs, can help a man discover who he really is and where he belongs in the world. And of course they also learned how to tell stories, and how to take care of the stories that others told them.

Go with Crow and Weasel as they leave their people and journey into uncharted lands. Share their adventures, their stories, and their friendship as they discover what it means to be a man.

—*J. R. B.*

Crying for a Dream   Grade 9–Adult
By Richard Erdoes

Native Americans, crying for a dream, for dreams are an essential part of the sacred path. "In the lost Eden of the human heart, an ancient tree of knowledge grows wherefrom the mind has not yet gathered more than a few windfalls."

"There was loud drumming and singing, getting stronger and stronger. Suddenly the lights went on. Their faces were ecstatic, their eyes bright and unseeing. They swayed back and forth to the rhythm of the song. I lost all sense of time and place."

Native Americans, crying for a dream, crying because of the waste. The waste of the earth, the waste of human lives. "You know what that culture deprivation is, that the anthros always talk about? It's being a white middle-class kid living in a split-level apartment with color TV. I'd exchange such a no-good apartment any time for one of our beautiful old Lakota tipis."

Native Americans, crying for a dream. Natives to the land. Worn by the wind. Fed by the earth. "The Earth is a living thing. The mountains speak. The trees sing. Lakes can think. Pebbles have a soul. Rocks have power."

Listen to the ceremonies, the dreams, the cries of a people deeply involved with the sacred. Absorb the photos that repeat the cry of the people of the land. A cry of wonder, of awe, of loss. Dream, and you may cry with them.

—Lesley S. J. Farmer

D, My Name is Danita — Grades 7–12
By Norma Fox Mazer

It seems every time Dani turns around she sees "Red sneakers. Bare ankles. No socks." This guy seems to be everywhere. He's at the mall each time Dani and her friend Laredo are there. He's leaning against a tree across the street from her house—and now Dani has been receiving peculiar phone calls.

Up to this point, Dani's life has been terrific. Her family is practically perfect, and her best friend Laredo is the greatest. But now this wonderful world looks unexpectedly shaky. All of a sudden there are too many mysteries, too many secrets—and not *nearly* enough answers!

—Bette DeBruyne Ammon

Dagmar Schultz and the Green-Eyed Monster — Grades 5–8
By Lynn Hall

Hey, if your hair was your best body part, and along came a new girl whose hair was longer, blonder, and prettier than yours (and naturally curly, too), wouldn't *your* nose get out of joint? Sure it would— especially if she also took your best friend and your boyfriend away from you! And right before the Eighth Grade Christmas Dance—the *worst* time of all for this to happen. There you are, feeling ugly and rejected, and with no one to take you to the dance. If you can't get rid of the new girl, at least you can get even, right?

Read *Dagmar Schultz and the Green-Eyed Monster* to find out how thirteen-year-old Dagmar gets revenge against pretty Ashley Fingerhut, and in the process discovers a few things about her friends, her family, and herself.

—Patricia Willingham

Dakota of the White Flats   Grades 3-6
By Philip Ridley

Dakota has a pet silverfish named Mint, a best friend called Treacle, and a mother who eats only dumplings. Dakota hates pink and girls' names, and would rather eat a stew of smelly socks than read a love story. This ten-year-old spits when she's angry, and she's *afraid of nothing*.

Whenever Dakota says "I want to find out!" Treacle knows they're off on another adventure. This time Dakota has a plan to see the "baby monster" that Medusa claims to have. (It's green). But when the baby monster vanishes, Dakota is onto a real mystery. Does her annoying neighbor Henry have anything to do with the disappearance? Why does he wear those strange pointy shoes? And where did he get that roomful of glittering jewels?

One dark night the girls follow Henry to Dog Island and come face to face with the mysterious recluse Lassiter Peach. To escape, they must climb a wall topped with barbed wire and broken glass, and row across eel-infested waters. (I told you, Dakota is afraid of *nothing*!)

To find out if she rescues the baby monster and who Lassiter Peach really is, read *Dakota of the White Flats*.

—Karol Schmitt Rockwin

Dancing on the Table   Grades 3-4
By Liza Ketchum Murrow and Ronald Himler

Jenny loves her "mischief days" with Nana, her grandmother. That's when they do special things, like going on night walks or collecting mussels. But then Nana tells Jenny she is getting married. "Grandmothers don't get married," says Jenny. But Nana is going to marry Charlie Streeter and even wants Jenny to be in the wedding. When Jenny finds a rabbit's foot, Mr. Streeter tells her she can make wishes on it. She decides to use the wishes so that Nana won't get married and move away. But what will it mean if her wishes come true?

—Melanie L. Witulski

Dark Horse: Grade 10–Adult
The Private Life of George Harrison
By Geoffrey Giuliano

In 1964, the Beatles hit the United States like a hurricane. There was Paul McCartney, John Lennon, Ringo Starr, and . . . wait a minute, who was the other member? [Pause] Oh yes! George Harrison. This "quiet Beatle" was the most enigmatic, elusive, and misunderstood of the Fab Four. *Dark Horse* will take you on an exclusive interview with the man who refers to his tour of duty with the group as "a nightmare." It will give you a chance to look into the life of a man whose public persona is that of a dark, brooding musician cloaked in the folds of Eastern mysticism. It takes you step-by-step through his world: his childhood and early teenage friendships, his passion for music and the forging of the Beatles' partnership, the skyrocket to fame, his much-talked-about spiritual quest, the complexities of his personal relationships, the ups and downs of his solo career, his experiments with hard drugs, and his intense fear for his own safety after John Lennon's death. George Harrison now lives in retreat behind the impenetrable walls of his estate in Henley-on-Thames, England. His life has been an unimaginable trip, and this book is your ticket to ride.

—Barbara Bahm

Darkling Grades 9–12
By K. M. Peyton

Darkling was all Jenny's. Murphy, her grandfather, bought him at the Newcastle horse sale. He was the meanest, wildest, most ill-behaved little thing that Jenny had ever seen. And he'd been injured, too. No one wanted him. Who would? So Murphy bought him as a gift for Jenny for next to nothing.

But Darkling behaved for Jenny, and Jenny loved him. The only problem was where to put him, but Murphy said not to worry, that he would figure it out. So he got twelve old toilet doors that were being thrown out and built Darkling a stable.

Murphy was always telling Jenny not to worry, that he would solve the problem, whatever it was. Sometimes his solutions were different or unorthodox, like the toilet doors. Who would ever think of making a stable out of toilet doors? But he did, and it worked. Murphy was an unusual sort. He lived in a run-down trailer next door to Jenny's family, with 3 dogs, 13 cats, 14 hens, 1 horse, 1 donkey, 2 cows, and 4 goats. They actually lived with him; he never shut his door. Yes, Murphy was definitely different.

Now there was another problem. Jenny's family was being evicted, kicked out of their house by Jackboots Strawson. He owned their house and the land under it, and he lived in the big house up on the hill. For some reason, he didn't like them. His sons did, though, especially Goddard. He and Jenny were a pair and had been for a long time. But Jackboots did not like them—at all.

Murphy told Jenny not to worry; he would figure it out. And his solution was to set up a horse race between Jenny riding Darkling against Goddard riding the best horse from Jackboots' stable. If Jenny won, her family would not be evicted. If she lost, her family would not only lose their home, she would lose Darkling—to Jackboots.

—*Margaret Butzler*

Darkness
By John Saul

Grade 9–Adult

There is a circle of candles, and there is also a circle of dolls. And the candles never flicker, and the dolls never weep. And only Old Clarey watches them all—Old Clarey, who is the Priestess of the Dark Man, but who refuses to give in to his enticements. She will not die, even though she has never taken the elixir that keeps the Dark Man and his friends alive and forever young.

And into this Southern swamp where Clarey and the children of the Dark Man live, come two teenagers who were never supposed to meet, who were never supposed to return to where the Dark Man practices his evil spells. Yet now they are here, and they have met and somehow recognized the emptiness and loneliness they both carry with them, the stigmata of the Dark Man. Soon they will learn of the power they have together, power the Dark Man never expected to confront.

Can he continue with his evil rites, with theft of things both seen and unseen? Or will Michael and Kelly be able to combine to form the catalyst that will end his evil reign forever?

The circles wait. Will the candles ever flicker? Will the dolls ever weep?

—*J. R. B.*

The Day That Elvis Came to Town   Grades 7–12
By Jan Marino

"Maybe *this* time it will be different. Maybe this time Poppa won't start drinking again. Maybe this time the new boarder won't be a grouch. Maybe the new baby will bring Momma and Poppa closer together. Maybe someday I'll be allowed to be me. . . .

What is it that makes Mercedes, our new boarder, so special? Did she really go to high school with Elvis? And what does she mean when she says, 'We got to sparkle and shine in this life, you in your way, me in mine'? Could Mercedes possibly help make my dream come true—to meet Elvis, to hear him sing?"

Wanda's life is full of questions, and they come to a focus as the new boarder enters her life. Mercedes appears to have a glamorous career as a jazz singer. She knows everybody and everything, so much about the world. Can she help Wanda through all the "maybes" in her own life? *Are* there answers to Wanda's questions? Find out in *The Day That Elvis Came to Town*.

—Anne Sushko

Dear God: Adult
What Religion Were the Dinosaurs?
By David Heller

Have you written any letters to God lately? If you find the idea intriguing (whether you've actually done it or not), you'll definitely want to read this latest book by David Heller, *Dear God: What Religion Were the Dinosaurs?*

One warning, however: don't read these letters simply to collect a bunch of cute quotes—a religious version of "kids say the darndest things." Because in spite of the fact that the letters collected here were written by children ranging from four to twelve years old, the questions raised and the feelings expressed are not just kid-stuff. Take the question fired by eight-year-old Camille: "Can a person have two religions? If they do, how do You decide on their fate at the end?" Written by a kid? granted; kid-stuff? I don't think so.

On the lighter side, Celeste, at the ripe old age of seven, is pondering a variation of the old how-many-angels-fit-on-the-head-of-a-pin theme which drove the medieval philosophers crazy. She writes God for the inside information on "What country has produced and made the most angels?" Some politicians might be interested in that answer.

While adults may talk about the apparent conflict between divine predestination and human free will, ten-year-old Sheila's question gets right to the heart of the problem. "Dear God: I read somewhere You know what we are going to do before we do it. How much advance notice do You get?"

Although we might not admit it, many of us adults would like to echo this direct question from a nine-year-old girl named Charlene: "How do you know Satan when you see him? Can You give me any clues?"

When you read these letters, you may find yourself reminded, as I was, of the passage in the Bible when Jesus rebukes his disciples for trying to stop a group of children from gathering around him. Jesus tells the disciples to let the children come to him because "the kingdom of God belongs to such as these." Virginia, age eleven, sums it up well in her letter: "Dear God: I feel that people would feel good if they said more prayers and did not forget their prayers ever. I wish that older people and kids would pray together more. That would make us feel like we are all part of the same generation. I feel that way since we are all children in Your eyes. Teach us to get our act together, God."

—*Margie Reitsma*

The Devil's Own   Grades 9-12
By Deborah Lisson

What kind of things do you think of when you hear the word "mutiny"? If you've read books like *Mutiny on the Bounty* or *Treasure Island*, or watched old swashbuckling movies, you might think of wicked captains clashing with heroic sailors, you might think of a beautiful island paradise, you might think of Errol Flynn or Douglas Fairbanks rescuing beautiful damsels from diabolical ruffians. Movies, and sometimes books, make a free-booting life on the high seas seem exciting and romantic.

But have you ever thought of the darker side of mutiny? Have you ever wondered what pirates had to do to become the outcasts that they actually were?

In 1629, the Dutch merchant ship *Batavia* was wrecked off the Abrolhos islands. The captain of the vessel took a boatload of his crew and went to get help from the nearby island of Java. They left behind the passengers, the rest of the crew, and several large chests of treasure. Also left behind was Jeronimus Cornelisz, a man who wanted that treasure, and who took it. Cornelisz was an evil man, and he knew that

there must be no witnessess to reveal his crimes when the captain returned. And so he planned and executed one of the bloodiest mutinies
in the history of the sea.

Three hundred and sixty-two years later, a yacht is anchored off the
Abrolhos islands. On that yacht, Julianna, bored and unhappy, wishes
she hadn't had to come on this trip with her family. She wishes that
something exciting would happen to her. And her wish is granted.

Julianna suddenly finds herself 362 years back in time, in a nightmare of mutiny and murder. Jeronimus Cornelisz is murdering his
shipmates. Can Julianna hope to survive the massacre? And even if she
survives, can she ever hope to see her family again?

—*Nancy A. Weitendorf*

Dew Drop Dead   Grades 5–12
By James Howe

Have you ever seen a boarded-up, abandoned old building and
had the urge to go inside and explore? Well, let me tell you
something—*don't.*

The three of us—David Lepinsky, Corrie Wingate, and me, Sebas-
tian Barth—got curious about the rundown, forlorn building known as
the Dew Drop Inn. Our curiosity got the best of us, and we climbed in
through a broken window.

What you expect to find in an abandoned building are a few old
things left behind when the owners moved out. What we found was
something else! There were still pictures over the fireplace. There was
a recent issue of a magazine lying open on the floor beside a chair.

We got an eerie feeling about that building, and we should have left
then! Instead, we went upstairs. At the end of the hall was an open doorway. From sheer anxiety, Corrie and I were laughing nervously, and
David started to hiccough as we reached the door. And when I pointed
the flashlight around the dark room, it caught something—*a body on
the bed*!

None of us remember racing back downstairs or out the window, but
I guess we did! And as soon as we were breathing again, we went to tell
the police. We were proud of ourselves for doing the responsible thing.
That should have been the end of our eerie adventure.

But what could we say to the police when they investigated and
didn't find a body, much less that recent magazine? How could we
prove the body we saw was real? What did the homeless people at Corrie's church have to do with this? And how was Corrie's friend, the sad

and disturbed man called Abraham, involved?

—Robbi Povenmire

Distant Fires   Grade 9–Adult
By Scott Anderson and Les C. Kouba

When I was young, my girlfriend and I used to pretend that we were
Meriwether Lewis and William Clark—we'd hike through the woods
to discover the wonders of the new Louisiana Purchase. Scott Anderson
and Steve Baker had similar dreams of adventure when they were boys.
They dreamed of taking a canoe trip from their home in Duluth,
Minnesota, over lakes and rivers to the shore of Hudson Bay, up near
the Arctic Circle. But Scott and Steve not only dreamed of the 1,700-
mile voyage—they actually lived it, just like the voyageurs of old. Well,
almost like the voyageurs of old! Their gear included a lightweight
Odyssey canoe, paddles, life jackets, sleeping bags, a tent, clothing, a
few tools and cooking utensils, and food—ten pounds of spaghetti,
twenty pounds of macaroni, and two pounds of Grape Nuts.

As for their trip, the two college students had planned to put the canoe in the water and never stop paddling until they reached their destination. Lake Superior had other plans. High winds and waves post-
poned their travels time and time again. As Scott says in the very first
lines of the book, "We did *not* tip over our first day out. Shoot, we
didn't even *leave* on our first day. We'd been gone five days before we
left, and it was on the second day, not the first, that we crashed our
foundering canoe onto the rocky Lake Superior shore."

Crashing, tipping over, fighting headwinds, waiting out storms, and
carrying the canoe overland in never-ending portages all became routine. And although the young men had planned carefully and armed
themselves against the creatures of the forests, they were not prepared
for the vicious, dangerous, bothersome, and ravenous mosquitoes they
encountered. In contrast to these nasty little companions, they made
other acquaintances, human ones, who were kind and helpful. Many
gave them shelter for the night and entertained them with their own
stories of life in the North Woods.

After three months of hardship and pleasure, paddle and portage, the
two men reached the shore of the great Hudson Bay. Reflecting on their
journey, Scott talks of distant fires: "Distant fires are around us everywhere. They do not burn just in the North. But in the lands, in the
woods, and among the lakes and streams they are easier to see, easier

to follow. Everywhere that dream is held and followed to its end, there the distant fires burn. "

—*Susan Weaver*

Note: A map with the route marked on it would be helpful to emphasize the length and difficulty of the trip.

Don't Rent My Room!   Grades 5-8
By Judie Angell

It really wasn't fair! Just because I was a kid my parents expected me to change my whole life so that they could live their dream. I mean, here I was about to start tenth grade and still it didn't matter to them that I'd have to leave my friends and school and start all over again if we moved to the country. They wouldn't even *listen*! No, they went right ahead and bought an old country inn hundreds of miles from the city, as if living and working together in the middle of nowhere would solve all our problems! Luckily, Grandma was as dead-set against the move as I was, so the two of us joined forces and somehow managed to persuade Mom and Dad to agree to a compromise: I would stay with the family during summer vacation, helping them get started as innkeepers. And when Labor Day came, if I didn't like being there, I could come back to the city and spend the whole year with Grandma. On my part, I had to promise to give our new home a fair chance.

Well, Labor Day is just about here, and I can honestly say that I gave country living my best shot. As for where I've decided to live this fall, and the mixed-up summer that led me to that decision, read *Don't Rent My Room!*. I think my choice will surprise you as much as it did me!

—*Sister Mary Anna Falbo, CSSF*

The Door in the Air   Grades 3-6
and Other Stories
By Margaret Mahy

A door in the *air* . . . ? Impossible, you say. No, it *is* possible, and you'll find it in one of the short stories in this book.

In "The Door in the Air" Aquilina is a young trapeze artist who performs for the royal family. Just before the circus begins, Aquilina notices a star on the prince's forehead. People say his nurse once let him wander into a place called Riddle Chase—could that have caused the star? Five years later, Aquilina sees the prince again; this time he wears a beekeeper's veil. When he removes it for a moment, there are many more silver stars, covering his whole face. The third time the acrobatic circus troupe performs in the town, Aquilina learns that now the prince must live behind a high wall, guarded by robots. Determined to visit him, she leaps across the tops of trees, avoiding the trails on the ground that are lined with traps. As she reaches the towering wall, she calls to the prince, "Climb the big tree there. Jump!" Aquilina snatches him at just the right moment, but as they flee, mechanical dogs, steel traps, and robot guards spring into action. Will the fugitives escape? Or are they trapped in the trees forever? Just step through *The Door in the Air* and find out.

—*Dorothy Davidson*

Downriver   Grades 7-12
By Will Hobbs

No permit, no river map, and no adults. Just the seven of us and the Grand Canyon, and the chance for lots and lots of adventures. That was *not* what my father had in mind when he sent me to Discovery Unlimited for a nine-week outdoor education course. If he had me in mind at all. My mom died when I was just five, and it was always just Dad and me—until Madeline. Now he'd sent me off for nine weeks so they could move into the new canyon house he'd designed with her. Everything I knew would be gone soon. My old life was slipping away— and he didn't seem to care. Well, if he didn't, neither would I.

That's one reason I went along with the others when Troy suggested rafting the Grand Canyon on our own. Our group had been together for weeks by then—we'd gotten to know each other, climbed mountains, made it through a set of rapids—and the counselor's plans for the next part of the course didn't sound nearly as great as going off by ourselves. So when he left the keys in the van while he went to make arrangements for a river trip, we just took off. On our own, with a full tank of gas, two rafts loaded with supplies, and nothing ahead but adventure and fun, without any adults to bug us or tell us we couldn't or shouldn't or mustn't. Just us—the Hoods in the Woods, off on our own, pirating the Grand Canyon.

I wonder if we would've gone if we'd known then what would happen before our trip was over. It was wild, it was fun—at least part of the time—but it was nothing like what any of us had ever expected.

It's hard to hide who you are in the middle of a river full of white water.

—*J. R. B.*

Dragon Cauldron Grades 5–8
By Laurence Yep

I tell this story because I am the cleverest. Not just because of who I am—a king and a wizard—but because of *what* I am.

My companion Shimmer spent years disguised as a beggar, but she's really a princess. And she too is clever and magical—but not so clever and magical as I. We argue about this a lot. Shimmer lost her home and people; that's why she had to wander as a beggar. We've found something that could save her clan, but it's broken. So now we seek the Smith and the Snail Woman; only they can fix it.

Civet has joined our quest as well. She was a witch before she lost her powers. Civet stole the inland sea Shimmer and her people lived in, and used its waters to drown a city. She would have killed the people there, too, if I hadn't stopped her. Now she's repented, and has vowed to help Shimmer get her home back. Shimmer doesn't trust Civet, but I say that, for all Civet has done, she's really only a teenage girl whose family sacrificed her, gave her in marriage to an evil river spirit. That's how she became a witch, why she became wicked. I believe she'll keep her vow.

Indigo is just a little girl, taken from her home, an orphan and a slave. Shimmer rescued her and feels sorry for her because the two of them have shared the same losses. But *I* worry about Thorn. After all, he's not much older than Indigo, and his life has been hard too. And Civet has had a vision, one showing that Thorn will become a creature of power—and that he will unloose a Great Evil on the world. Well, visions are what we make of them. And yet. . . .

It would surprise my friends to know how much I think and worry. Shimmer, especially, thinks I'm just a clown and a practical joker. She's filled with such grand, dramatic ideas, and speaks in such pompous language, it's hard not to try and deflate her. Her notions of honor, too. . . . It's easy to be grand and noble when you're like Shimmer. But my people have always had to sneak around and be nosy and play tricks. We're small and delicate: trickiness is the only protection we monkeys have.

And as for Shimmer—well, after all, *she's* a Dragon!

—Rene Mandel

Dream Teams: Grades 5–Adult
Best Teams of All Time
By Michael Benson

Put away your baseball cards; there're more home runs, touchdowns, goals, and scores between these covers than in anyone's card collection!

You can be there, as Roger Maris breaks the Babe's record for home runs. You can feel the excitement as the 1980 Olympic Hockey Team dreams of miracles and then proceeds to make them happen! Dribble with a pro basketball team as they set a record of 33 straight wins and remain at the top for almost ten years. Sprint with the San Francisco 49ers as they break record after record, including the most points ever scored in a Super Bowl. Travel to Munich, Germany, for the 1972 Olympics and discover just what a "perfect 10" is, and who or what was the "Munchkin of Munich."

Everyone dreams of being the best, the champion. If you'd like to explore the best of the *very* best in the world of sports, read *Dream Teams*.

—*Suzi Smith*

Drummond: The Search for Sarah Grades 3–4
By Sally Farrell Odgers

Drummond, a spiffy teddy bear in a red, white, and blue striped blazer, vest, straw hat, and watch chain with a *real* gold watch, woke up from his long hibernation when he heard Nicholas calling, "Sarah!"

Why, this Sarah might be *his* Sarah from long ago, Drummond thought, the Sarah he had come to Australia with in a big boat. He had been her constant companion on the trip, but then he had lost her. And he still hadn't found her. "Your name might be Sarah, but you're not *my* Sarah," complained Drummond to the girl who had lifted him up. Then he drooped lifelessly in the astonished girl's hands and said no more.

Sarah and Nicholas went on unpacking the box of old toys for the Village Fair, but they both knew they had heard the teddy bear speak. When they looked for him, though, he was gone! Then they saw him crawling away very quietly, obviously trying to avoid being seen, going off on his own quest for his own Sarah.

They picked Drummond up and decided to keep him, but he had his own ideas about that!

Where *is* Drummond's Sarah? Does she exist? How did he lose her, and will he ever find her again? See for yourself in *Drummond*.

—*Nadeane Silbernagel*

Eben Tyne, Powdermonkey   Grades 5-8
By Patricia Beatty and Phillip Robbins

Jamie was frowning as he went to meet Eben. Once they'd been mortal enemies, but ever since Eben had approached Jamie about becoming a powdermonkey on the secret ship in Norfolk, they'd become friends. Jamie had slung a hammock right in the shipyard rather than return across the harbor to his shabby, crowded home each evening. He'd been asleep in the hammock last night when something had wakened him. Lying quiet in the dark, Jamie saw three men hunkered down by the lamp in the powder magazine. He couldn't tell who they were, but he could hear them whispering and see them drawing lines on the deck.

"Tomorrow night for sure. We'll do it right here. That'll be the end of her." Jamie suspected his ship was in danger, but what should he do?

When he talked it over with his friend, Eben said they should tell one of the ship's officers—but who was going to believe them? They had no proof. They were only thirteen, and they'd probably be laughed off as excitable boys, seeing imaginary enemies in the dark. Eben and Jamie decided to hide right in the powder magazine the next night and learn who the saboteurs were.

It was hard for the boys to stay awake, lying hidden among the flannel bags of gunpowder, but at five bells (2:30 AM) a noise roused them. The saboteurs were back. One of the men was so close he nearly touched Eben, but luckily he didn't see the boy. Piling some bags of gunpowder on the deck, the men lit a long fuse and prepared to leave the doomed ship.

"We'll blow her sky-high, lads," one said. "The *Merrimack* will never go out to fight. Fewer lives will be lost, and our *Monitor* will be invincible!"

Eben and Jamie held their breaths. Would they be able to put out the lighted fuse before it reached the powder? Would they have time to reach their captain before the traitors escaped?

—*Kristina Peters*

Echoes of War   Grade 7–Adult
By Robert Westall

Five stories of war, a war long past but still echoing from one generation to the next. In one story, ghostly memories are strong enough to turn a quiet air-freight flight over present-day Germany into the heart-wrenching sights and sounds and smells of a bombing run forty years in the past.

Then there's Zakky. He's a thirteen-year-old killing machine. He lives only to kill Germans. The Home Guard in the quiet English countryside is far too tame for him. And what will become of him after the war, when there are no more Germans to kill?

In "The Making of Me" a small boy fears his formidable, shell-shocked grandfather until the day he is left alone with him. Granda hauls out a big old tea chest and shares the story of each object inside—a rusty hammer, a weird knife, a huge brass tap, and a short brass cylinder. And the boy never views his grandfather—or himself—in the quite same light again.

These, and a story about a man who could be Adolf Hitler and another about a boy whose passion for souvenirs of the Blitz leads to a grim discovery, make up the *Echoes of War*.

—Diane L. Deuel

Eenie, Meanie, Murphy, No!   Grades 3–6
By Colleen O'Shaughnessy McKenna

Have you ever kept a diary? For me, that was the place where I could write down all the things I really thought about people but didn't have the courage to tell them—especially boys! My diary was the most personal and private thing I owned, and I remember the night I opened it and discovered that my worst enemy had somehow gotten hold of it, read it—and written in her own comments in the margins. But there was no way to prove who'd done it, and I sure didn't want her to know how upset I was, so I just acted as though nothing had happened. But after that I was very, very careful about where I left my diary! And by the way, I still keep a journal or diary—and where I keep it is still a secret!

That's why, when I read this book, I knew *just* how Colette felt when she heard Peally reading her very own diary aloud to the whole camp! She wanted to run up to her and snatch the pages out of her hand—and

snatch the hair out of her head, too, for good measure! But she didn't—
she didn't want anyone to know that she was the one who had said all
those things about Tommy, the cutest boy at camp—and Peally's exclusive property, according to Peally, even though Tommy seemed kind
of interested in Colette. And when Colette confronted Peally alone afterwards, Peally just said, "Give it back? Like you and your two friends
gave me back my cabin? No way!"

It looks like a stalemate—Colette, Sarah, and Marsha have Cabin
Seven, the one Peally and her friends always had before, and they aren't
going to give it up, not after they had to fight so hard to keep it, and
Peally has Colette's diary and she's not about to give that up, either.
Camp's supposed to be fun—no school, no parents, no little brothers
and sisters, just lots of fun and lots of neat stuff to do with your friends.
But with Peally around, it isn't fun at all. It's war!

Can Colette actually win, or will she lose not only her diary but Tommy too? Do nice guys—and nice girls—*always* have to finish last?

—J. R. B.

Encyclopedia Brown's
Book of Strange but True Crimes
By Donald J. Sobol and Rose Sobol

Grades 3–8

The law finally caught up with Cristina Echvarria, a lady of many
addresses. Among her offenses: practicing medicine without a license
and billing Medicaid for treating a 220-pound football player for diaper
rash!

For two years Astred Greene flew the world free, saving herself an
estimated $40,000 in air fares. She masqueraded as a flight attendant.
Greene got aboard overseas flights by walking past the gate agent, who
took her for a member of the crew. But one mistake did her in: she was
too good at the job. Passengers wrote letters to the airline praising her
helpfulness. An office worker decided to start putting the letters in
Greene's personnel file. Whoops, no file!

Have you heard the one about two women who selected $419
worth of clothes in a department store in Heath, Ohio? They paid with
a fake $1000 bill—a fairly obvious fake, bearing the signatures
"A. Phony-bill" and "U. Cantcashit." The store didn't have change for
$1000, so a clerk took one of the women to a neighboring store. No one
there noticed anything unusual either, and the two women walked off
with their new clothes and $581 in real-money change!

Strange, but oh-so-true. Encyclopedia Brown has done it again, and this time he's gathered stories of strange but true crimes that will make you wonder why anyone would ever try this—or how on earth they got away with it!

—*Betty A. Holtzen*

Escape from Slavery: **Grades 3–6**
Five Journeys to Freedom
By Doreen Rappaport

Think back a moment, back to the last time you were scared. *Really* scared. Scared right down to the tips of your tingling toes, with your breath fast and soft, and your heart pounding against your ribs.

What would you do if you were a slave, to be free? Would you dress up like a man, if you were a young girl? Would you let yourself be nailed into a shipping crate with a little food and water? Could you cross a river on ice floes? That's what Eliza and her two-year-old daughter do after Eliza overhears that she is to be sold within the next few days.

Eliza, carrying a sleeping Caroline, steals away from her Kentucky plantation. At daybreak she comes to the river and discovers that it is not solidly frozen but has already started to thaw. Quickly she finds shelter for the day, but by dusk the slave catchers are out looking for her. Returning to the riverbank, she's dismayed to see that the spaces between the huge ice chunks are getting wider and wider.

Eliza steps out onto the ice. It holds. Another step, and then another. But now the chunks are not as steady, and they begin to groan and move. Cold water rushes up around Eliza's ankles. A minute later, the water is up to her knees, and then to her chest.

Only thirty feet from the Ohio border, Eliza puts Caroline down on an ice floe and tries to swim ashore, pushing the floe before her. About ten feet from land, the icy water begins to numb Eliza's limbs, and the air is filled with Caroline's screams. All of a sudden, ten feet looks like a very long way to swim.

Discover what it is like to be an escaping slave. Meet Eliza and Caroline; Dosha; Cornelia and Selena; Henry and Jane and Ellen and William in *Escape from Slavery: Five Journeys to Freedom*.

—*Susan Trimby*

Note: Eliza's story was told by the abolitionist Harriet Beecher Stowe in her novel *Uncle Tom's Cabin*.

Everywhere   Grades 5-8
By Bruce Brooks

During the night my grandfather had a heart attack. I didn't know
exactly what that meant, and I didn't know what to do, either, when
my grandmother sent me outside. So when Lucy Pettibone, the nurse,
arrived with her nephew Dooley, they found me just sitting in the
backyard, thinking about how much my grandfather meant to me.
Well, Lucy went upstairs to take care of Grandpa, leaving Dooley
behind with orders to cheer me up. He took one look at me and figured
that the only thing that would make me feel better would be the
knowledge that my grandfather would live. You know what Dooley
did? He talked me into trying out some strange ritual he'd read about
in a comic book, something called "soul switching." Dooley was *sure*
it would save my grandfather! I'd never even heard of such a thing, and
if you haven't either, come along and join us in a soul-switch I'll never
forget!

—Sister M. Anna Falbo, CSSF

Expedition: Grade 9-Adult
Being an Account in Words and Artwork
of the 2358 A.D. Voyage to Darwin IV
By Wayne Douglas Barlowe

[Show pictures from the book as you describe the various animals.]

New York, March 24, 2366: Five years to the day after his return to
Earth, Wayne Douglas Barlowe has published a collection of the sketches, drawings, and paintings he made during that first manned expedition to the planet Darwin IV.

This is your opportunity to view the incredible variety of fauna and
flora that inhabit Darwin IV, much like the great variety of species that
once lived on our own Earth. Of course, most of Earth's species have
been destroyed, and our planet is now almost devoid of life. It is only
because of the intervention of the Yma, a benevolent starfaring people
who came to our aid, that we are still able to live on Earth ourselves.
When the Darwin star-system was discovered, the Yma saw a chance
for humanity to re-educate itself, and planned a bi-species expedition.
Barlowe went along as the expedition's wildlife artist to record what the
group found on this unique, untouched planet. This book contains his
records.

Here you will meet the animal that Barlowe describes as the "most bizarre creature I had ever laid eyes upon"—the Rayback [p. 24-25]. The Rayback is very bad-tempered and will go after anything that moves, using sonar to locate its prey. When Barlowe first saw it, it was chasing another animal of the grasslands area, one he called a Gyrosprinter, a strange, two-legged creature built for speed. The fleeing Gyrosprinter had one especially odd feature—a pair of post-like organs that stayed horizontal to the ground no matter how its body moved, probably helping it balance as it raced for its life [p. 30-31].

Here [p. 38-39] you see a group of three-legged Thornbacks being pursued by what Barlowe called an Arrowtongue, "as lethal and as threatening as any predator I saw on Darwin IV." The Arrowtongue kills with a long, red, arrow-like tongue that darts out from its head. Like all the liquivores, it consumes its prey by first injecting it with strong digestive juices and then sucking out the liquified tissue.

Other creatures on Darwin IV look *nothing* like animals. This big "tree" [p. 42-43] is not a tree at all—it's an animal, and the smaller, leaf-like organisms sprouting around it are its offspring, still being fed by their parent. And these [p. 58-59] are the Flipsticks, that move by launching themselves into the air and turning over in midflight to land on their other end.

This [p. 68-69] is a Gulper, luring a Spade-nose into its huge, translucent body, where it will be trapped and digested alive, one of the more hideous kinds of predation that Barlowe witnessed. Other predators fill the skies with death, among them the gliding Daggerwrist, which lives in the forested areas of the planet and spends the time between meals honing its daggers on the branches of trees [p. 72-73]. These are only a few of the many creatures Barlowe discovered, sketched, and named while on Darwin IV. I am amazed at the variety and complexity of life that he found there, and invite you to share in his adventures and discoveries on the planet Darwin IV.

—*J. R. B.*

Face the Dragon   Grades 7-12
By Joyce Sweeney

Eric, Paul and Melanie are guinea pigs. They were "chosen" as part of a program for gifted students. A test was given to all the eighth graders at Coral Springs Junior High—a test to determine skills in "adapting to challenging learning environments"—and only Eric, Paul and Melanie scored high enough to participate. Now the three of them will be skipping the ninth grade and entering high school a year ahead of their classmates.

They're all a bit nervous, to say the least. Starting high school is scary enough, let alone starting with an entire group of strangers who seem to have already mastered high school, or at least the social skills bit.

Eric decides right from the beginning to approach this experience as the challenge it was designed to be. (After all, aren't his test scores proof enough that he can stand up to a challenge?)

First challenge: Stop competing with Paul. That'll be a tough one, since Eric and Paul's four-year relationship has been based almost entirely on Eric's shadowing of Paul.

Second challenge: Win Melanie's heart. Maybe the high school guys will consider Melanie too young for them and leave her all to him. (Now there's a thought!)

Third challenge: Kick butt in class. Especially in Mr. Gregory's tenth-grade English. There they will be studying *Beowulf,* and like the mythical dragon-slayer of that story, Eric decides that he too will face up to the dragons that are cluttering his life.

Just when it seems that Eric has his challenges beat, a new "dragon" appears—a gigantic fire-breather the likes of which Eric has never imagined. But this new challenge won't be *his* to deal with. This time, it's Paul's turn to *Face the Dragon.*

—*Rebecca E. Jenkins*

The Faces of Ceti   Grades 7-12
By Mary Caraker

Six years we've been on Ceti. Six years living on food supplied by the settlement on Arcadia, six years never seeing the sun set, six years of hard work and despair.

When we came to Ceti, we were so hopeful. We had been in space for five years, coming from Earth to a new solar system, hoping to find a world we could inhabit. And the Tau Ceti system had two worlds that seemed promising. It was a good thing there were two, because not all of us settlers liked the repressive plans that Captain Fauss had for the planet Arcadia. When we discovered that Ceti could support human life, my family and others jumped at the chance to have our own world, away from his domineering ways.

But that was a long time ago. At first Ceti held such promise. But the jade plants that we had hoped to eat proved poisonous. Our animals and our Earth grain died. And now Arcadia says it will no longer supply us with food. The Arcadians say, "If you are hungry, why don't you eat the animals that live on your planet?" But we don't kill the Hlur—the

native creatures—because we have seen them working, much the same
way humans work, to harvest the jade plants, which are not poisonous
to them. If they proved to be intelligent, how could we ever forgive ourselves?

The Arcadians want us to return to their planet. They need us to help
them fight the war that has been raging against Arcadia's native life-
forms ever since the settlers landed there six years ago. We don't want
to go, but we may have no choice.

Word had just come to me that our youngest children have disappeared. Did they leave on their own, or did someone take them? Somehow, I know the Hlur have them. We must go to the Hlur to save the
children, and maybe, just maybe, to save all of us on Ceti.

—Nancy A. Weitendorf

The Farewell Kid   Grades 7–12
By Barbara Wersba

"It was the year I swore off men, and the year I decided not to go to
college. It was the year that my mother went to Europe with her best
friend Bobo Lewis, and the year I realized that my true mission in life
was to save every stray dog in New York. In other words, it was the
most important year of my life, and its hallmark was that I was saying
good-bye to everything. Good-bye to the male species, who had caused
me nothing but pain, and good-bye to adolescence—which had been
like a long illness—and goodbye to living on Manhattan's Upper East
Side. I was seventeen and a half, and putting my old life behind me in
every possible way. I was getting good at the word 'farewell.'"

Thus begins the summer after high school for Heidi Rosenbloom.
It is a time for farewells, but also a time for new, if uncertain, beginnings. A time for starting a new business, even if things are slow at first,
and it is hard for Heidi to give up the dogs she has rescued to adoption.
A time for a first apartment—just an old barbershop, but it's cheap and
there is room for the dogs. And to Heidi's surprise, it is also a time for
love. To learn more about "the most important year" in Heidi's life,
read *The Farewell Kid*.

—Linda Olson

Fast Talk on a Slow Track   Grades 7–12
By Rita Williams-Garcia

Denzel Watson has never failed. Through all twelve years of school, Denzel has come out on top, ending his senior year as both class valedictorian and class president. And then while attending a summer preparatory program at Princeton, Denzel discovers that his fast talk and easy methods won't always work. He can't risk failure, but he can't face telling his proud family that he's decided not to go to Princeton in the fall, either. So to escape from his worries, Denzel finishes his summer as a fast-talking door-to-door salesman. Once again he gets caught up in competition, this time with a fellow salesman, Carmello, who comes from a world much rougher than the one Denzel's used to. Carmello, a school dropout, can't read and has a police record, but he also has the ability to be the top salesman of the group. Caught up in rivalry, Denzel doesn't have time to look at his fear of failure. How far will he go to win? And what's he competing for, anyway? What will it take to put Denzel back on the track?

—Terri Summey

Fatso Jean, the Ice Cream Queen   Grades 3–4
By Maryann Macdonald

Nine-year-old Jean's Inside Voice tells her that the world is divided into Hot Shots, Normals, and Nerds, and that she is definitely a Nerd! Jean can't dive into a pool, can't do a wheelie on her bike, and every time she tries to hit a softball, she misses. Definitely a Nerd! The only thing Jean can do well is eat ice cream. She will never give it up; so what if the Mean Team calls her "Fatso Jean, the Ice Cream Queen"!

When Jean reads an advertisement for Kamp Klutzo, an expensive camp for fat kids, she decides that's where she has to go. But Jean's parents don't seem to be able to manage it, so secretly Jean develops a plan to turn her craving for ice cream into a money-making business. Does Jean's plan work? Will she make it to Kamp Klutzo, or will the Mean Team cause a break in the action?

—Anne Liebst

Fiends   Grade 9–Adult
By John Farris

It is the paintings that make him different, unique—those horrible eerie paintings, all so dreadfully similar, all revealing the inferno seething beneath the mute calm exterior of the artist. Using white shoe-polish and charcoal, he paints the same face over and over again, the white face of a hairless woman with black staring eyes. There is no explanation for his fixation. He is mute and does not read or write. He has lived almost his entire life at the state mental hospital. His name is Arne Horsfall, and the story starts with him.

It began when he was a child on a farm, almost sixty years ago. A horror took over that farm, an evil took control of first his mother and then his father. Arne could not fight it, could not even understand it, could only flee. So he did—and he forgot, at least most of the time, until he would see again the face that he paints over and over. The face of evil, of fear, of terrible, terrible danger.

He'd hoped he'd outrun it, that he would never have to fight it again, but the moths showed him that it was still alive, waiting, waiting. So again he did the only thing he knew how to do—he ran.

Enid Weller, who worked at the state hospital and had gotten to know Arne through his paintings, had invited him over to her and her sister's house for dinner. It was there that he saw the moths and knew he would have to flee. The evil that had roamed the earth so many years before, that had destroyed the entire town of Dante's Mill, was back— and it wanted, it needed, to be fed. And its food had always been the lives and souls of human beings.

Arne was old and frail, in no condition to fight, but was there anyone else who could recognize the danger? And even if they saw the danger, how could they fight the evil, the undead, the Huldufolk?

—J. R. B.

Finding Signs   Adult
By Sharlene Baker

"You are a different breed, Brenda Bradshaw."

I've heard those words my whole life. Not that it bothers me. I take it as a compliment. After all, not everyone can be a different breed. I've spent my whole life proving that.

When you're my kind of different breed, only two things matter in life—love and adventure. Not necessarily in that order. Finding adventure was practically impossible when I worked in the San Diego Safeway. It's hard enough just staying awake when you're cashiering, much less thinking about adventure. And as for love, I had already found it in Al. Sweet, loyal Al. All I had to do was get to Spokane, Washington, where Al lived. And that's when the adventure part began.

There really wasn't any hurry. It had been five years since I had seen or heard from Al, but neither of us was much on long-distance communication. I knew he was in Spokane—and madly in love with me. He knew I was somewhere—and madly in love with him. What more did we need? But when his postcard arrived at my brother's apartment, I knew it was time to see him again. I can tell you exactly what it said. "Visit me, visit me, visit me. Al." Not hard to remember, is it? *I* sure got the message.

So I went to Spokane. Sort of. Trouble is, when you travel by thumb you don't have much control over your schedule, and a three-day trip can stretch out to three months. That's because when I hitchhiked from San Diego to Spokane, I wound up in Arizona. Then Philadelphia. Then Boston. Then Reno. Well, at least by then I was headed in the right direction. And because I took the scenic route, a shock awaited me in Spokane. How could so much have happened in just a few months? I'd finally reached Spokane, but the adventure was far from over.

—Nancy L. Chu

Fire Mask   **Grades 5–6**
By Charles L. Grant

The fire mask. The first time that Cliff saw the fire mask was in a dream. It was an upsetting dream, but then it had been an upsetting night. Rushmore was a quiet town, a peaceful town, and to tell the truth, a boring town. But that night there had been a fire. A huge fire. And Cliff was there. Not only was he there, but he saw the man who set the fire, right before he died. Is it any wonder that Cliff had the dream? But sometimes, and this was one of those times, Cliff was scared by his dreams. They had an eerie way of coming true. Not all of them, but if *this* dream was one of *those dreams*, Cliff was in for trouble.

The fire mask. The next time that Cliff saw the fire mask was late at night. Strange things had been happening to Cliff ever since the night of the fire, and now a strange man was chasing him through the dark streets of Rushmore. A man hidden in the shadows. A man who couldn't quite catch up. A man Cliff couldn't see—until the man reached out to grab him, and Cliff saw that he was wearing the mask.

The fire mask. The third time that Cliff saw the fire mask was at the party. The very strange party at the house of the man who had owned the hotel that burned down. Some of the guests were wearing fire-mask pins or necklaces. Not all the guests—just the strange ones. Cliff was not having fun at the party. The place felt familiar, as if he had been there before. But he knew he hadn't. It was like a place out of a dream. Then, later that night, Cliff saw the fire mask again. For the final time.

—Marijo Duncan

First Wedding, Once Removed   Grades 5–8
By Julie Reece Deaver

Pokie stares at her reflection in the full-length mirror. She's wearing a lacy, lime-green bridesmaid's dress, high-heeled shoes, and a wide-brimmed picture hat. She looks absolutely ridiculous—she could just barf! This nauseating costume was selected by Nell, the bride-to-be, and Pokie's own brother Gib went along with it.

He's going to be the groom. All summer long, it's been nothing but Gib and Nell, Nell and Gib. It never used to be that way. Last summer, for instance, it was always Gib and Pokie. They went everywhere together. But now Pokie can't go with Gib. Once he marries Nell, he'll be gone forever, and Pokie's life will never be the same. She isn't gaining a sister, she's losing a brother! She's never been without Gib before. How can she stand such a drastic change?

—Kaite Mediatore

Fling   Adult
By John Hersey

Finally! A collection of short stories from John Hersey! And, as expected, they're insightful glimpses of strange and marvelous people.

Take Billy, for instance. His father had been a missionary in China. To the community, Dr. Wyman was a brilliant man with a laugh as loud as Niagara Falls. By contrast, Billy was washed-out and obedient, with sad bloodhound eyes and scuffed black shoes. Billy could be counted on to be bullied into adventures, as long as his father didn't catch him. So it wasn't surprising that Billy cried until his lungs almost burst when his father swooped down on him sleeping in the family's prize aboretum. What *was* surprising was Billy's reaction when a thunderstorm uprooted the aboretum trees—and killed Dr. Wyman.

And there was Miss Peg, the pastry cook, with a coffee eclair hovering in her fingers. She got all gussied up one day to meet her new beau, but she had to run a small errand for the family first. That small errand turned out to be a substantial smelly salmon. And she had no time to deliver her bundle before meeting her merchant marine. Nor would any checkroom relieve her of her smelly burden—no way! The package seemed like all the unhappiness she would never get rid of in this life, until her marine said, "Miss Peggety, three's a crowd, but let's face facts, he goes where we go. What's it to be, steak or little twinkletoes?"

Fascinating people await you in this collection of Hersey's short stories.

—Lesley S. J. Farmer

For Laughing Out Loud: Grades 3–8
Poems to Tickle Your Funnybone
Jack Prelutsky, sel.

If you have got a funnybone,
and I've no doubt you do,
then this completely silly book
is sure to tickle you.
I've filled it full of dizzy rhymes,
the wildest I could find,
and if it makes you laugh out loud,
that's what I had in mind.

With that invitation, come into a world of silly stories, tongue-in-cheek tales, and goofy characters. Make fun of such serious and sober subjects as homework, parents, and hot dogs. Only strong and solemn souls will be able to keep straight faces when reading about Friendly Frederick Fuddlestone, who could fiddle on his funnybone, or Chester Lester Kirkenby Dale, who caught his sweater on a nail. For those whose hobbies run to recipes, there are "Rhinoceros Stew," "Snowflake

Souffle," and "Garbage Delight." The weird, wild, and wonderful are waiting to be discovered in *For Laughing Out Loud: Poems to Tickle Your Funnybone.* You'll never think about poetry without laughing again!

—Nancy L. Chu

Forever's Team   Grade 10–Adult
By John Feinstein

Juice, Captain, Charlie Manson, Fonz, H, Klinger, Johnny Gun, Mikey, Coach Benny, Preacher, Tinkerbell, Dirty Dog, Jewish Mother, Little Buckaroo, Wenz.

They were innocent, they were unique, they were going to be the greatest team ever.

They were the Duke University basketball team that went from last place in the ACC to within seconds of winning the NCAA championship game of 1978.

They were one of the great Cinderella teams of all times.

They were a team with only one senior, led by two freshmen forwards, a sophomore center, and a junior guard. A team that an entire nation took to its heart, and expected to found a dynasty.

They came from New Jersey, North Carolina, Kentucky, Pennsylvania, Georgia, and Connecticut, from the inner city and the family farm. They were the sons of lawyers, coaches, farmers, and clerks.

Their extraordinary success was followed, in many cases, by extraordinary adversity: cancer, heart attack, brain tumor, automobile accident, and failure.

They were a team of boys destined for success, and twelve years later, they are individual men coping with dashed dreams, with truth, with life.

They were the Duke Blue Devils. They are *Forever's Team.*

—Barbara Bahm

Fourth Grade Rats   Grades 3–6
By Jerry Spinelli

First grade babies!
Second grade cats!
Third grade angels!
Fourth grade rats!

Rats don't cry, and they aren't afraid of spiders! Rats eat meat, not peanut butter and jelly! Rats are mean to little kids! *Real* rats say No to their mothers! Only problem is, Suds Morton doesn't want to be a rat. Being an angel was so much easier for him. His best friend Joey says being a rat is part of growing up and becoming a man. (Joey, of course, thinks it's great being a rat.)

Judy Billings thinks rats are great too. And since Suds likes Judy and being a rat is the only way he can get her attention, then a rat is what he'll have to be! Will Suds survive crawly spiders, baloney sandwiches, and total embarrassment just to become a full-fledged rat and the love of Judy's life? Watch out, world, this isn't going to be easy for Suds!

—Anne Liebst

The Foxes of FirstDark   **Adult**
By Garry Kilworth

He murdered my babies and swore that I'd be next. I know I should find a place to hide, but where can I go? No one living in Trinity Wood can protect me against Sabre. They are all terrified of him, and rightly so. He is known as the most deadly hunter in the area, and he kills without mercy. Unlike the other hunters here in the Wood, Sabre kills for the pure enjoyment of it. I have even heard him brag that he lives to kill.

How could any creature turn so monstrously unnatural? It must come from living with humans and serving them. After all, humans also kill us and even their own kind just for the thrill of it. I can't understand it. Camio, my friend, says that not all humans are cruel. He claims that when he was traveling across the country he met some who tried to be kind to other creatures. But I think such talk is dangerous. Why, next Camio will try to make me believe that not all dogs are traitors to the rest of animalkind. *I* know better. If we animals didn't have to worry about humans and their dogs, life would be much easier. Then we could concentrate on finding mates and raising children, and live like normal creatures.

But enough of such thoughts. If I want to live at all, I have to find a way to outfox Sabre. And that won't be easy—even for a fox.

—Margie Reitsma

Fresh Brats
By X. J. Kennedy   **Grades 5–12**

For his mother's mudpack Brent
substituted fresh cement.
Mom applied it; in a while
Found it hard to crack a smile.

But you'll find it easy to smile, and even laugh out loud, at the havoc
these fresh brats wreak upon themselves and their poor, long-suffering
families. Listen to what one brat does for dear old Dad:

Sheila, into Dad's right shoe,
squirts a blob of Superglue,
does the same thing to the left,
thus discouraging shoe-theft.
Stuck on fast, they're hard to lose—
Still, who'd rather be in Father's shoes?

Brats all—from Steffan, who puts a dead mouse in Mother's rising
bread, to "rotten Ross," who puts Tabasco in the mouthwash. I'm sure
none of you would ever consider such dastardly deeds as dipping your
baby sister in glow-in-the-dark paint. Or waving a rubber rat around
at the 4-H bake sale. But you can have almost as much fun by reading
about kids who do in *Fresh Brats*.

I'll leave you with a tip on how to get great grades on your next report
card:

On report-card day Spike Sparks
scores incredibly high marks.
Is Spike smart? Has he a tutor?
Nope—he's cracked the school computer.

—Diane L. Deuel

Friend of My Youth
By Alice Munro   **Adult**

Alice Munro's stock-in-trade is people. Here are a few choice
characters in her collection:

Matilda was a captive-princess beauty. Long, floating, light brown hair, pink-and-white skin, the milk of human kindness. Known as a champion speller. And soon as she could, Matilda would do her best to get rid of or camouflage that beauty—it isolated her, more severely than a mild deformity, because it could be seen as a reproach. Captive princesses exist to be rescued, but who would dare confront Matilda's monstrous mother?

Maya's home was considered "your friendly neighborhood fortress." Maya the gatekeeper wore a long shapeless robe of coarse brown cloth; her skin was rough and pale with marks like faint bird tracks. The only thing she did to her face was paint her plucked eyebrows blue, "just a little daub of blue over each eye, like a swollen vein." At dinner parties, Maya served indifferent food, nothing special, and set the table with faintly tarnished family silver. She seemed devoted to her husband, hanging on his every word—or was that just a cover-up?

Almeda Joynt Roth was the sort of woman who aged well. She wore a tucked and braid-trimmed jacket, accompanied by a soft beret that signaled a shy, artistic eccentricity. Almeda lived in a fine old house, right up the street from one of the roughest neighborhoods in town. All the changes and storms around her can be borne only if channeled into a poem. One very great poem that will contain everything.

Alice Munro's Canadian world, depicted in her short stories, will surprise you. You may not like all her people, but you'll certainly recognize them—they're your neighbors, seen more sharply than you'd ever imagine.

—Lesley S. J. Farmer

Friendship Across the Arctic Waters: Grades 3-8
Alaskan Cub Scouts Visit Their Soviet Neighbors
By Claire Rudolf Murphy

What would it be like, being a Scout in Siberia? Eleven American Cub Scouts from Nome, Alaska, had a chance to find out when they were invited to travel to Provideniya, across the Bering Strait, and visit with the Young Pioneers, the Soviet equivalent of Scouts.

It's only 250 miles from Alaska to the eastern edge of Siberia [show map, p.1]. It doesn't sound like a very long trip, but for more than forty years people were not allowed to travel from one side of the strait to the other, even to visit relatives.

At first the Cub Scouts were excited and only a little nervous about meeting the Young Pioneers. Then, when they arrived and saw Soviet military planes and helicopters, the red hammer-and-sickle insignia, Russian-language signs, and uniformed guards with guns, the boys were really scared! But finally they spotted three smiling women waving a sign written in English as well as Russian: "Welcome!"

Let these Alaskan Cub Scouts tell you all about the gifts they exchanged with the Soviet boys and girls and the problems they had pronouncing "thank you" and "you're welcome" in Russian. You'll find out about Russian homes, the jobs the young people have, and some of the games that both groups play: Duck Duck Goose, Musical Chairs, and Simon Says. Frisbees, transformer toys, softball, and wiener roasts were new to the Young Pioneers, but not for long, thanks to the Cub Scouts!

After you read *Friendship Across Arctic Waters*, I think you'll agree with the Scouts: "We're so much more alike than we ever imagined, aren't we? . . . People are people, no matter where you go."

—*Dorothy Davidson*

Full Moon Soup, or The Fall of the Hotel Splendide
By Alastair Graham

Grades 3-8; Adults

It was the night of the full moon when things began to go wrong at the lovely Hotel Splendide. Just as the chef took a sip of the soup he was to serve that night for dinner, strange and frightening things began to happen. The monsters in the cellar and the ghosts in the attic came out to play, and suddenly nothing was as it should be!

Discover how mayhem and madness combine to change these scenes [show inside front cover] into this [show inside back cover], and transform the Hotel Splendide [show first double-page spread of the hotel] forever! [Show the final spread, or one of the illustrations near the end.]

—*J. R. B.*

A Gathering of Flowers
By Joyce Carol Thomas

Grade 7-12

Have you ever wanted to take a peep into the lives of other teenagers—people like yourself, and yet different? In these eleven short stories, you'll get a quick glimpse of events in the lives of Mexicans, blacks, Indians, Japanese, Koreans, and whites—all American-born teenagers, who tell about happy, sad, and weird feelings or experiences in their lives.

You'll probably be puzzled by "Almost a Whole Trickster," and haunted by "Harrington's Daughter"; you may travel through Zee's mind in "Going to the Moon," or feel Rose's love in "Autumn Rose." And guys, especially, will understand Alfonso's "First Love."

However, one thing for sure, the flowers of youth gathered in these short stories can tell you a little something about yourself, and maybe about someone else as well—someone you see every day but do not really know. Meet a few new friends in *A Gathering of Flowers*.

—*Faye A. Powell*

George Washington's Socks   Grades 3–6
By Elvira Woodruff

It is a warm, moonlit night when Matt and his friends make camp in Tony's backyard. Little do they know that this will be a night to remember!

It's hard to say just when it all begins. Perhaps when they decide to hike down to Levy Lake, formerly known as Levart Lake. Or perhaps it begins when Tony tells them the legend of the lake, and of the mysterious disappearances, and how those who returned were never the same—and then there were those who *never* came back. Or maybe it begins when Matt's little sister discovers an old rowboat with the name *Emit Levart* etched on the side, and they step into it, one by one, only to find themselves in the middle of the icy, rushing Delaware River.

As they look out over the river, they see a boat coming toward them. At the bow is a tall, stately gentleman who looks a lot like George Washington. Matt can't believe it and neither can his friends, but here they are—crossing the Delaware with George Washington's army, preparing for battle during the American Revolution. Soon the five friends are faced with the life-and-death realities of war as they search for a way out of the eighteenth century.

Will they ever return to the twentieth? Read *George Washington's Socks* to find out all about Matt and his friends' adventure, and the mystery of Levart Lake.

—*Cara A. Waits*

Germy Blew the Bugle   Grades 5-6
By Rebecca C. Jones

Any sixth-grader worth his weight in Big Bubba bubblegum knows that bloody worms and gelatin salad filled with grass clippings are just a few of the revolting meals served in the grade-school cafeteria.

Sixth-grader Jeremy Bluett, nicknamed "Germy Blew It" by his peers, thinks he knows all about the garbage the cafeteria serves. He intends to run the whole ghastly story in the newspaper he wants to publish for profit at Dolley Madison Elementary School.

Who cares that Germy can't type, assigns himself all the best stories, and tries to sell ads while using the school's supplies, time, and students to get the newspaper started? His family cares, and so do Ms. Morrison, the hugging principal, and pushy Margaret "Mouth" MacElroy, a fifth-grader who talks way too much but has a computer with desktop publishing capabilities.

Undaunted by his problems, Germy jumps into the newspaper business with both feet and soon discovers he's up to his eyebrows in a lot more than disgusting food. His friends don't want to write stories but like to cut class for staff meetings. Squirrel, his buddy, wants help with his love life in exchange for reporting class news, and "Mouth" MacElroy wants her own column—or maybe two!

Is the glory of being Jeremy Bluett, Editor, worth the static Germy has to take from his classmates, teachers, and cafeteria workers for distorting the facts? Can he be rescued from this mess, or has Germy really blown *The Bugle* once and for all?

—Suzanne Bruney

The Ghost in the Attic   Grades 5-8
By Emily Cates

When Dee Forest went to spend the winter on Misty Island with her Aunt Winnefred, she never imagined that she would become friends with Louisa Lockwood, the ghost of a girl who died in a fire in 1897 at the age of thirteen. Louisa, trapped between the land of the living and the land of the dead, wants to rejoin her parents and her brother, who also died in the fire. But before she will be allowed to rest in peace, she must help four living family members. So Dee and Louisa set out to find four of Louisa's relatives who are in trouble today. Little do they suspect that they will become involved in burglary and kidnapping in the process.

What happens when a ghost tries to help the living? Find out in *The Ghost in the Attic.*

—*Kathy Ann Miller*

The Girl with the White Flag   Grades 5–8
By Tomiko Higa

Imagine you are seven years old and live on the island of Okinawa. It is June 1945. For weeks you have been wandering around the island, dodging bombs and grenades, eating out of dead soldiers' knapsacks. You sleep in caves during the daytime and move about only at night, when you can't be seen. This is how Tomiko Higa lived for three months in 1945, during the battle for Okinawa.

The Japanese army on Okinawa was a hundred thousand strong, and it took the Americans months of fierce fighting to overcome them. Many lives were lost. The entire island was a battle zone. But when the fighting was over, to celebrate, a young Army photographer took a remarkable picture. It showed a little barefoot girl in tattered clothes waving a piece of white cloth tied to a crooked stick. She had come along the road all by herself, carrying her white flag.

That photograph is the reason this book was written. Many years later, while browsing in a bookstore, a much older Tomiko Higa came across the picture of that little girl with the white flag, and her wartime memories came flooding back. She finally had the courage to put her story into words. Here is an account of the battle for Okinawa, as seen through the eyes of a seven-year-old child.

—*Blair Reid*

A Graveyard for Lunatics   Grade 9–Adult
By Ray Bradbury

Have you got a few minutes? I have a *great* idea for a new film. Here's the basic outline of the script: *Location*— Hollywood, the city built on fantasies and dreams. *Time*—1954, on Halloween night, a time when magic and nightmares reign. *Cast*—a newly-hired science-fiction scriptwriter; his best friend, the famous special-effects genius Roy Holdstrom; the apparent corpse of James Charles Arbuthnot, who was the head of Maximus Films twenty years ago; an ominous but elusive beast-creature; and of course the studio's usual cast of thousands. *Story line*—The science-fiction writer is lured via an anonymous note to the graveyard attached to Maximus studios on Halloween night, where he sees—or thinks he sees—the corpse of the long-dead studio executive Arbuthnot. When the writer tries to discover who sent him to the graveyard and whether what he saw there was really a corpse or some kind of dummy, the people he contacts begin dying and/or disappearing.

Suddenly the writer doesn't know what's reality and what's illusion. Life has become one big Hollywood fantasy. Is someone really killing these people who are disappearing, and if so, why? Was he lured to the graveyard and shown a glimpse of what looked like Arbuthnot's corpse as part of some blackmail scheme against the studio? And if it is a blackmail scheme, does that mean that Arbuthnot didn't really die in a car crash twenty years ago? Was he murdered and the car crash arranged as a cover-up? And finally, who or what is the frightening beast-figure that the scriptwriter and his friend see disappearing into the graveyard at night?

Well, is that enough to give you the general picture? It has a little bit of everything: mystery, horror, fantasy, and humor. Wait now; before you tell me whether you like it or not, you should really read the whole script. And I just happen to have a copy with me! Here it is: *A Graveyard for Lunatics*. When you finish, give me a call. We'll do lunch and talk details.

—*Margie Reitsma*

The Greatest Idea Ever   Grades 3–6
By Joan Carris

Gus Howard is an energetic fourth-grader with lots of good ideas. Some of them earn him praise, like the new way he ran the student art show, but most of them get him into trouble. For instance, there was the time he set up a "bendy" pencil business in the boys' bathroom to earn money to support his new puppy, or the time he wowed his cooking class with a cockroach omelette. But the most difficult idea to come up with is how to get even with the class tattletale, Nanny Vincent. Accomplishing this and staying out of trouble at the same time will require the help of his friends Pep and Buzzer, and—*The Greatest Idea Ever*!

—*Monica Carollo*

Growing Up Isn't Hard   Adult
To Do if You Start Out as a Kid
David Heller, comp.

"Once you start being grown up, there's no way to quit or stop and try it all over again." So speaks ten-year-old Blaire, one of the children interviewed in David Heller's latest book. Well, maybe Blaire is right. We adults can't turn back into kids, even if we'd sometimes like to. But Heller's book lets us do the next best thing: it lets us look at our grown-up world and behavior through children's eyes, and the change of perspective can be quite revealing. Take six-year-old Eric's description of marriage: "Marriage is when you get to *keep* your girl and don't have to give her back to her parents." No subtle beating around the male chauvinist bush for Eric! On the other side of the discussion, Lynnette, age eight, thinks that "Dates are for fun, and people should use them to get to know each other," adding thoughtfully that "even boys have something to say if you listen long enough."

But marriage and dating aren't the only topics these kids want to talk about. We also get to hear their opinions on adults: their weird tastes in food and clothing, why they're always working, what being a parent involves, and why so many adults become parents in the first place. Some of these quotes are startlingly perceptive. Eight-year old Sheila's comment on television sitcoms is an example: "Most of the parents on TV are getting paid to be parents. Mine do it because they love me!"

Remarks like that can make a parent feel that it's all worthwhile, but other observations may make us wince. When asked how being a parent was different in ancient times, eight-year-old Dana delivered this analysis: "There was no television or computer games, so the parents were forced to talk to the kids more, and the kids were forced to listen."

No one is going to force you to read this book, of course, but I strongly recommend it—especially if you're ready for a radically different perspective on the world around you. As Heller's book shows, being grown-up doesn't have to be dull and predictable, not if we keep in touch with the kids. After all, *we* started out that way too!

—Margie Reitsma

Gruel and Unusual Punishment　　　Grades 5-8
By Jim Arter

Arnold Dinklighter wasn't sure what Mr. Applin, the detention room teacher, meant when he wrote "Welcome to the Gulag" on the board. If Arnold had known about the Soviet prison camps where people serve out life sentences at hard labor, he would have understood, and sympathized. There were times when Arnold felt as if he'd been given a life sentence to South Kenton School. He was repeating seventh grade, and he was in detention so often that he had his own reserved chair.

And what had he ever done to deserve all this detention, anyway? All he'd ever tried to do was liven up the place a little bit. What's the harm in a little bra-snapping, or a few practical jokes, or a little disrespect for teachers who deserve it?

Arnold seems doomed to solitary confinement in the Gulag until a new kid named Edward moves in. Finally! Someone who can match Arnold prank for prank, detention slip for detention slip.

But Arnold soon discovers that Edward has some serious problems and that his newest scheme involves killing Mr. Applin. Arnold has to make some serious moves fast, before he earns himself a *real* prison sentence, in a Gulag that won't be a joke.

—*Jeff Blair*

The Half Child　　　Grades 7-12
By Kathleen Hersom

Everyone said that my little sister Sarah was a changeling, because of the way she looked and talked and behaved. They said the only way to get my real sister back would be to treat Sarah so badly that the Little People would have to come and rescue her, and undo the swap they must have made. In Yorkshire, England, in 1644, a lot of people thought this way. I didn't believe them, but just in case, I made daisy chains for Sarah to wear to protect her from the Little People. I loved her, and I didn't want them to take her away.

But on the night a new baby was born in our house, the night Cromwell's men destroyed the church, Sarah disappeared forever. People whispered that the Little People had finally come for her.

I still didn't believe them. I want so much to believe that she was found, and that someone cares for her and loves her as I did. I want to believe that someone else is making a daisy chain for her to wear. I think about seeing her again one day and asking her where she's been— and hearing her answer, "Not telling!"

—*Donna L. Scanlon*

Halsey's Pride   Grades 5-6
By Lynn Hall

March Halsey is keeping a secret. When she goes to live with the father she hasn't seen in years, she doesn't tell him about her epilepsy, and she doesn't tell the kids at her new school, either. The secret keeps her from making many new friends, so she spends her free time helping her father with his collie kennel, especially with Pride, his prize-winning dog. But Pride is more than a show dog to March. Pride gives her the love she craves, and it is Pride who stays by March when she unexpectedly has a seizure. But one day a puppy is found dead in the kennel. Rumors start to move around show circles that Pride has "bad blood." When March's father discovers this gossip is hurting his business, he knows he has to get ride of Pride. Now it is up to March to save a dog who, like herself, cannot help what he is. Will March have enough of *Halsey's Pride* to stand up to her father?

—*Kaite Mediatore*

A Hand Full of Stars   Grades 9-12
By Rafik Schami, translated by Rika Lesser

Uncle Salim is my best friend. He's not even my real uncle and he is seventy-five years old, but it's because of something he said that I keep this journal.

I have discovered what I wish to do with my life. I want to be a journalist. But will my father allow it? He's always making me leave school to help in the bakery. It does not matter to him that I don't go to school. How can I be a journalist without a proper education?

In my city of Damascus, journalists are not very popular. The government is always arresting people, especially those who speak out, tell the truth—and that is what a journalist must do.

The government is also always changing. First there is a coup, then a new government. And my girlfriend Nadia's father always works for the latest government. As a spy. We have to be careful.

I have found a good friend who will help me become a journalist.

Habib is a great writer, and he pushes me to do my best. He forces me to re-examine and re-write my thoughts until the words say what I mean. Habib is not an easy teacher. Then he is arrested.

How can my friends and I—mere teenagers—combat the military, avoid Nadia's father, and get the news to our people? Then suddenly I know. We'll distribute the news in socks sold in the market. The "sock-newspaper" will show the military how many Habibs the imprisoned journalist has brought into the world.

—*Barbara Diment*

Hank   Grades 7–12
By Jim Sauer

Hi, my name is Richard. I want to tell you about my younger brother Hank. You see, Hank marches to a different drummer. He believes in getting things right. He has this idea that everything has a way it's supposed to be. A right way that may not be easy or even appreciated, but is right just the same. Even if doing something the right way could get you killed.

It's because of Hank that I got to know Allie and her sister Emily better. It all happened the first day of school. Hank and Emily were painting when Seth Thompson started picking on Emily, which is definitely not right in Hank's book. Well, to make a long story short, Hank dumped paint on Seth and was sent home from school. As part of his punishment, Dad said he had to help out with any chores Seth's father happened to need done, but Seth's father wasn't taking any chances on a repeat performance. So Hank ended up painting the garage for Allie and Emily's father instead. And *guess* who had to supervise? But it turned out OK because, after many false starts, Allie and I got together.

It was also because of Hank that we got to know Arthur, who was one of the local street people. Arthur came around, poking through the garbage looking for pop cans. Hank didn't think this was right, so he put our pop cans in a separate bag, to give Arthur when he saw him in the back alley by the garbage.

Hank lives by his philosophy of doing it right, no matter what. If doing something right meant you'd have to die, I'd do it wrong. But Hank always does it right, even if he's the one who has to pay the price.

—*Linda Olson*

Hannah Grades 3-6
By Gloria Whelan

Have you ever had something wonderful happen to you that changed your whole life? I did! It happened in the fall of 1887, when the new teacher came to board with my family. We were all looking forward to having her stay with us, especially since there were hardly any neighbors living near our farm in northern Michigan. I was nine years old then and had never been to school, because I'm blind, and my parents figured it'd be a waste of time. After all, how could I read schoolbooks if I couldn't see? Still, it hurt me so to have my brother and sister go without me, leaving me to keep my mother company! Well, when Miss Robbin arrived and convinced Mama and Papa to let me attend her classes with the other boys and girls, I was thrilled. Learning how to read and write was my dream! Little did I know how far I still was that day from making my dream come true!

—*Sister M. Anna Falbo, CSSF*

Happy Endings Grades 7-12
By Adele Geras

Two-faced, shallow, rotten little cow! Oh, I was taken in at first. Dinah definitely has acting talent. She had me thinking she was an innocent, sweet little thing. But I started to see through her facade on that visit to her house. Talk about indulgent parents! Her room was crammed full of anything and everything her little heart desired and though her parents may be deluded fools, they're sweet—her mother did *not* deserve to be shoved off rudely when she offered to help with the costumes at the theater. That was when I began to realize what Dinah was *really* like, when I saw how she put down her mother.

Oh, my name is Mel. All right, my full name is Melusine, but heaven help the soul who calls me that. I got to know Dinah through the theater group. We're putting on Chekhov's play *Three Sisters*. Why do I dislike Dinah so much? You mean, besides knowing that she's cruel to her parents and shallow and greedy? Well, it's because of Chris and Clare. Chris is the director. He's good, even if he is stupidly blind about Dinah. Clare was the costume and set designer. They (Chris and Clare) *were* in love. But then who comes prancing along, flapping her eyelashes, wiggling like an eager puppy, but Dinah. I've got to hand it to her. She's not just beautiful, but a terrific actress; ambitious and ruthless, to be sure, but she knows what she wants and she gets it. And when she decided she wanted Chris, there was no way to stop her—she got him. She says she loves him, but I know she's just using him to get ahead. We'll all no doubt be seeing her on the silver screen some day. Rotten little. . . .

And Clare? She's gone. She destroyed the model of the set, and she's gone. I'm really worried. Anyone who would break something up like that has got to be awfully upset and depressed. If I don't hear from her soon, I'm going to find her. Maybe I can help. Or maybe I'd better stay out of it. I wish life were more like a play! Then I could read ahead and find out if there's a happy ending.

—Julie Bray

Harry and Catherine   Adult
By Frederick Busch

Harry and Catherine. Catherine and Harry. Their names were once inseparable. But twelve years have passed since they parted. Catherine's sons, the little boys that Harry once pulled in a coaster wagon, are now young men. Catherine has changed too, though not in the ways that really matter. Her gallery business is doing well, especially with tourist trade from New Yorkers heading upstate to find rural treasures. She is still strong, regal, and independent. And, unfortunately for Harry, her love life isn't bad these days either.

But it's not as if Harry has been sitting around for all those years. As aide and speechwriter for a New York senator, he's comfortable in Washington—not excited, but comfortable. Things are getting more interesting now that the senator's name is often mentioned in the same sentence with the words "White House" and "presidential material." Harry can look forward to new projects that will add variety and maybe even prestige to his job. Such as going on a fact-finding mission to find out about the pre-Civil War cemetery threatened by the construction of a new shopping mall. Local legend has it that the people buried there were fugitive slaves, heading north on the Underground Railroad when they died in an epidemic. Luckily for the senator, they died in his home state where he can get political mileage from every special-interest group on the East Coast.

It's even luckier for Harry, because the trip will take him practically into Catherine's backyard. To her front door, actually. Maybe farther. They can be Harry and Catherine again.

Only, when Harry gets to Catherine's front door, he doesn't meet Catherine. He meets Carter, her lover and the contractor whose asphalt will cover the long-forgotten but politically critical graves. Harry has the power to save Carter from bankruptcy or send him into financial ruin. Which will get Catherine back? Or is Catherine through with Harry forever, no matter *what* he does?

—Nancy L. Chu

Harry Kaplan's   Grade 9–Adult
Adventures Underground
By Steve Stern

In the night from a raft, Memphis' Beale Street looked enticing and somehow glamorous. But in daylight, the other side of the tracks looked kind of threatening. As Harry boldly walked into a black barbershop, one of the local teens who had floated him "down the river," so to speak, came to his rescue: "He ain't white. He's Jewrish."

From that point, Harry began to sneak out of his parents' apartment two, sometimes three nights a week. His family had their own affairs to attend to, and they never missed him. His father was busy tracking the personal history of each item brought into his pawnshop, which was a lot of items, the Great Depression being what it was, and his mother was busy with Uncle Morris trying to get Grandpa put away in an asylum.

Harry's two black buddies were twins, a loquacious Lucifer and a mute Michael—"Our daddy named us after angels." They showed him Memphis' gambling spots, non-kosher eating holes, the Baby Doll Hotel with its unsavory lovelies. Harry was their shadow. In return for all this education, Harry had to get books for Michael. It was hard to know what Michael made of them—he damaged any books he *did* get beyond repair—but Harry kept his side of the bargain.

The problems really began when Harry started borrowing books from his romantic cousin Naomi. She gladly parted with the volumes, booktalking with the best. Unfortunately, when Michael saw the shiksa Cotton Queen, he suddenly began ranting love lines and never stopped. Desperate, Harry figured the one way to stop Michael was to get Naomi to dress up and shock him back into silence. Oh, boy—"Love on a coffin with Huck Finn's Jewish cousin!"

—Lesley S. J. Farmer

Harvey's Wacky Parrot Adventure   Grades 3–4
By Eth Clifford

Hi, I'm Harvey. My cousin Nora has to stay with us over the Christmas holiday. As usual, whenever she is around all sorts of weird things happen. This time it involves Sinbad, a talking parrot.

Sinbad belongs to my Uncle Buck. He used to belong to an old friend of my uncle's, Captain Corbin. But Sinbad would get seasick whenever he went on a trip with the captain, so now he stays on dry land with Uncle Buck. Captain Corbin still comes to visit Uncle Buck whenever he can. He and Uncle Buck play tricks on each other. The Captain's last was to hide a treasure, and now that the Captain has been lost at sea, only Sinbad has the clue.

But that bird can say lots and lots of things. How are you supposed to know which one is the clue? I'm not even sure there *is* a treasure! That could be the Captain's finest trick yet—telling Uncle Buck that there's a treasure when there's not. That's why Uncle Buck never hunted for it. But now Nora is here, and I know *nothing* will keep her from that treasure hunt. So why don't you join us? Like I told you, whenever Nora is around all sorts of strange things happen—maybe there *is* a treasure, after all.

—Frances W. Levin

He Came from the Shadows   Grades 7–12
By Chris Westwood

Eastfield was a slowly dying town when the stranger arrived. The mines had closed two months before, leaving most of the men in town without work. Some people were moving on to other places, but most couldn't afford to, so there they were, stuck in Eastfield, with nothing to do but watch the place fall apart.

The stranger came out of nowhere. His name was Stands, and he said that he had been called—that someone in the town had wished him there.

Granting wishes was Stands' business, you see. He started off small, but the more wishes he granted, the stronger he became. And as he became stronger, the wishes he was able to grant became bigger . . . and more frightening.

At first people got things—new appliances, new cars, fur coats. Somebody won the lottery. Kids got bikes, and their toy stuffed animals became real, live pets. The list went on and on.

And everyone was delighted, thrilled, grateful to the stranger—
everyone except Jules. He was frightened. Why couldn't anyone see
what was really going on, who Stands really was, and what he was doing? Oh, Rachel and Steve agreed with Jules, but who were they against
the whole town?

The day will come, however, when Jules and his friends have to act.
For, inch by horrible inch, Stands is taking control of the town and everyone in it. Pushed to the limit, Jules and his friends decide to take
on Stands and try to stop him—even if they die in the attempt.

—*Melinda D. Waugh*

Hey Little Walter,   Grades 7–12
and Other Prize-Winning Plays
By Wendy Lamb, ed.

"These young playwrights are the theater's future." So says Stephen
Sondheim. Six young playwrights, aged 15 to 18, had their plays
produced by the Foundation of the Dramatists Guild. Now *you* can be
the judge. Look at these characters:

There's Doris, feeling somehow "different" from her friends. Even
her efforts to put on a really rad party fizzle rather than sizzle. Maybe
those people aren't her friends. Maybe her friends are out of this world,
literally. Would you rather stay on Earth or swing on a star?

Or Opal. Her mom is always nagging her. She's not trying hard
enough. She needs a boyfriend. Well, Mom isn't so happy when Opal
does dress up and find a boyfriend. Maybe it's because Klaus was Momma's boyfriend first!

And take Little Walter. He's a good-enough kid, trying to make it in
the Brooklyn slums. But it's hard with brothers and sisters, constant
bills, and no dad. And it's harder when he knows buddies who are driving well and looking good. It's no big deal to deal, right?

That's only half the cast. By the time you finish these plays, you may
want to create a drama of your own!

—*Lesley S. J. Farmer*

The Hideout   Grades 5–8
By Eve Bunting

Forty-five dollars and a burning desire to see his dad were all that
twelve-year-old Andy had going for him when he ran away from home,
away from his mother and the new stepfather he'd nicknamed "Paul
Paws" because the man couldn't keep his hands off Andy's mom.

That's all he had until he reached the Countess International Hotel, not far from his San Francisco home. With some quick maneuvering, Andy picked up a hotel key that a careless doorman had dropped when reaching for a tip and traced the letter "T" on the key label to the hotel's posh tower suite.

From this perfect hideout, he telephoned his friend Leah, who came over with food and other supplies. When Leah left, she gave Andy her Easi-Talkie (smaller than a Walkie-Talkie), so he could contact her if he had to leave the hideout. The cops were looking for him, Leah reported.

It was all a great set-up, but when Andy tried to call his father in London, he found his dad was off on an archaeological dig and wouldn't be back for several weeks. So Andy hatched a crude plan to get money and travel out to the dig himself. And just when he was about ready to execute the plan, he got careless—and then everything got crazy.

Andy always slept under the bed for safety, but that night he left his Reeboks out in plain sight. Fred the hotel maintainance man and his date decided to use the suite for a midnight picnic. They saw the shoes, hauled Andy out from under the bed, and threatened to report him for breaking and entering.

Badly frightened, Andy blurted out his money-making plan, and Fred turned greedy. Andy found himself bound, gagged, and thrown into Fred's van for the most terrifying journey of his life. His only hope was the Easi-Talkie hidden under his sweatshirt.

—*Suzanne Bruney*

High Cheekbones   Grade 7–Adult
By Erika Tamar

Fourteen-year-old Alice Lonner lives with her mom and her little brother Jamie in a run-down old building in New York City. There's not a lot of money to go around, so Alice and Jamie sometimes earn extra money helping people carry their bags home from the grocery store. One day they carry some bags for a pretty, dark-haired woman who stares at Alice all the way to her apartment. It really makes Alice feel uncomfortable, but then the woman tells her she has good bones, and that she could model if she wanted. She gives Alice her card and tells her to call if she's interested. Alice has always known she's pretty, and that's nice, but getting through school and into a good job so she can support Jamie has always been more important to her.

But on a whim she calls the woman, who turns out to be an assistant for one of the biggest modeling agencies in town. Alice doesn't feel as if she can ever be as beautiful as the models she sees in the photos on the agency's walls, but once again it's her high cheekbones that get her through the door. As soon as she starts going out on shoots, Alice is a hit. One of the best photographers in town befriends her, and almost immediately her face is on magazines all over the country.

But being a big star and having lots of money for the first time in her life doesn't make Alice as happy as she'd always imagined. Modeling isn't all fun—it's a lot of sitting around, and then working with rude, arrogant people, and always having to watch her diet.

Alice has to drop out of her school, and she doesn't seem to have much in common with her old friends any more. Worst of all, she doesn't have much time to spend with Jamie. But it's not until tragedy strikes that Alice really begins to take charge of her own life and her career.

—Susan Dunn

High Trail to Danger   Grades 5–12
By Joan Lowery Nixon

Sarah Lindley is on the adventure of a lifetime, doing things she never dreamed she would be doing; things that at one time she would have been scared to even *think* about doing. But now there's no time to think . . . she must act!

It's 1879, and Sarah has traveled from Chicago—away from safety, security, and civilization—to Leadville, Colorado—to the Wild West, with its gunfights, outlaws, thieves, and cold-blooded murderers.

She has come to Leadville to find her father, a man she barely remembers. He left the family ten years ago, and she hasn't seen him since. His last letter came from Leadville, but she doesn't know if he's still there or even if he's still alive.

But she must find him. Now that her mother is dead, Sarah has got to bring her father back to Chicago, or her aunt and uncle will steal the family home.

But Sarah's in for a few surprises. Finding her father and taking him home is no simple task in the lawless town of Leadville. In fact, as Sarah soon discovers, there are people who are quite willing to kill her in order to stop her search.

Sarah is alone in Leadville, up against some very dangerous and desperate people. If she doesn't find her father soon, it will be too late.

—Melinda D. Waugh

Home Sweet Home, Good-bye   Grades 3-6
By Cynthia Stowe

I was having one of those perfectly horrible, no-good, very bad days. You know, the kind that ought to be happening to somebody else. The fact that Mom had spread marmalade on her toast should have been an indication that something positively terrible was about to happen (she hates orange marmalade). Then she told me that she had found a new house, and my whole life turned upside down. I couldn't believe what I was hearing—a new house? The one we'd been living in for the last ten years was just fine, and I told her that in no uncertain terms before I left for school. Who needs a new house anyway?

From then on my day went from bad to worse. I got into a fight with David, the class thug, had to report to the principal's office, and told my best friend, Mark, to mind his own business. I was having a very bad day! But by third hour I was starting to feel better and was actually thinking that perhaps my mom wouldn't go through with this plan. Wrong thinking! My pleasant thoughts were rudely interrupted by Mr. Aberdinian, who got upset when he found out I hadn't been paying attention. I was sent to the principal's office again, but this time I didn't report. I figured he wouldn't want to see me twice in one morning.

Or would he?

What more could possibly go wrong? Read Cynthia Stowe's *Home Sweet Home, Good-bye* to find out.

—Paulette Nelson

The House in the Woods   Grades 5-8
By Isabelle Holland

The minute we got here, I just knew this was going to be the worst summer of my life. Daddy had insisted that we come to this cottage on Badger Lake instead of going to our usual vacation home on the Maine coast. I said, at least in Maine we were right near town and there was plenty to do—bookstores, a movie theater, and an ice-cream shop. But no-o-o-o, Daddy insisted, and our new nanny, super-organized, super-thin, super-athletic Ingrid, agreed that this would be a better place to help Morgan improve.

Morgan doesn't talk, you see, but he understands just fine. And I'm probably—no, definitely!—the only one who understands him. Maybe he would have started to talk if Mother hadn't died five years ago. I don't know. But Daddy's fed up with doctors, so here we are.

Morgan and me, we're the different ones in the family. You already know about Morgan. But I'm different because I'm adopted. It's easy to tell, because I don't look like the rest of the family. I'm fat. And Daddy and Ingrid and the twins take every opportunity to remind me of that fact.

Just today Ingrid made a big salad for lunch. For my benefit, I'm sure. Then she suggested skim milk, when I wanted a Coke! Morgan hates salad, and there was no peanut butter (which is the only kind of sandwich he likes). He threw his plate on the floor and ran out of the house. I ran after him, and soon we were lost in the woods.

We came upon a spooky-looking, broken-down old house, but somehow I wasn't afraid. In some strange way, I knew that this had once been a beautiful home, where people loved each other. We found a nice lady inside, drawing pictures, and she said the house had been abandoned years ago. She was only using it now because it was quiet and she could work in peace on her art. I didn't want to ask too many questions, so I just wandered around. When I went upstairs, I got a horrible feeling, like something awful had taken place there! I ran down, grabbed Morgan, and we raced back home.

Now Morgan and I can't wait to sneak out again and go back to that deserted house. I'm sure this sounds really weird, but I feel that I *know* this house, or that maybe it has something to do with my birth parents. Isn't that crazy? What do you think I should do?

—Susan R. Farber

I Am Leaper   Grades 3-6
By Annabel Johnson

Leaper, a small kangaroo rat, lay curled up with her tail over her nose in the laboratory cage. It was a nice cage, with food, water, wood chips, and an exercise wheel, but Leaper did not care for these things. She just watched and waited. She knew escape would be easy, but that was not an option right now. She had been appointed by the desert animals to find help to fight the monster that was terrorizing them all. Leaper could only hope that these two men in white coats could help her.

The door to her cage was opened. Leaper ventured out on the table to the round gray tube with a wire at one end. She assumed this must be the ear of some strange creature, for she had seen one of the men speak into it. She cautiously squeaked into the ear and saw the creature's face light up. One of the men made adjustments with the square buttons on the creature's chest. Leaper again squeaked and twittered into the ear. One green line appeared on the creature's face.

The scientists were shocked and amazed as the words "I am Leaper" appeared on the computer screen. Leaper spoke into the ear once more. The computer again translated her squeaks into the words: "I am Leaper, I have come to talk to you about a matter of life and death." But Leaper soon realized that the scientists, although very excited about being able to talk with her, had no intention of helping her *or* of letting her escape.

Read *I Am Leaper* and discover who she finds to help her, and just what the monster is that has terrorized Leaper's desert friends.

—*Linda Olson*

I Bet You Didn't Know That Fish Sleep with Their Eyes Open and Other Facts and Curiosities

Grades 3–6

I Bet You Didn't Know That Hummingbirds Can Fly Backwards and Other Facts and Curiosities

I Bet You Didn't Know That There Are Golf Balls on the Moon and Other Facts and Curiosities

I Bet You Didn't Know That You Can't Sink in the Dead Sea and Other Facts and Curiosities

By Carol Iverson

It's possible to see a star that has already exploded and disappeared. . . . In Appin, Scotland, in 1817 it actually rained fish. . . . The yo-yo was invented in the Philippine jungles, where it was used as a weapon.

How do I know all these weird and startling bits of trivia? I read the "I Bet You Didn't Know That" books. Do your parents say you ask too many questions? Do you actually *like* to read the *Guinness Book of World Records*? Then you'll love the amazing facts and figures in these four books. An ear of corn always has an even number of rows (can you prove it?); you are taller in the morning than at night (why?); the names of twenty-six states are on the back of a five-dollar bill (check it out!); and a baby has over sixty more bones than an adult (where do those baby bones go?). Fool your friends, stump your teachers, and drive your parents crazy with questions from the "I Bet You Didn't Know That" books!

—Jan L. McConnell

I Can Hear the Mourning Dove   Grades 7–12
By James Bennett

Dear Diary:

Dee Dee, my lab partner from school, stopped by today. No one ever comes to see me, so I didn't really know what to say or do. Even before we moved here, I didn't have many friends. Mostly Dad and I did things together after school and on weekends, but he died a little over a year ago. Mother thinks that maybe things will be different now, but I doubt it. I figure Dee Dee will spend just enough time with me to find out how weird I am and then she'll avoid me, so I decided to save us both the time and trouble—I told her that I had been in a mental hospital most of last year for depression, and that I had tried to kill myself. She looked uncomfortable and turned red in the face. Then she told me that she hadn't actually come to visit on her own. Miss Shapiro, the guidance counselor, had asked her to come. That figures. Why would a girl like Dee Dee want to be friends with me? I watched her walk down the street through our kitchen window. She walked past Mr. Stereo and his loud, surly friends without batting an eye, utterly beautiful, utterly confident. It's totally intimidating, yet I really would like to be her friend. If only I could be a normal person. . . .

—Kathy Ann Miller

I Hate Camping!   Grades 3–4
By P. J. Petersen

Dan is going camping with his mother's boyfriend Mike and Mike's two children, Raymond and Kim. The problem is, Dan *hates* camping! And what's more, he can't stand Raymond or Kim! Dan tries all the usual excuses to get out of going—there'll be snakes in the sleeping bags, bears that eat campers, mosquitoes everywhere, forest fires, no pizza, and worst of all, no TV! But nothing works—he has no choice.

Once they reach the campground, it's just as he feared. The tent keeps falling down, the canoe overturns, and then, late that night, Raymond and Dan hear growling outside their tent!

Can it get any worse? Read *I Hate Camping!* and find out.

—*Cara A. Waits*

I Have Words to Spend: Adult
Reflections of a Small-Town Editor
By Robert Cormier; edited by Constance Senay Cormier

I'd like to introduce you to a friend of mine. He's a slight, silver-haired man who doesn't really stand out in a crowd. He doesn't push himself on people, and although he's become a well-known and highly respected writer, he remains just as down-to-earth as he was that first day I met him, back in 1977, when he was a fledgling novelist. When the spotlight falls on him today, he is at first awkward, but then rises to the occasion with a graceful phrase or two before stepping away, back into the role that is most comfortable for him: an observer—of life, of people, and of the details that most of us never take the time to notice.

That's another thing about my friend. He always takes time, even when others don't or won't, to respond to someone else's need or cry for help. When he needed a phone number for a character in his second book, he put in his own number, because, he said, "they will know if it's a fake number—I'd have to start it with 555." So for years afterward, when the phone rang and a young voice asked for Amy, the response in his family was, "She isn't here right now. Would you like to talk to her father?" The callers almost always did—and ended up talking to my friend, who is in truth Amy's father, since he created Amy. Not all of those phone calls were brief.

He also remembers people. Years after our first meeting, he knew who I was as soon as I spoke to him, and in the years since then he has never failed to greet me by name. But in all that time, I never read anything of his that was not part of a book. Now, finally, his newspaper columns have been collected, and I can see the man behind the novels and discover the beliefs and philosophy that led him to write them. Now I know even more clearly why being "Amy's father" was not an option but an obligation.

But I want you to meet him through his own words, speaking as he does face-to-face—open, direct, not pulling punches, and from the heart.

"I have words to spend and sometimes spend them foolishly . . . squandering verbs and nouns, sending metaphors askew . . . using similes like fireworks whose sparks often fail to flame . . . There are certain words I love to use over and over again, words like 'marvelous' . . . 'stunning' . . . 'wonder' . . . 'September' . . . 'remember.' And then there's 'cellophane.' 'Cellophane,' said slowly. . . . [But] there's one word that is both splendid and terrible, and I often ponder its mystery. The word is 'but.' A traffic cop of a word. A word of terror and beauty. For instance: 'I'd love to go with you, but . . .' or 'It was a lovely Christmas, but. . . .' But—and there's the magic of the word—it can [also] be used in marvelous ways: 'I had planned to go away this weekend, but . . .,' or 'The x-rays do show some shadow there, but. . . .' Thus it can [also] be a word of hope."

Watching a man try and fail to ring the bell to prove his strength at the local carnival: "I watched him and [his wife] strolling [away] hand in hand. And I thought, How precious are these women who love their men so much they turn small tragedies into triumphs. Ringing a bell has nothing to do . . . with what a man is, and what he knows he is to his wife and children." On giving up smoking: "It's ten years ago today that I gave up smoking, and I'm happy I did. But there's a part of me that will be sad forever." How many of us give up things for all the right reasons, and yet a part of us mourns forever for what we have sacrificed . . . .

He talks about goodbyes, taking a boy—no, a young man—to college for the first time, and then watching him marry and move away. And he remembers the times they talked while the boy was growing up, the late-night talks, because he had insomnia and was always up when the boy got home. "Those were the best times of all. There's an intimacy in the night, and you can say things to each other at that hour that would be impossible at three o'clock in the afternoon."

He shares times of going away and of coming back home, the people he's met and the ideas he's wondered about—which may turn out to be things you've wondered about as well. There seems to be no part of life that he has not subjected to his own personal microscope, including what he worries about: "Know what worries me? This is what worries me: I pick up the *Times* and see a sample of handwriting . . . and the [text] says that [it] is that of a schizophrenic. And the handwriting looks almost exactly like my own . . . I worry [about] what to do when the repairman comes . . . whether I should stand there and watch . . . or leave him alone . . . . I worry about seeing [a UFO] . . . because I know that I won't be able to keep quiet about it . . . and it will lead to all sorts of complications . . . . I also worry when I tell people what

I'm worried about and they say 'Funny, *I* never worry about that.' . . . I worry when people take me seriously when I'm trying to be funny and think I'm being funny when I'm being serious. I worry because sometimes I'm not sure of myself. Like today. And I keep thinking of that handwriting sample."

Robert Cormier has words to spend, words to make you chuckle or sigh or consider; to make you feel happy or sad or nostalgic or warm inside. Words that let you know there are other people who think and wonder and care about the same sort of things you do.

Let him spend some of his words on you.

—J. R. B.

The Importance of Being Oscar   Grade 3–Adult
By Oscar Wilde (selected by Yvonne Skargon)

To quote Lazarus Long (with thanks to his creator, Robert Heinlein), "Anyone who doesn't believe in protocol has never had to deal with a cat." Oscar, who is the subject of this book, would certainly agree— after all, he *is* a cat. He is also a fan of Oscar Wilde, and shares with us some of his favorite quotations:

On killing a mouse: "In nearly every joy, as certainly in every pleasure, cruelty has its place."

On work: "Industry is the root of all ugliness."

On life: "One's real life is so often the life that one does not lead."

On wisdom: "To look wise is quite as good as understanding a thing, and very much easier."

On journalism: "There is much to be said in favour of modern journalism. By giving the opinions of the uneducated, it keeps us in touch with the ignorance of the community."

And finally, on himself: "Oh, he is better than good—he is beautiful!"

Discover for yourself what other things Oscar has to say about Oscar. Lazarus Long would have loved him!

—J. R. B.

In Caverns of Blue Ice   Grades 7–12
By Robert Roper

"It sometimes happens in the mountains that you live . . . or you don't. All you can do is pray." Louise's father had said that many times. Now, as she dangled in midair with the belay line cutting into her flesh and the avalanche crashing down around her, her father's words echoed through her mind.

Louise had grown up in a family of mountaineers, so it was only natural for her to become one too. She had been one of the first female guides, leading people up into the high peaks, and Louise was good. She was agile and clear-headed, had a sure sense of direction and excellent judgment. So it wasn't surprising that she hesitated when it was suggested she accompany a group of climbers up Devil's Slide. This expedition just wasn't safe. Some of the climbers weren't very experienced, the weather was bad, and it was the wrong time of year for this sort of climb. But it would be a challenge and Louise wanted to try it, so she finally agreed.

In the end, high up in the mountains, it was only Louise and Lawrence. They were at the Devil's Slide itself. The sun had gone down, and the evening chill had frozen the surface of the snow. It was easier to move around now; sometimes they could walk, sometimes they could "swim," and sometimes they would still sink down through the crust but find solid footing beneath. The avalanches had finally stopped. Louise was going first now; she situated herself in a good belay stance and tugged the rope three times, a signal that it was safe for Lawrence to move. As he came slowly closer, she gathered up the slack in the rope. A little flock of sparrows appeared, fluttering around and lighting on the snow. Just as Lawrence came into view, the birds took off high into the sky. She barely had time to tighten her grip on the rope and yell "Avalanche!" before the entire mountain let loose beneath her feet.

With her ax holding her onto the mountain wall and the rope tightening around her waist, Louise thought she was being cut in half. The wall of snow had surely killed Lawrence, and the weight of his body on the ropes was choking the life from Louise. Her only hope was to cut the rope and let his body fall free. She reached for the knife but couldn't get it. No matter how she twisted or bent, she couldn't reach it. "Oh well, we'll die together," she thought, as her world went dark.

—Margaret Butzler

Into the Dark   Grades 5–8
By Nicholas Wilde

When someone is blind, darkness can mean more than just not being
able to see. Sometimes it can mean feeling lonely or afraid. Twelve-
year-old Matthew is blind, but he manages to cope with his handicap.
The hardest thing to deal with, though, is not having friends.
Sometimes it seems to Matt that his mother is the only person in the
world who cares about him. Matt lives with her in a small flat in
London, and they have never had a real vacation, until now. Matt's
mother is a cook and doesn't make much money, but she's finally able
to afford a week at an old cottage by the sea. Matt is tremendously
excited about the trip—anxious to smell the sea air, hear the rushes
blowing in the breeze, and feel the sand beneath his feet for the first
time. What he doesn't expect to find there is his first friend, a friend
he meets in the most unusual place.

On the day after their arrival, Matt learns to maneuver on his own
along the path near the cottage. As he is exploring, he comes upon an
old graveyard. He finds it fascinating—he can read the engraved letters
on the headstones with his fingers. He is drawn to a certain headstone
and begins to feel the letters: "Rupert Oliver Latimer. Died August
29th, 1887." With a kind of sadness, he traces the final line: "Aged 12
Years." Then he is so startled he nearly falls over when a sudden voice
beside him says, "Hello. What are *you* doing?" The boy who is speaking
catches him from falling and apologizes for scaring him. Matt tells him
it's all right, he's always tripping anyway because of his eyes. "Yes, I
know," the boy says. "You're blind, aren't you?" Matthew is taken
aback. Most people can't tell right away that he's blind, but this boy—
Roly—can. Soon they are chatting away about all sorts of things, and
they quickly become fast friends. With Roly's help, Matthew is able to
explore the seaside and even the mysterious old mansion at the edge
of the village. But Matthew becomes uneasy when he notices some
strange things about Roly and realizes he is hiding something. Matthew
soon learns the "something" involves Matthew himself, and a secret
that takes him beyond his blindness, *Into the Dark*.

—*Diane P. Tuccillo*

Jeremy Thatcher, Dragon Hatcher   Grades 3–6
By Bruce Coville

It is Midsummer Eve. The fog is getting thicker, muffling the sound of my footsteps. I am waiting for something to happen, for the second part of the prophecy to be fulfilled, the part that says, "Midsummer Night will break your heart."

Despite everything that has gone on—my stumbling upon that magic shop I'd never seen before, Mr. Elives' strange instructions about the full moon's light, the mysterious marbled orb itself—I never really believed anything exotic would hatch out of that egg. Yet, a month ago, in the the moonlight, I watched spellbound as first the egg cracked, then tiny claws chipped away at the shell, then a thumb-sized green head appeared, then red wings . . . . It was a tiny dragon, just as Mr. Elives had foretold. So the first part of the prophecy—"Full moon's light to hatch the egg"—had come true.

I named my dragon Tiamet. Mrs. Priest, the librarian, gave me a book, *On the Nature of Dragons*, and that's where I read about the ancient Company of Hatchers. That's how I learned *why* I was given the egg, and what I must do tonight, on Midsummer Eve.

Now I am here alone, waiting for someone . . . or something. And wondering about the rest of the prophecy. "Midsummer Night will break your heart," it says, but then it goes on: "All Hallows' Eve may patch it."

—Karol Schmitt Rockwin

The Jewel of Life   Grades 7–8
By Anna Kirwan-Vogel

It was the third day of the late summer Poke Fair. The last of the year's harvest hiring had been done, and the last crop of apprentices were being signed on to the guild lists, their keep paid out to craftsmen and merchants who would train, feed, and house them until they could pay their own way. Master Humphrey had herded all the orphans from the almshouse—including young Duffy—into a rope-ringed booth at the edge of the market.

For three days prospective mistresses and masters inspected and estimated the meager worth of the untaught youngsters. And for three days no one had looked at young Duffy. Duffy didn't much care what manner of master he got, so long as he need not stay another day—for another beating—with Master Humphrey at the almshouse.

On the third day the apothecary Crowe came looking for an apprentice. Even though Crowe had really hoped to take an older child into his service, because his work was difficult and sometimes decidedly peculiar, he saw something special in Duffy's remarkable eyes—something alert and inquisitive—and decided to take him instead.

Duffy was relieved to see Crowe sign the apprenticeship papers, even though he knew people said strange things about the old apothecary. They said he did black magic. They said he had powers.

And Duffy saw some of those powers on the first morning he served his new master. Crowe performed an experiement in which he *seemed* to change wine into water, and then into fire! But the lesson Crowe taught Duffy that day was that things are not always what they seem. Duffy also learned that Crowe was more than an apothecary: he was also an alchemist. And as an alchemist, Crowe had some ideas about where to look for the great treasure, the Jewel of Life, the Philosophers' Stone, which promised power and wealth to the one who could find it where it nestled among the commonplace.

If you too wish to learn where to look, you can join in the magical adventures of Duffy and old Crowe as they do battle with the serpent, the cockatrice, and the horned dragon in their quest for *The Jewel of Life.*

—*Olivia D. Jacobs*

Jilly's Ghost   Grades 7–12
By Dian Curtis Regan

There's a ghost in the backyard of Jilly Milford's house. He has been there for at least fifteen years, pacing from the toolshed to the canal to the gazebo, and then back to the toolshed. Most of the time his image is shadowy, but on some nights he looks almost real. When Jilly was little, she tried to tell her parents about the ghost, but they didn't take her seriously. They would refer to "Jilly's imaginary playmate" or "Jilly's ghost." Jilly's best friend Amanda is the only one who believes her. And now Amanda thinks Jilly should write an article about the ghost for the school newspaper! That could mean stirring up things better left alone. And to make matters worse, Jilly's nosy neighbor Russell has seen the ghost too, and wants to expose him to the whole world. How can Jilly stop Russell? Should she warn the ghost? What if the ghost is basically evil and decides to turn on *her?* In all these years, Jilly has never even tried to talk to her ghost, and she has never been afraid of him, either. Until now!

—*Anne Liebst*

Journey   Grades 3–6
By Patricia MacLachlan

Journey lost his family when his mama left. Oh, he still had his sister, Cat, and Grandfather and Grandma. But his mama had taken away his past, his memories, when she went.

Grandfather discovered the camera first, discovered what the pictures told. He took pictures of everything—cow pies, chickens, but mostly the family. "Things don't look the same through the camera," Journey said, "Not the way they are in real life." But sometimes the pictures showed what really was there. Could they help Journey find his past again?

—*Melanie L. Witulski*

Journey from the Dawn: Grade 9–Adult
Life with the World's First Family
By Dr. Donald C. Johanson and Kevin O'Farrell

Have you ever heard of Lucy? No, I don't mean Lucille Ball, of "I Love Lucy" fame. This Lucy's real name is Dinquinesh, which means "thou art wonderful" in Ethiopian. "Lucy" is just the nickname given to her by the scientists who found her in the desert of the Great Rift Valley in 1974. These scientists estimate that Lucy is about three million years old. Her partial skeleton is the most complete example of the hominid known as *Australopithecus afarensis*, or "the ape that stood up."

However, the most interesting fact about Lucy is that she was not alone. About one year after her skeleton was discovered, further explorations in the same area located fossil remains of thirteen other hominids, including young children as well as male and female adults. Along with Lucy, they have become known collectively as the World's First Family.

And this book is a journey into their lives. Based on scientific research, it presents a fictionalized account of what one day in the life of the First Family might have been like. We flee with the Family from a volcanic eruption, experience birth in the wilds as Lucy delivers her third child, and get a taste of the first cooked egg, accidently roasted in volcanic ashes. Along with the fictionalized story, there is a scientific text describing the environment that probably surrounded the Family, and there are full-page illustrations as well.

But this is more than just another coffee-table book. It's an opportunity to experience the life of a family from an entirely different time. So if you haven't heard about Lucy—or the World's First Family—here's your chance. All you have to do is take an exciting journey back to the dawn of civilization.

—Margie Reitsma

Journey Home   Grades 3–6
By Isabelle Holland

Now that both their parents are dead, twelve-year-old Maggie and her seven-year-old sister Annie are all alone. Maggie knows that the streets of New York City are a terrible place for orphans to be. So even though she's frightened and hates the whole idea, she feels she has to keep her promise to her dying mother: Take the Orphan Train to the newly opened West. There, with any luck, a good family will adopt them and keep them safe from the cruel world.

However, Maggie has heard horrible things about non-Catholics: how they don't like poor Irish immigrants, and how they'll make her give up her faith. And Maggie remembers what happened back in Ireland when she was six years old: the Irish Protestants burned down her family's cottage and killed their livestock. Her family were forced to escape to America, to live in poverty and sickness. After all that, how can she and Annie survive with such people?

When the two girls are at last taken in by a family in Kansas, Maggie is surprised and jealous at how quickly Annie seems to adjust to the wild prairie and the local people, with their prejudices against newcomers. Even when Maggie herself begins to fit in, she fights the feelings of comfort in order to stay true to her religion and Irish heritage. But when she's faced with losing this strange new place, she begins to realize what her promise to her mother really meant. . . . If someone cares about you, any place can be a *Journey Home.*

—Faye A. Powell

Junkyard Dog   Grades 3–6
By Sandi Barrett Ruch

Toad had lived in the junkyard for a long time. It was the perfect place for a toad to be. Then *he* came! He was a massive dog, broad-shouldered and square-muzzled, with saliva dripping from his mouth.

His grizzled black coat was tattered and ragged, hanging in ropy tangles under his belly and down his heavy legs. Mr. Zlotnick had bought him to guard his junkyard, and named him Slobber.

When Toad first saw Slobber, the dog was chained to the fence, with his feet braced wide apart and his head lowered, ready for whatever might come next. Would this dog ruin Toad's wonderful opportunities to hunt all those delicious bugs, crickets, beetles, and slugs that lurked in the junkyard clutter? Could Toad hunt for all those juicy creatures with that great savage beast pacing back and forth on his chain?

And there might be another, more serious problem with the dog. Slotnick's five children—Crystal, Frieda, Pearlie, Huey, and Melba—had the run of the yard now that they stayed with their dad. Toad was particularly worried about Huey, a chubby, red-cheeked four-year-old terror. He'd scamper across the junkyard, searching for new exciting places to hide. He couldn't seem to stay out of trouble, and Toad knew that this big dog with his teeth bared in a fierce silent snarl was more trouble than Huey had ever run into. But when Huey had one too many adventures and disappeared, Toad discovered some special things about that dog. What made Slobber special? Read *Junkyard Dog* and find out.

—Robbi Povenmire

Jurassic Park   Grade 9–Adult
By Michael Crichton

Come one, come all! See the wonder of the 1990s—the most amazing spectacle you can imagine—the world's newest, most original theme park! This is Jurassic Park, where you can see real, living dinosaurs, recreated from the fossilized remains of their DNA. With your own eyes you can see dozens of species, hundreds of animals, just as alive as they were when they ruled the earth millions of years ago!

Yes, you can actually *see* living dinosaurs close up, almost close enough to touch. And of course, it's all perfectly safe—they are contained in pens with electrically-charged fences, controlled by computers. There's *no* way they can get loose.

What did you say? The extra bars and fences around the lodge? Oh well, we just want to make sure that you'd be *totally, completely* protected. There is, I assure you, absolutely *no* danger.

And now that the park is open, all our exhibits are accessible for your pleasure—well, all but two, actually. The aviary and the jungle lagoon ride still need some refining. You see, the pterodactyls have an annoying way of dive-bombing anyone who enters the aviary. We hadn't realized that they were so *enthusiastically* territorial. And the jungle ride? Well, that was another unexpected complication. The Dilophosaurus was commonly believed to have been a scavenger, but we have now discovered that it is a predator, and poisonous besides—just as venomous as a rattlesnake, a Komodo dragon, or Gila monster. Dilophosauruses spit at their prey, paralyzing or blinding it—and of course, to a dinosaur we *all* look like prey! So you can see that while these are among the most beautiful of our dinosaurs, we can't allow you to get as close as you can to the other species. Your view of the Dilophosaurus will have to be through binoculars, which we will provide for you on our train trip through the park.

However, the Tyrannosaurus rex, one of our most popular dinosaurs, can be seen quite close if you're lucky, since our tour route runs right by the edge of that pen. We have two lovely specimens, an adult and an adolescent, which is quite small for a T-rex—he weighs only about a ton or so and is just about twenty feet high.

How do we run the park? I'm so glad you asked that! We have a computer system that's second to none. In fact, the entire park can be run by a staff of twenty-odd people, and we have every possible fail-safe device built into the system. You will be *completely* safe during your visit here, no matter what part of the park you enjoy.

Or will you? Computers have glitches, programmers have their own agendas, and chaos theory points out that no living system is permanently stable or static. Do you dare visit Jurassic Park, and indulge in a little modern-day, genetically-engineered time travel? It's not too hard to get into the park, but when computers break down, the programmer disappears, and chaos reigns supreme it may be difficult, even impossible, to get out!

Ever wanted to see a dinosaur *really* close up? Are you *sure*? Come to Jurassic Park—it's your big chance, the chance of a lifetime, *but* . . . it may be the *last* chance of your lifetime!

—*J. R. B.*

Just a Dream   Grades 3-Adult
By Chris Van Allsburg

Walter couldn't wait for the future to get here—he just *knew* he'd have his own robot, like the boy on his favorite TV show. He didn't pay a lot of attention to the present . . . or to the trash he dropped on his way home from school, or the garbage he was supposed to sort before he dumped it in the can. He was thinking about the future.

But then one night while he was sleeping, Walter traveled into the future he'd been waiting for. He woke up in the middle of the a huge dump—but the street sign said Floral Avenue. *He* lived on Floral Avenue. "This can't be the future," he decided, and pulled the covers over his head and went back to sleep. "This is just a dream."

The next time Walter woke up, he was in a tree that two men were about to cut down. They said they needed it for something important—and then Walter saw the writing on their jackets: they worked for a toothpick factory. Walter traveled on—to a factory, a snow-covered mountain, an ocean, and a crowded freeway. But nowhere did he find the friendly little robot he'd seen on TV. In fact, he didn't see anything that looked anything like what he'd always expected the future to be.

Will he be able to find the future he's looking for? Travel with Walter and discover what the future may really be like.

—*J. R. B.*

Kidnapping Kevin Kowalski   Grades 5-8
By Mary Jane Auch

Not too long ago, my friend Kevin came home from the hospital with a plate in his head. No, not a dinner plate, the kind of plate doctors put in to protect your brain after a car has knocked you off your bike and dented your skull. Ever since then, Kevin's mom has been treating him like such a baby that he's starting to act like one, and it's driving me nuts! I think it's about time Kevin got back to normal. So Mooch and I decide to kidnap Kevin with a four-wheel all-terrain vehicle and take him into the woods for an overnight sleepaway.

Nobody knows what we're up to—not our parents, not his parents, not even Kevin himself! Great idea, right? And everything goes just right—we're out in the woods, it's dark, and we've got the tent all set up near the lake. Even Kevin is having fun. But then we hear noises. People noises. The people stop near our tent, but they can't see us. One of these people starts to strip. This person is *not* a boy. She's wearing a bikini. It looks like this trip is gonna be even better than we expected.

—*James Witham*

Kisses   Grades 7–12
By Judith Caseley

Hannah Gold heard the alarm clock go off in her parents' bedroom. She was already awake and had been for quite a while, but she didn't get up. It was audition day for the all-state orchestra, it was raining hard, and she was nervous. She got up finally when her father called out, "It's time!" He made breakfast while she dressed, but she could only eat a bite. When it was time to go, she wrapped her violin in her raincoat and got into the car. She jumped when the radio came blasting on; her father quickly turned it off. She tried to concentrate on her music, but the tempo of the windshield wipers messed her up.

With her father's "Good luck" ringing in her ears, Hannah entered the school where the auditions were being held. She made her way to room 213 (cursing unlucky thirteen) and practiced a little; her throat was tight and her hands clammy. Then Hanna heard her music being practiced by someone else—the piece she had worked on every day for thirty weeks. It sounded so beautiful—and so much better! She vowed she wouldn't look at the player, but she couldn't resist a peek. It was a girl with flowing red hair. Hannah then glanced down at the girl's number and sighed with relief. The girl's number was forty-three, Hannah's was forty-two; Hannah would play first.

Forty-two was called, and Hannah entered the classroom. She pressed the violin tightly against her chin to keep it from trembling. She played her scales, her solo piece and a sight-reading test. Then suddenly it was all over, and she was accepted into the all-state orchestra.

But the luck of acceptance hasn't spilled over into other areas of Hannah's life. For one thing, she is still flat-chested, with no improvement in sight. And the blind date she has with a friend of another orchestra member is the pits. Even a date with the boy she has had a crush on all year doesn't turn out right. Meanwhile, her best friend is involved with a boy who is nothing but a bully, and Hannah is worried. Then she starts receiving love-letters signed "RM." Is Hannah's luck about to change? Read *Kisses* and see.

—Linda Olson

The Kite That Braved   Grades 5–12
Old Orchard Beach: Year-Round Poems for Young People
By X. J. Kennedy

Poems use high-falutin' language to talk about important things like Love and Nature, right? Wrong! Here's a helpful poem about how to work a jar lid:

> The way hands move around a clock
> Is how hands make a jar lid lock.
> Hands must go backwards, if they are
> To make a jar lid come ajar.

Think you can remember that? And if the jar should contain popcorn, here is another helpful hint:

> How suddenly each tiny seed
> Into a puffball grows!
> A ping, ping, ping within the pan
> Accelerates, then slows—
> I like to lift the lid and look,
> But if I do, it snows.

Poems about friends and family, about small-time fun and big-time dreams, about seasons and holidays, and about the birds and the beasts—they are all to be found in *The Kite That Braved Old Orchard Beach*. I'd like to leave you with two verses of a poem called "Cricket":

> Imagine—what if you or I
> Were laid out like a cricket
> And had an ear beside our knee?
> That might be just the ticket,
>
> For if you didn't want to hear,
> The loudest band that rocks,
> Why, all you'd do to shut your ears
> Is yank up both your socks.

—Diane L. Deuel

Larger Than Life: Grades 3–4
The Adventures of American Legendary Heroes
By Robert D. San Souci

What could be "larger than life?" Well, let me tell you about Old
Stormalong. He was a sailor from Maine who was twenty-four feet tall
when he was grown—about four times taller than anybody you know.

Even as a child, Stormalong loved the sea, and sometimes he'd swim
a hundred miles just so that he could play with his friends. When he
became a sailor, an octopus once entwined its arms around the anchor,
preventing the sailors from raising it. Old Stormalong fought the octopus and tied each one of its eight tentacles into a different sailor's knot!

While serving on John Paul Jones' ship in the Revolutionary War,
Old Stormalong fired the cannon from his shoulder like a rifle, and if
that wasn't enough, he'd *throw* the cannonballs with his bare hands.

Then, when his own huge ship, the *Albatross*, was blown off course
during a storm and got wedged in the English channel, he had to devise
a way to get it out. Read about his solution in *Larger Than Life: The
Adventures of American Legendary Heroes*. You'll also enjoy the other
tall tales: about John Henry, the steel-driving man; the Texas heroes
Slue-Foot Sue and Pecos Bill; mild-mannered Strap Buckner (who
loved a good fight); and the great logger Paul Bunyan.

—Dorothy Davidson

Lark in the Morning   Grades 9–12
By Nancy Garden

Gillian Harrison's vacation gets off to a bad start when her family
arrive at their home and find unmistakable signs of a break-in. Not
many things have been stolen, but Gillian's diary is among them.
Concerned over who might be reading about her private feelings for her
best friend Suzanne, Gillian goes hunting for the thieves—and gets a
surprise when she stumbles upon twelve-year-old Lark and her brother,
five-year-old Jackie. Lark and Jackie are hiding out in the woods, living
on what they can find. They've run away from their abusive father. And
Gillian can't blame them—who could? Soon she finds herself taking
responsibility for the runaways, against her better judgement and,
eventually, against the advice of her closest friends, Suzanne and Brad.
As the police close in on the children and begin to suspect Gillian's
involvement, she faces a tough decision.

—Kim Carter Sands

Last Chance Summer   Grades 7–12
By Diana Wieler

I am a runaway. Not a typical runaway, because I don't have family to run away from. I compare myself to the runaway train that keeps recurring in my dreams. It chases me and I run as fast as I can. The train never catches me because I wake up, out of breath and drained, drenched with sweat, just before it is about to run me over. And in real life I run whenever the going gets tough. I don't have a destination when I start, and I never get very far because I'm always picked up by the cops or someone in the social services system. I've been in and out of foster and juvenile homes ever since I can remember. I never station myself anywhere, so I can always escape when trouble seems to be looming. I don't know anything about my background, and all I know about myself is: I'm thirteen; my skin is golden brown; my hair is coarse; my eyes are slanted; I can't read; and if I run away one more time, the authorities are going to send me to Ryser—a juvenile's darkest pit.

My social worker Cecile, the one positive person in my life, says, "Mark, this is your last chance! I had to beg, plead, and pull strings to get you this last chance of living in society, and if I hadn't you'd be on your way with a one-way ticket to Ryser." I really want to please Cecile! I have let her down so many times before.

This last chance is on a farm near the Canadian Badlands, a farm run by Carleton Jenner and a cook named Vilda. Other juveniles live here, too—like Topa, Goat, Rayo, and Len. I'm really going to try to fit in. I really am, for Cecile. I am going to beat this train ride.

Read *Last Chance Summer* and learn what it's like to have only one last chance.

—Cathy Crowell

Last Chance to See   Grade 9–Adult
By Douglas Adams and Mark Carwardine

Douglas Adams, in his *Hitchhiker's Guide to the Galaxy* series, has taken his readers on some wild and woolly trips through time and space. But this time the places he takes us are on Earth, right now, and the tales he tells are all true. There are hundreds of endangered species of animals—birds, primates, fish, and creatures of all kinds that soon we may be able to see only in the history books. Adams introduces us to some of them, as he travels the world looking for animals that it may be our last chance to see.

The first creature he introduces us to is one of the most horrible—the Komodo dragon, a huge lizard so poisonous that once you're bitten, death is almost inevitable, because the wound simply will not heal. The bacteria in the dragon's saliva prevent it. A Komodo dragon is not exactly something you'd want to meet unexpectedly, especially if it was in a bad mood. It's not very attractive looking, either—and it is "big. Very big. There's one . . . over twelve feet long and . . . a yard high, which you can't help but feel is entirely the wrong size for a lizard to be, particularly if it's a man-eater, and you're about to go and share an island with it."

The next animal Adams encountered was a contrast in every way to the Komodo dragon—a silverback mountain gorilla. These animals have become used to people, and one older male let Adams get quite close. "At last we came across a silverback lying on his side beneath a bush, with his long arm folded up over his head . . . while he watched a couple of leaves doing not very much. It was instantly clear what he was doing. He was contemplating life. He was hanging out."

Adams also found one of the rarest and most amusing birds I have ever heard of—the kakapo, one of the flightless birds of New Zealand. "The kakapo is a bird out of time. If you look one in its large, round greeny-brown face, it has a look of serenely innocent incomprehension that makes you want to hug it and tell it that everything will be all right, though you know that it probably will not be. It is an extremely fat bird . . . flying is completely out of the question. Sadly, however, it seems that not only has the kakapo forgotten how to fly, but it has also forgotten that it has forgotten how to fly. Apparently a seriously worried kakapo will sometimes run up a tree and jump out of it, whereupon it flies rather like a brick and lands in a graceless heap on the ground."

And these are only a few of the wonderful and hilarious animals Douglas Adams introduces you to. By the time you have met them all and heard their stories, I'm sure you too will agree that "the world would be a poorer, darker, lonelier place without them."

—*J. R. B.*

The Last Defector   Adult
By Tony Cape

Headline News! CNN Special Report: "The United States and the Soviet Union have agreed not to destroy each other . . . ."

So we will *not* be blown to Kingdom Come—what a relief! Now we can dismantle all those nasty warheads, make some money in Eastern Europe, and sleep safely in our beds at night . . . .

"Not so fast, comrade," says Tony Cape in his latest novel. There are bound to be people who don't agree, in both the East and the West. Troop reductions, strategic warheads, second-strike capacity, security zones—these are the hot topics as the world prepares for a superpower summit meeting in Oslo. But will the leaders of the great powers hold sway at the conference, or will fringe groups embarrass them and insert their own agendas?

Into this delicious mix drop one Derek Smailes, a mid-level security officer at the British mission at the United Nations. Derek is a likable plodder, in charge of electronic surveillance and the carpool. But suddenly he is given an unusual assignment: to recruit an informer from the Soviet U.N. mission. For a while things go well—the Brits are learning a lot. But when they learn that the Soviets are hiding their missiles instead of destroying them, bodies begin to fall, and Derek is thrown into a frenzy of mistrust. Who is manipulating whom? Where do the Americans fit in? Is he getting real information, or disinformation? Who on Derek's own staff could be a traitor? Even Derek's girlfriend is suspect—what does he really know about her, anyway? Isn't her father a high-profile right-winger in England? What sort of secrets could Derek have spilled to her unwittingly, perhaps even in the throes of passion?

If the deceit and play-acting are this intense for mid-level players, imagine the games that are going on in the real seats of power!

And we find out. Not only do we hustle with Derek from a U.N. reception to a grisly murder scene outside London, we follow the parallel plot of Soviet leader Rostov, ever-cautious in his retreat deep in the forest outside Moscow. Does Rostov know that as long as one Stalinist is alive he is not safe? Does he dare deal with the U.S. president *before* the summit? Does he know what a panic the British are in?

What will happen to *The Last Defector*?

—*Mark Anderson*

The Last Seven Months   Grade 9–Adult
of Anne Frank
By Willy Lindwer

Anne Frank did not survive the death camps. Her familiar narrative voice cannot describe the horrors undergone by people packed into cattle-cars, forced to strip in front of armed Nazi guards, and living with the constant threat of death, either from starvation, typhus, or the gas chambers. Instead, we hear six other voices describing these experiences, the voices of women who knew Anne Frank. Some of them were her childhood friends before the war; but for most of them, Anne Frank was simply a fellow victim in the death camps, someone they knew briefly as a fellow sufferer. Each of these voices varies in its individual reaction to the daily encounter with pain and death. Yet they are all similar in one respect: all of their stories reveal something about the will to survive. One story describes an incident when several French prisoners were shaved completely bald by the Nazis; the prisoners maintained their sense of personal dignity by wrapping scraps of cloth around their heads and using dirt to emphasize their eyebrows. They refused to be dehumanized.

Such stories show us the backbone of survival in the camps. This was the spirit of resistance; this is the same spirit found in Anne Frank's diary, and it is why she has become a symbol for both the unimaginable suffering of the Jews during the war and the unexplainable will to survive even in the face of such suffering. That is why this book is important to read, even though it is not relaxing or pleasant or even composed by Anne Frank herself. It is a moving tribute to her suffering and to all the victims who survived in Hitler's camps—whether in body or only in spirit.

—Margie Reitsma

Last Summer with Maizon   Grades 5-6
By Jacqueline Woodson

> My pen doesn't write anymore,
> It stumbles and trembles in my hand,
> If my dad were here—he would understand.
> Best of all—it'd be last summer again. . . .

and thus begins the poem that Margaret writes for class. A poem that expresses how she feels about last summer.

Last summer, a time that Margaret would love to erase. A time of pain for Margaret and her mother as they face the death of Margaret's dad. A time when Margaret realizes she may lose her best friend who's accepted a scholarship to a private school. A time for Margaret to discover her inner strength and courage.

It's not always easy when you promise to be best friends forever.

—Susan Wolfe

Leap Year   Adult
By Peter Cameron

The marriage is over, and the final divorce decree is hammered out. The papers are signed, the lawyers count their money, and everyone is resigned to going on with their now-separate lives. There are no bad feelings, no bitterness, just the realization that the marriage was never meant to be. No adjustments, no more having to fit your life into someone else's. An amicable, civilized divorce. At least, that's what Loren and David think when their marriage ends.

But after a year, both Loren and David begin to realize that you must work at a successful divorce just as you work to build a successful marriage. At first their lives intersect because of their daughter Kate. Then Lillian, a mutual friend, unexpectedly draws Loren and David together in her struggle to undergo in-vitro fertilization and become a single parent. To complicate matters further, the decision to divorce—so right a year ago—now doesn't seem so right after all. Loren and David wonder—could they make it work again? Strange things do happen during leap years. Rules change for a time and then right themselves as the calendar regains its balance. Nineteen eighty-eight was another leap year. What did it hold for Loren and David?

—Nancy L. Chu

The Leaves in October   Grades 3-6
By Karen Ackerman

Poppy had promised that when the leaves in October turned red, they would go home. Livvy whispered the promise in the dark, and then the tears rolled down her cheeks. She turned on her side and looked at Younger and Poppy sleeping a few steps away and she thought about that promise. Livvy longed for a home—a place of their own where they could be together and safe. But Livvy knew that grown-ups didn't always keep their promises. She remembered how it had all begun, over a year earlier when the factory where Poppy worked shut down. At first it was fun having him home all day—they'd done so many special things. But then Poppy's unemployment ran out, and Livvy watched as each day he became quieter and sadder. She knew something bad was going to happen when she saw him sitting in his chair with his face in his hands, shaking his head and talking to himself. That something happened when the manager of their trailer park knocked at their door and told them they would have to leave because their rent was still unpaid. They'd lived at the Fourth Street Shelter for the homeless ever since. Poppy had promised that they'd have their own place again, but she could see that Poppy was not himself—once again it looked as though something bad was going to happen.

Livvy, Younger, and Poppy have already lost their home and all they own. As the leaves in October turn red and events close in around them, Livvy looks for something she can do to make sure they'll still have each other. Will she find it?

—*Helen Schlichting*

Libby on Wednesday   **Grades 5-8**
By Zilpha Keatley Snyder

"I've decided to quit school again." Now *there's* a surefire way to get your family's attention! After all, the only reason Libby is attending Morrison Middle School, an eighth-grader at age eleven, is to be "socialized," and six months ought to be long enough for that. So surely her rather eccentric family will agree to let her go back to being taught at home.

It's all because of the FWW. Being the granddaughter of a famous writer doesn't win friends in middle school, nor does knowing things no one else knows. But the last straw for Libby was the FWW, the Future Famous Writers group. When Libby won a creative writing contest, her English teacher had a brainstorm: Libby and the four other winners would meet weekly to read and critique each other's work. Every Wednesday? And with *those* four in particular! Alex twitches when he talks; Tierney has pink hair and wears safety pins for earrings; Wendy looks like a plastic prom queen; and G.G.—well, he's the kind you don't want to be alone with.

But Libby the writer becomes intrigued as she begins to glimpse the personalities—and the pain—behind those faces. Making a friend, Libby finds, may not be so hard after all. It's being a friend that gets tricky.

—*Kathleen Beck*

Line of Duty   **Adult**
By Michael Grant

At first glance, the dead men had nothing in common—an art dealer, an attorney, and a Harlem drug supplier, all murdered in the past month. The tie that bound them was a lonely death with a bullet hole between the eyes.

As information about the murders was slowly unearthed, Detective Brian Shannon noticed the similarities between the three killings. And when he discovered a possible link to the police department, he was ordered to conduct an off-the-record investigation and assigned a partner from the hated Bureau of Internal Affairs, Alex Rose.

Working together despite their mutual distrust, Rose and Shannon uncovered a chain of criminal activities reaching into one of the top agencies of the New York City Police Department, the Narcotics Enforcement Team, an elite anti-drug squad commanded by Patrick Stone. One of New York's finest, Patrick Stone was an ambitious career police officer with his sights set on the future.

But Stone's past had caught up with him in the form of a Peruvian drug kingpin, who was now manipulating Stone *and* the narcotics squad for his own gain. Unless Shannon and Rose can unravel the twisted chain before the next killing, the shockwaves will rattle the NYPD from top to bottom.

—Jeff Blair

Long Time Passing   Grade 9-Adult
By Adrienne Jones

It is said that there are moments in everyone's life that will come rushing back in memory, as crystal-clear as if they had happened yesterday. All it takes is a letter, or maybe a song.

For Jonas Duncan, that was exactly how it happened. A letter and a song carried him back in his memories twenty years ago to the summer of 1969. That summer, when Jonas was eighteen years old, he lost his mother in a tragic car accident. His Lieutenant Colonel father shipped out for Vietnam. And he was sent to live with a cousin he barely knew. He hated those changes. That summer, when Jonas was eighteen years old, he met Auleen Delange, the first girl he ever loved. With her he joined a commune. He marched and carried signs in the peace demonstrations at Berkeley. His mother would have been proud.

That summer, when Jonas was eighteen years old, it took only one phone call to change his life completely. The call reported his father missing in action. He knew then that he would have to go over there. So he became a Marine and was sent to Vietnam. His father would have been proud.

It was a world in turmoil, it was a country in turmoil, it was a young man in turmoil. It was a *Long Time Passing*.

—Linda Olson

Looking Inside: Grades 3–4
Machines and Constructions
By Paul Fleisher and Patricia A. Keeler

Everyone who loves a mystery, hands up! I love mysteries of any kind. Would it be exciting to be involved in a mystery, trying to find out about the hows and whys? But look around you—there are lots of mysteries! Are there any real detectives out there? Did you spot any mysteries? No? Take another look—I'll bet you see a couple every day.

How about the telephone? Why is it that when you press some buttons or dial some numbers you can talk to a friend who lives miles away? Sure, the phone company connects you, but how is it that you can hear your friend's voice? All that's really there are some wires. That's a mystery.

How many of you have used a key to open a door? Well, why does one key work and not another? They all look pretty much alike. That's another mystery.

Now if I point a camera at you and press a button, I will eventually get a picture. Why? I know how it works on the Flintstones! But somehow I don't think that's how it works today.

One way to solve these mysteries would be to look inside. That could be a problem, since most of us probably couldn't put these things back together again! So do the next best thing and read *Looking Inside*. It will help you to solve all those mysteries. By the way, any one know how a toilet flushes? That's one more mystery!

—*Paula Paolucci*

Losing Joe's Place   Grades 7–12
By Gordon Korman

Have you got plans for the summer? How many of you are going on a trip? A trip to Europe? You know the only thing better than going on a trip to Europe? Well, it's having your older brother go on a trip to Europe. A brother who gives you the key to his Camaro. A brother who gives you the key to his great apartment—filled with stereo equipment, big screen TV, Nintendo, and a VCR. That's what sixteen-year-old Jason Cadone has lined up for his summer. It sounds so easy, so great . . . so what's the problem? It *is* great . . . except for his two invited roommates—Don, aka Mr. Wonderful, and Ferguson, aka The Dork. Except for the other crazy people in the building, who include the Stripper, The Phantom, and The Assassin. Except for the landlord, Mr. Plotnick, who hears everything. Except for the last words Jason's brother Joe spoke before he left for Europe: "Don't lose my lease!" Easy enough, until Joe's friend—the kind of guy whose knuckles drag on the ground and who needs to shave his back daily—arrives on the scene to hang out in the apartment. He gets his kicks by letting people hit him in the stomach with a two-by-four and wrestling alligators. Sound like fun? [Pull out a key and toss it up and down in your hand, or throw it to someone in the first row.] Here's the challenge—can you have the time of your life without *Losing Joe's Place?*

—Patrick Jones

Loving Someone Else   Grades 7–12
By Ellen Conford

I was shocked when my mother told us the news. Thanks to a hostile takeover, my dad was out of a job. Now Mom would have to go back to teaching, and they wouldn't be able to pay my sister's tuition at Yale or mine at Sarah Lawrence. Mom suggested I attend Unity, the local community college, but I had no desire to go to a school whose only entrance requirement was being free of communicable disease. I decided I would get a job and earn my tuition money.

When I saw the ad for a companion for two women at $8.00 an hour, I thought I had found my dream job. It started out closer to a nightmare. Their house was on an island and would have made a good setting for a horror movie. Only the thought of earning money for school kept me from leaving when I met the two weird old ladies who lived there. But after I met their gorgeous nephew, I had another reason for staying on.

That summer was an eventful one—I didn't know my job would involve driving a hearse, speaking Esperanto, attending seances, and watching *Divorce Court.* And of course I never suspected the *really* important lesson I would learn during my summer as a companion. What was it? Join me for a most unusual summer and find out.

—Terrie Ratcliffe

Lyddie   Grades 5–8
By Katherine Paterson

How many hats can one girl wear? By the time she was fifteen, Lyddie had been a bear-fighter, a bread-winner, a farmer, a servant, and a factory girl. After Lyddie's father left his wife and the four children, Lyddie's mother went a little "strange in the head," and so, being the oldest, Lyddie assumed the role of the mother for the younger children. It was the winter of 1843, and Lyddie and her brother Charlie did everything they could to hold onto their Vermont farm and keep food on the table. But finally the two youngest children and their mother had to go live with relatives, while Lyddie and Charlie were "rented out" to help pay the debts. Charlie became an apprentice in a sawmill, and Lyddie went to work as a servant at a roadside inn.

Lyddie had always been strong, but she was scared and lonely under the harsh treatment of the inn's mistress. When she was suddenly and unfairly fired, it was her determination to earn enough money to save the farm and re-unite her family that gave her the courage to travel to Lowell, Massachusetts, and become a factory girl.

The life of a factory girl was nothing like anything Lyddie had ever experienced. She and the other girls lived in dormitories and were expected to dress properly and behave like ladies (which included going to church every Sunday). On weekdays (which included Saturday) they rose before dawn to begin their thirteen-hour work day in the textile mills.

Perhaps what surprised Lyddie the most about the mills was the noise. Clatter and clack, great shuddering moans, groans, creaks and rattles. The shrieks and whistles of huge leather belts on wheels . . . all this coming from the giant looms of the factory. But Lyddie adjusted quickly. And she made good friends, though her heart was still in Vermont. Eventually it became sadly obvious that her dream of re-uniting the family could never come true . . . her beloved Charlie and her sister Rachel had settled in with a family who loved them and treated them well, her mother and her other sister had passed away, and the farm was finally sold. At that point Lyddie had to make some very important decisions. Should she return to Vermont and marry the young man who still loved her, or should she wear one more hat before she became a wife? This hat was one that in the past had been worn only by men, yet it would bring her pride and self-fulfillment. This was a hat made for only the most modern and dedicated of women. Would Lyddie be able to fill the bill and wear the mortarboard, that funny-looking square hat with the tassel, the one that is reserved for scholars?

—*Susan Weaver*

Macdonald Hall Goes Hollywood   Grades 5-8
By Gordon Korman

Bruno and Boots are used to being the centers of attention at their prep school, Macdonald Hall. But now, with a motion-picture production crew and teen heart-throb Jordie Jones on campus to make a movie, the dynamic duo are forced to take a back seat. But anyone who knows Bruno and Boots knows *that* situation won't last long.

In the course of their attempts to get into the film, the boys discover that in spite of their preconceptions about him, Jordie Jones wants nothing more than to be treated like a normal guy. And so the boys try—they invite him to late-night poker games, smuggle him into mixers at the girls' finishing school, let him join the hockey team, and so on. But like most escapades involving Bruno and Boots, something always seems to go wrong.

Will Macdonald Hall survive the making of *Academy Blues*? Will *Academy Blues* survive Macdonald Hall? Find out, in *Macdonald Hall Goes Hollywood*!

—*Jeff Blair*

Make Four Million Dollars   Grades 3-6
by Next Thursday
By Stephen Manes

[For this talk, you'll need two props: a facsimile of the book *Make Four Million Dollars by Next Thursday* by Dr. K. Pinkerton Silverfish, and an article of clothing (jacket, vest, or pullover) with pieces of paper marked with large dollar signs safety-pinned all over it. Put on the jacket just before you start this talk.]

I'll bet you're wondering just why I'm wearing all these dollar signs. Well, it's a secret! . . . Do you really want to know? Well, okay. . . . The other day I found this incredible book called *Make Four Million Dollars by Next Thursday*. The fine and distinguished author, Dr. K. Pinkerton Silverfish, lists step-by-step ways to become a millionaire, and this jacket [pullover, vest] is just one of them. But wait, I'm getting ahead of myself—you really need to read Jason Nozzle's story first. After all, he found the book before I did. In fact, this is all very secret stuff, and the only way you can *really* find out is to read *Make Four Million Dollars by Next Thursday* (the one by Stephen Manes).

—*Bette DeBruyne Ammon*

Make Like a Tree and Leave   Grades 5-8
By Paula Danziger

As chairman of the Mummy Committee, I was convinced that I, Matthew Martin, could lead Brian Bruno, Billy Kellerman, and Joshua Jackson to immortality. I knew we would make our teacher proud of our contribution to the sixth-grade Egypt unit. Only problem was, we used too much plastic gauze to wrap up Brian, and by the time we got through, we had to take him out of the house on a dolly, load him into the back of my mother's station wagon, and haul him to Billy's dad's office to get him cut out of his "all-body" orthopedic cast. Billy's dad was great, though. He's got such smooth technique that he was able to remove Billy and save our mummy. So our teacher really was impressed. Everyone was, including Mrs. Nichols. Mrs. Nichols is really neat—she's seventy-eight years old and has been our class volunteer since we were in kindergarten. She always lets us go sledding and skating on her property and makes hot chocolate and cookies for us.

Only now Mrs. Nichols has broken her hip and is in the hospital. And people are saying she'll have to sell her place because she needs the money. And Cathy Atwood's father wants to buy it so he can build a shopping center and a housing development!

Even barfy Vanessa Singer agrees with me that something has to be done. Some of the adults are talking about setting up a thing called a conservancy. Their idea is to raise enough money to buy Mrs. Nichols' land and give it to the town to keep. After my great success on the Mummy Committee, I'm confident that I, Matthew Martin, can handle *this* project too!

—*Kim Carter Sands*

Making History   Adult
By Carolyn See

Spoiled rich kids, spectacular car crashes, a new-age seeress, a philandering businessman, and blended families are all part of this quintessential California tale.

Jerry, who is trying to pull off the deal of a lifetime by enticing investors into a Pacific resort, fantasizes about his blond stepdaughter Whitney, the stereotype of a privileged California girl. Wynn, his wife and Whitney's mother, is only slightly disconcerted when Whitney is banished to a remote apartment at the family home. After all, Whitney is the daughter of the previous marriage, and the two new children conceived with the current husband do seem to take priority.

Unexpectedly, all their lives are touched by a former Australian housewife who can see into people's past lives and discern their current problems—and sometimes she can even foretell what is to come.

—Di Herald

The Man from the Other Side Grades 7–12
By Uri Orlev (translated from the Hebrew by Hillel Halkin)

Marek's stepfather, Anthony, is a smuggler. He smuggles food and now guns to the Jewish people imprisoned in the ghetto by the Nazis. The Germans have closed off the ghetto so the Jews can't get out, and nobody else can get in. But Anthony has found a way. He goes underground through the sewers of Warsaw to meet his contacts. When he comes home his clothes really stink, but he has lots of money. Those Jews are desperate—they'll pay unbelievable prices. Of course what Anthony's doing is illegal, and it's also very dangerous. No one must ever know. If the Germans found out, they'd shoot Anthony immediately, and probably his family too.

On Marek's first trip with his stepfather, another man follows them into the sewers. He says he's been watching and he knows what they are doing. He wants a cut of the money to keep his mouth shut. What do you do with a blackmailer who can turn you in to the police? While Marek is watching, the man suddenly falls, and only then does Marek see the knife in Anthony's hand. Anthony wipes the blade on the dead man's clothes and kicks him into the gutter so that he floats off in the current of sewage. No one must ever know.

Marek and Anthony aren't taking these chances for the sake of the starving Jews—they're doing it for the money. As a matter of fact, they both hate Jews. One day Marek helps two of his buddies rob a Jew who has escaped the ghetto. They get all his cash, and Marek puts his share in his pants pocket. His mother discovers the money and is furious when she finds out how he got it. She is so upset she cries. That's when she tells Marek that his real father was Jewish. How can this be? How could Marek be part of what he despises? Did his father have a beard and sidelocks, did he wear black clothes like the men of the ghetto? His father was killed because he was a Jew *and* a Communist. Could this really have been what his father was like? Should Marek start caring about these people he has always hated? Will it be different, the next time he smuggles food—and guns—to the other side?

—*Maggie Carey*

Masquerade   **Grade 10–Adult**
By Janet Dailey

When she woke up, she didn't know where she was, what she was doing there, or even what her name was. The doctor told her she was in a hospital in Nice, that she had been brought there by the police, and that she had been seen arguing with a man, had fallen or been pushed against a tree and knocked unconscious. The man had run off when two other men saw her fall. She had a row of stitches across the back of her head and a dark bruise by her mouth. She could remember many general things, but nothing that would give her any clue to her own identity. Until the doctor brought her a mirror, she didn't even remember what she looked like. Gazing into the mirror, she saw a stranger's face—tawny shoulder-length hair, pale skin, refined features, hazel eyes with flecks of amber, an image that looked proud and strong, with a hint of daring, that somehow seemed to challenge the world. Is that me? She didn't know—there was nothing familiar about the face.

The only thing that she could identify as something that belonged to the her that she couldn't remember was an urgency, a feeling that she had something to do, something that she had been about to do when she was struck down. But other than that, nothing.

She'd been wearing a designer evening gown and valuable topaz and diamond jewelry when she was found—did that mean that she was wealthy, or had they been gifts from a generous lover? There was no way to know. Inquiries were fruitless. No one had asked about her, no one had missed her. Finally the police inspector who had been trying to help her discover her own identity said that they would put a picture of her in the local paper, in hopes that someone who knew her would see it and come forward.

It was an awful picture, but it worked. A man came to get her—tall, lean, handsome, well dressed . . . and somehow hauntingly familiar. "Remy!" he said when he saw her, and at first she didn't realize he was talking to her, that Remy was her name. But before she could do anything, he had pulled her into his arms and was holding her close. And suddenly she was aware of a feeling as strong and real as the urgency she'd been feeling—the feeling, no, the knowledge that it was right for her to be in his arms, that it was where she belonged.

But once Remy began to find out more about her family, and just who Cole Buchanan really was and why his arms felt so familiar, she began to wonder: how could being with him feel so entirely right, when all the evidence pointed to him as a liar and a fraud who was trying to ruin her family's business—and her family itself?

Who was really the fraud? Who were the people who said they loved her? Did they wear masks? Did Cole? And what would she find out if her memory returned, the memory that her family was so strangely reluctant to help her recover?

—J. R. B.

The Matter Is Life
By J. California Cooper

Adult

The matter is life. Not wistful maybes or glamorized memories, but the stuff of rock-hard, take-the-consequences life. In short stories that range from early this century to late last night, Cooper's narrators describe the lives they have built or destroyed with their own hands. "Everyone wants to matter," says Cooper, and in that striving for significance her people either break out of the prisons of their lives or build new ones and throw away the keys. Few of her characters can attribute success or failure to overwhelming tragedy or amazing luck. It's the little, everyday, moment-by-moment happenings of just living that mold or twist. The poisoning of a destructive animal awakens a fascination that leads to murder. An abusive husband's delight in doing what his wife pleads against becomes the means for her revenge and freedom. A ninety-seven-year-old woman revels in the love of family and friends which the words "I ain't ready" can draw out. An aged Don Juan wonders if his early-marrying, hard-working brother was really so stupid after all. Cooper's storytellers speak in a direct, pared-down vernacular that feels like intimate, front-porch gossip. So lean back, chile, and set a spell. You might learn something about life, even at your age!

—Pamela A. Todd

Matthew Jackson Meets the Wall   Grades 3–6
By Patricia Reilly Giff

"Matthew sat back. . . . He took a breath. It was time to think about. . . . the New Matthew plan. He was going to start all over in this place. He was going to be a new Matthew, a different Matthew. He was going to be tough. . . . He was going to be smart."

Can Matthew Jackson adjust to life in a tall, pointy house with skinny windows that looks kind of haunted? Without the Beast or Emily Arrow or the rest of the kids of the Polk Street School? Especially when, as luck would have it, Matthew's new room is in the attic, his cat Barney turns up missing, and the town bully lives right next door!

Matthew and his family have moved from New York to Deposit, Ohio, and if Matthew is going to survive here, he has a lot to learn!
— *Glenna Hoskins Seeley*

Maxie, Rosie and Earl—   Grades 3–6
Partners in Grime
By Barbara Park

"The principal looks like a green bean in that suit," Rosie was thinking. Maxie was muttering to himself, "It's not fair!" and Earl was giggling, as he usually did when he was nervous.

All three of them had been sent to the principal that Friday afternoon: Rosie, because she tried to keep the teacher informed at all times about things he should know, like how Jennifer had cheated on the test, and how Michael had sneaked into the girls' bathroom. Mr. Jolly called it *tattling*, but Rosie was just trying to *help*. Earl had been sent to the office because he refused to read aloud when the teacher called on him. Earl couldn't help it—the kids had laughed and laughed at the mistake he made the first time he read aloud. He hadn't planned to refuse today . . . it just happened! And Maxie was here once again because he was *so* tired of sitting in alphabetical order—which put him in the last seat of the last row. Daniel W. always sat in front of him, so today Maxie just cut a hole in the back of Daniel's T-shirt.

When the principal had to leave his office before he could see the trio, both he and his secretary told them to return to class and come in to the office again on Monday morning.

As they left, they thought, "Why go back to class?" Walking toward the outside door, they had to get past a suspicious second-grade teacher and a prissy little girl who wanted to show them how she could skip down the hall. Just as they left the building, the bell rang—no, it was a fire drill! What to do now? No choice but to jump in the Dumpster!

Yes, the Dumpster was smelly and had gooey stuff in it; yes, the kindergarten kids beat on it while they waited for the all-clear bell; yes, one boy threw his gum in, and, yes, the gum landed on Earl's arm! When Rosie decided it was safe to leave, twenty-eight minutes after the all-clear bell had sounded, the three fugitives climbed out, free at last—or were they? The janitor had seen them climb from their hiding place and *this* was the janitor with the bleeding dragon tattoo on his arm, the one who had a skull painted on his mop bucket! Would he tell?

—*Dorothy Davidson*

Mayflower Man   Grades 5–8
By Jean Adair Shriver

In the evening twilight, thirteen-year-old Caleb Brewster stands in the barnyard and gazes at the old yellow house. Built in the late 1600s, the Brewster place is a piece of living history. But now this Massachusetts family farm has been sold to Mike Kelso and his family—from California. Up till now, Caleb had been a somebody in the eyes of the community. Dorothy Brewster, his grandmother, had been a somebody, too.

But now he is a nobody, invisible to his classmates and the people in the community. With Gran gone, there is no prestige and no money. No money for Caleb to attend a private boy's school, no money for the upkeep of the family farm. That's why the farm was sold, and why Caleb and his mother had to move into town and live in a cheap apartment complex.

Caleb needs a plan. A plan to get the farm back from the Kelsos and save it from the developers. He starts by accepting a job working for Mike Kelso as a handyman around the farm. Next, he develops a cautious friendship with Mike's step-daughter Mose. And now Caleb has the Massachusetts Historical Society on the bandwagon to help save the Brewster Place. The Mayflower Man, as Mose calls Caleb, is on a roll. Everything is falling into place. Who cares if he loses his only friend? Who cares if people get hurt? The most important thing in Caleb's life is the family farm. Or is it?

—*Mary Ann Capan*

Mississippi Bridge
By Mildred D. Taylor

Grades 5–12

"I ain't liked the way Pa done talk to Josias. Josias was a nice man. He wasn't hurting nobody. But I knowed that was the way, for Pa and the other men to talk like that to Josias and for Josias to take it. Colored folks seemed always to have to take that kind of talk. One time I seen Pa and Melvin and R.S. and a whole bunch drag a colored man down the road, beat him till he ain't hardly had no face on him 'cause he done stood up for himself and talked back. That ain't never set right with me, the way Pa done. It wasn't right, and I just knowed that."

That's the way it is in Mississippi in 1930—"niggers don't have no say 'bout nothin'. They ride in the back of the bus, and if that bus is full up they have to get off so's the white folk can ride."

Jeremy Simms, a ten-year-old white boy, doesn't feel the way most other white folks do towards the colored people. He wants to be their friend.

About once a week the bus comes down this way from Jackson, makes a stop in front of the general store to pick up folks, then goes on west over the bridge that crosses the creek. The next day, it comes back again heading north.

Josias, one of Jeremy's black friends, has a lumbering job waiting for him, and he has to be on that bus. But before the bus leaves another white family arrives. The driver makes all the blacks get off to make room for them. Moments later the bus crashes through the bridge railing and sinks in the rain-swollen river.

Josias and Jeremy are the first to arrive to pull out the bodies. Jeremy shakes his head and asks, "But how come, Josias? How come?"

Josias shakes his head and gives a mighty sigh. "Ain't for me t' know. Can't go questionin' the ways of the Lord. Onliest thing I know is that the Good Book, it say the Lord He work in mighty mysterious ways."

Discover what it's like to live in the Deep South in the 1930s—it's not easy whether you're black or white.

—Betty A. Holtzen

Molly by Any Other Name   Grade 7–Adult
By Jean Davies Okimoto

Molly Jane Fletcher looks into the mirror and wonders: Who do I look like? She sees high cheekbones; straight, shiny black hair; and dark Asian eyes. Molly's parents, Ellie and Paul, adopted her as an infant and have always been open and honest about her beginnings—at least as far as they know. But at seventeen Molly is beginning to have more questions than they can answer, especially after a speaker comes to her school to talk about the Northwest Adoptees Search Organization. Her best friend Roland assures her that it's obvious who she is—"a whole Molly, all Molly." But her friendship with Roland is changing, now that he acts interested in that boy-chasing Megan Lee. And Molly's feelings about Roland are all mixed up with a reluctant attraction to fellow cheerleader Joe, who is very open about his feelings for her. Add to all this two hurt and confused parents who can't understand Molly's sudden desire to discover her past. But Molly can't help wondering: Who is my birthmother? Why did she give me away? What is my true heritage, and my real name? When Molly turns eighteen her adoption records can legally be opened, and maybe then she'll find some answers. Or will she simply discover that *Molly by Any Other Name* is still Molly?

—Bette DeBruyne Ammon

Monster of the Year   Grades 5–8
By Bruce Coville

What would you think if all the monsters you have ever read about or seen in old movies—a vampire, a Frankenstein monster, a creature from the black lagoon, a werewolf, all those guys—showed up at your house? And it wasn't even Halloween night! Well, that's what happens to Michael and his best friend Kevver.

It all starts because they are bored during summer vacation—the old "nothing to do" syndrome. So they convince Michael's mom to let them work at her advertising billboard company. And they like being gofers and learning about the business. They like it so much they decide that for their shared birthday they want a billboard of their own for a month. Michael's mom finally agrees. Michael and Kevver are monster fans—and they want to poke a little fun at an anti-billboard campaign called BAM, for Billboards Are Monstrous—so they design a billboard announcing a Monster of the Year contest. The day after the billboard goes up, it and the contest are the talk of the town. But then Michael starts receiving telegrams—from Transylvania—announcing the arrival of a Count, and of someone called Igor who is bringing a contest entrant. Before he knows it, the house is filled from the basement (where the Count has moved in, coffin and all) to the attic— with monsters! And each one expects Michael to name *him* the Monster of the Year. What can Michael do? He sure doesn't want all those monsters mad at him! Would you?   —*Diane L. Deuel*

The Moon Clock   Grades 3-6
By Matt Faulkner

I tell you, it was the greatest adventure anyone could ever have! There I was, leading an army against enemies who could wipe us out with just one look from their evil eyes. Was I scared? Oh, maybe a little. But what else could I do? When you're the leader, everyone looks to you for courage.

Sounds good, doesn't it. You'd believe me, too, unless you knew what everyone at school called me: 'Fraidy Cat Robin, the world's biggest crybaby. Yeah, well, maybe then. But that was before I met Mr. Kolshinsky and had the most frightening, exciting, wonderful adventure ever. Read about me and Mr. Kolshinsky in *The Moon Clock*, and see why no one will *ever* call me a coward again!

—*Nancy L. Chu*

More Stories to Solve: Grades 3-9
Fifteen Folktales from Around the World
By George Shannon, retel.

It has been said that it takes no exceptional intelligence or super-special powers to solve riddles. It just takes looking at the problem from a different angle—a fresh approach. Listen carefully to this riddle [from pages 35—37], and see if you can give me the solution:

Long ago, many kings would compete with riddles instead of fighting wars. After solving a riddle the Egyptian king Nactanabo had sent him, King Lycurgus of Babylon decided to send him a riddle in return. So he choose the cleverest man he knew, Aesop, a former slave, to bear his challenge.

Aesop quickly outwitted King Nactanabo, but the king would not let him go. He hoped to defeat Aesop and send him home in disgrace. He tested Aesop with riddle after riddle but Aesop easily solved each one. Finally Nactanabo came up with an impossible task.

"If you can bring me something that I've never seen or heard about," the king told Aesop, "I'll send one thousand dollars as a tribute to your king. If you fail, you must leave and admit both your and your king's defeat."

Aesop begged for three days to think of something. "Take your time," said Nactanabo. He knew that no matter what Aesop came up with, all he had to do was say he'd already seen it. His advisors were ordered to say the same thing.

When Aesop returned, he handed King Nactanabo a small piece of paper. Just as planned, the king and his advisers all said, "We've seen this before. We know all about it. You have failed."

"That's good," said Aesop. "Now I'll take the one thousand dollars for my king."

"No!" said King Nactanabo, "I've never seen this paper before."

"Good," said Aesop. "I've passed your test and will accept the one-thousand-dollar tribute for my king."

There was no way King Nactanabo could win. If the king said he *had* seen the paper, he had to pay King Lycurgus one thousand dollars. And if he said he had *not* seen the paper, he had to pay King Lycurgus one thousand dollars. What words had Aesop written on the paper?

Now think about it for a minute—what was written on the paper Aesop gave King Nactanabo? [Let the audience try to guess.] The note said, "I, King Nactanabo, owe King Lycurgus one thousand dollars to be paid to Aesop." No matter what answer King Nactanabo gave, whether he said he had seen the note before or not, he would still have to pay the other king a thousand dollars.

You see, if you let a riddle tease your brain for a while and look at it from different angles, you too are likely to find the solution. If you're a riddle buff or if you're trying to stump a friend, you'll want to read the other fourteen tales in *More Stories to Solve*. And just in case one of these riddles has you stumped, the solution is given at the end of each story.

—*Sandra Carpenter*

Most Precious Blood   Grades 5-12
By Susan Beth Pfeffer

Boy, was Michelle mad! But Val Castaladi knew that if she just let her cousin blow off steam, it would be over, and then she could walk away from all the kids who had gathered around the lockers to find out what all the yelling was about. Val was thinking she should have gone over to her cousin's house for dinner yesterday, the way she was supposed to—maybe then Michelle wouldn't be so ticked. When Michelle started yelling about her father not being her *real* father, Val was stunned. What? What was she talking about?

"It's true," Michelle said. "And it's about time you knew it. He isn't your father. Everybody in the family knows. You're not really family. You don't really count." How could this possibly be true? It had to be a lie; Michelle never lied, but she had to be lying now. Wasn't she? Someone tell her it's a lie!

When Val got home, she remembered that her mother had written her a letter—Mom had told her this several months before she died. Should she open it? It said not to open till she was eighteen—well, she'd just have to; maybe the answer was in the letter.

It was. What Michelle had said was true. Val is an adopted child. Rick is not her real father—either that, or she is his daughter by another woman. Where did Val come from? Where did Rick get the tiny baby he placed in his wife's arms as a gift? And if he isn't her real father, how did he get hold of her? Could she have been kidnapped, as her friend Caroline once suggested? Would Rick have had her real mother killed to get the baby? It's possible—after all, *his* father had been involved with the mob; everyone knows about the powerful Castaladis and their mob connections.

And why does Val have to have a bodyguard drive her every place? Why can't she just walk home from school or over to a friend's house? Why are two housekeepers always with her—do they have anything to do with her past? Can she ever find out the truth about who she is? She can't bear to ask Daddy—Rick—for the truth. How can she believe him now, when he's been lying to her for sixteen years?

—Maggie Carey

A Mouse in My Roof   Grades 3–9
By Richard Edwards

Have you ever heard of a monster called the Sliver-Slurk?

> Down beneath the frogspawn,
> Down beneath the reeds,
> Down beneath the river's shimmer,
> Down beneath the weeds,
> Down in dirty darkness,
> Down in muddy murk,
> Down amongst the sludgy shadows

Lives the Sliver-Slurk.

Lives the Sliver-Slurk,
And the Sliver-Slurk's a thing
With a gnawing kind of nibble
And a clammy kind of cling,
With a row of warts on top
And a row of warts beneath
And a horrid way of bubbling through
Its green and stumpy teeth;

With its green and stumpy teeth,
Oh, the Sliver-Slurk's a beast
That you'd never find invited
To a party or a feast—
It would terrify the guests,
Make them shake and shout and scream,
Crying: "Save us from this loathesomeness,
This monster from a dream!"

It's a monster from a dream,
Haunting waters grey and grim,
So be careful when you paddle
Or go gaily for a swim:
It is down there, it is waiting,
It's a nasty piece of work,
And you might just put your foot upon
The slimy Sliver-Slurk.

Can you see in your imagination what a Sliver-Slurk looks like? Could you draw one? (Would you really want to?)

The Sliver-Slurk is just one of the strange phenomena you'll meet in this book. You'll find all kinds of things here, a carrot named James, and paint that makes things disappear, Tarzan's cave behind a waterfall, and a mouse in the roof. Poor Henry can't sleep as the mouse scampers and creeps, gnaws and squeaks. He moves to a new house, then to a hotel, a tent, a hammock, a cave. Always there is a mouse in his roof, even when he *has* no roof. Henry does not like the mouse in his roof, but you will.

—*Diane L. Deuel*

The Mozart Season   Grades 7–12
By Virginia Euwer Wolff

I'm Allegra Shapiro. I know it's a weird name, but my parents are
both musicians, so I got a musical name. And I'm a musician, too. I'm
supposed to play Mozart's Fourth Violin Concerto in the Ernest Bloch
Young Musicians Competition next fall. In Oregon or anywhere else,
that's a big deal. Only six kids get picked for the competition, and I'll
be the youngest. I'm twelve. And I'm not sure I'm happy about this.
Why not?

Number 1: Nobody told me I was a finalist until school was over.
They said they didn't want to distract me from softball playing or
school. But that leaves only eight weeks to get ready for the contest.

Number 2: I'll be the youngest. That means everybody will be expecting a child prodigy or something.

Number 3: Steve Landauer. He's sixteen, another finalist, and one
of the greatest-looking guys I've ever seen. He's also insufferably con-
ceited and arrogant. And I sit next to him in the Youth Orchestra.

Number 4: I have other things going on in my life. Like finding Mr.
Trouble's waltz. Mr. Trouble? Oh, he's the dancing man at all the outdoor concerts. I promised I'd help him find a waltz he knew thirty years
ago. It's turning into a full-time job!

And finally I have to look for me. I mean, find out what it means
to have had a Jewish great-grandmother who died in Treblinka. Who
was she? Was she like me?

So I don't know if I really want to be in the Bloch competition, but
I guess I don't really have a choice. Maybe if I do it for my great-
grandmother. . . .

—Julie Bray

Mummy Took Cooking Lessons   Grades 7 –12
and Other Poems
By John Ciardi

Life is full of trouble. And danger. It's also a lot of fun when you look
at it through the eyes of John Ciardi, your poet and guide through some
of the strangest experiences you will ever encounter. Take weather, for
example:

The morning after the night before,
The wind came in when I opened the door.

It blew the "Welcome" off the mat.
It blew the fur right off my cat.
It blew my shirttail out of my pants.
It grabbed the curtains and started to dance
Around and around and around about
Till I opened a window and kicked it out.

Or cooking:

This is Little Betty Bopper.
She has popcorn in the popper.
Seven pounds of it! Please stop her.
That's more popcorn than is proper
In a popper. Someone drop her
Just a hint! Mommer! Popper!
Betty's going to come a cropper!
Look, it's starting! Get a chopper.
Chop the door down!
                                    . . . Well, too late.

Oh, well. Those things happen when you aren't careful. Meet a crowd
of strange, funny and intriguing characters in *Mummy Took Cooking
Lessons and Other Poems* by John Ciardi. And then hide the cook-
books.

—*Nancy L. Chu*

My Aunt Ruth   Grades 7–12
By Iris Rosofsky

How could my Aunt Ruth change so much? I thought acting was
everything to her, but now she was suggesting that it *wasn't* the only
thing in life. Just being alive—able to walk and talk and breathe the
fresh air and feel the raindrops—that was more important, she said.

I couldn't believe it. Would I feel the same if I had been through all
that surgery and had my body so totally changed? And yet I knew that,
even with her disability, Aunt Ruth still planned to go on with her acting career. She was tough. She wasn't a quitter. So why did she imply
that acting wasn't all in life? It was certainly everything to me, especially now that I'd finally won the part of Juliet in our school play.

A few months ago Aunt Ruth had seemed to be the luckiest, happiest woman in the world. A beautiful, talented actress, she was living in Hollywood with her husband, a handsome actor. None of us were prepared for the nightmare that would begin with some routine medical tests.

The more I thought about Aunt Ruth's words and watched those raindrops hitting on the pavement below the hospital window, the more I wanted to write about that scene, so vividly etched in my mind. But I could hardly keep up with both my acting and my writing. What did I really want most? Sometimes it seemed as if Aunt Ruth had discovered the secrets of life, but other times it seemed as though we were only scratching the surface together.

My Aunt Ruth is still very special to me. I'd like you to get to know her too.

—Sharon Thomas

My Crooked Family   Grades 7–12
By James Lincoln Collier

I'm not the kind of guy that goes around looking for trouble. But once you get a taste for having a few bucks to spare, it's hard to keep your nose clean. It all started the night I stole some fried pork and rice from the Chinaman's. Ma was drunk, and Lulu, my sis, and I were hungry. I tried to hit Pa up for some change, but he wouldn't part with a nickel. He said it wouldn't do no harm for us to miss a meal now and again. It was Lulu's idea to beg food from the Chinaman. I knew the Chinaman wasn't into handouts, but I decided we should give it a try. I was getting ready to ask him if we could pay tomorrow when Lulu handed over Pa's lunch bucket and asked for two orders with lots of glop. When the Chinaman came back with the food and demanded sixty cents, I tried to explain that we couldn't pay until tomorrow. But the Chinaman said, "No money, no food." That's when I grabbed the bucket and ran for it. A cop caught up with me a block later and hauled me into the station house. That's where I met Circus Penrose. I asked him why he was there. He said he'd been in a crap game where a third die with shaved corners had mysteriously turned up. It seemed there had been some gunplay over the matter. Shortly after that, Ma came and talked the sergeant into letting me go. Outside, she told me that Pa had been shot, and that they didn't know if he'd live. That's why, when Circus showed up outside of school the next day and offered me a chance to earn some dough, I agreed. The idea of going crooked scared me, but I was tired of being hungry and looking like an orphan in a movie. But I never thought things would turn out the way they did.

—Kathy Ann Miller

My Name is Sus5an Smith. Grades 7–12
The 5 is Silent
By Louise Plummer

Imagine being an artist in Utah . . . kind of difficult, isn't it? Then try being named Susan Smith . . . dull, isn't it? Now imagine the worst possible: how about being a seventeen-year-old artist named Susan Smith in the middle of Utah's most ordinary family . . . it boggles the mind!

Susan was desperate for a life of her own. She wanted to distinguish herself, to be a famous painter and have her talents recognized and appreciated. A silent 5 in the middle of her name was to be the grabber, a real visual statement, and just the right touch to set her apart as she struggled toward fame and independence.

Sus5an's family were at once her greatest help and her biggest hindrance. They loved her, but what did they know about being an artist? The only one who might understand would be Uncle Willy, wherever he was. He was the man who had abandoned her aunt right after the wedding ten years ago. Willie had always made Sus5an feel special, most of all when he gave her a silver armadillo necklace on her eighth birthday. Her family had never forgiven him for walking out, but Sus5an had never forgotten his kindness, his imaginative present.

It was another relative, Aunt Libby, who finally offered Sus5an a chance to escape, when she invited her to stay in Boston for the summer. Sus5an grabbed the opportunity to begin a new life.

Boston did provide all sorts of interesting people and situations for an apprentice artist, starting with Sweeney, the blushing usher, and Grace, the eccentric lady in a neigboring apartment who hadn't thrown away a thing in forty years, and going all the way up to stupid pet tricks on TV. The one thing Sus5an didn't count on was finding Willy again, and discovering for herself just who he really was—the hard-hearted rat her family detested, or the caring, attractive man *she* remembered.

Spending the summer in Boston would be the time for Sus5an to find out all sorts of truths, with or without the 5.

—Sue Young

My Sister Is Driving Me Crazy · Grades 5-8
By Mary E. Ryan

Mattie was sick and tired of being a part of some one else. Mattie and her sister Pru were identical twins. When they were younger it was fun to dress alike and do their hair in the same style. No one could tell them apart, especially not their teachers. They could trade classes and no one would suspect a thing. But now they were growing up and it wasn't fun anymore. Mattie was tired of friends calling her one of the Twinkies. And she was tired of people asking, "Well, which one are you?" More than anything Mattie wanted to be different. She wanted to be an individual with her own identity and personality. This year, Mattie decided, was the year she was going to be her own person. But just how far do you have to go to be an individual when you're an identical twin?

—Linda Olson

The Mysterious World   Grades 9-12
of Marcus Leadbeater
By Ivan Southall

They tell me that losing someone you love is never easy. Well, Gramps' death has certainly left things in turmoil in my life. It was bad enough being there when he died, but knowing that I might have prevented his drowning makes it worse. I've clung to memories of the happier times we had together, and I planned to share them with Gran during my visit. But instead of being a time for remembering the man we both loved, my visit began with another shock: Gran was selling the house, Gramps' house, the house I was supposed to inherit. How could she get rid of something that contained so much of Gramps? It's like she never cared about him. Or about me. There *must* be an explanation. But what?

—Terrie Ratcliffe

Naked in Winter   Grades 7-8
By Jerome Brooks

Mrs. Heegard called him "an omphaloskeptic," Coz called him "the Jedge," and his folks called him "Junior." At school the kids called him "Jake" and the teachers called him "Jacob." Funny, he had almost finished his junior year at Crane Tech before he realized that they were all right—each of the names fit part of him.

"Junior" placed him in the family; "Jake" was the comfortable, well-used public name. But "Jacob" was a name to grow into—a slow and unsteady process. It was like instantly falling in love with Roberta Hubbard and not having a clue what to do about it. Like watching Roberta flee from him because he knew Coz. Later on, it was talking to her and finding out what they had in common. It was the total anguish after he made a wrong move. It was his return to Adrienne Himmel because she wanted him so much and it was so easy to be with her.

His whole life he had known Coz and Benny and the Moose. They were his best friends. Oh, there were times when Coz's "lay the lady" stories were too much, or when three of them ganged up on the fourth, but they were a kind of family, a kid family. That was why it was so strange that it took him so long to accept the truth behind their name for him—"the Jedge." He was beginning to understand that somehow human need and decision-making were connected, and that he didn't always have the right to judge others.

His English teacher explained to him that "omphaloskeptic" meant "introvert," literally someone who bends over and studies his or her own belly-button. Mrs. Heegard went on to say that Jake was showing only a part of himself, and that part, she felt, had scars. Maybe that's what started his odyssey, looking for connections, discovering who he was and where he fit in.

—Barbara Hawkins

The New York Times Book   **Adult**
of Sports Legends
Joseph J. Vecchione, ed.

Read this book and you will live fifty lives. *The New York Times Book of Sports Legends* is a wonderful collection of short essays about historic achievements on the fields of play and also about the broad fabric of the American experience in the first sixty years of this century.

Skip around! You don't have to read it straight through! Choose favorites, or read about the personalities of first one sport, then another. Share it with your friends, because part of the charm of such collections is . . . "Look who was left out!"

Let's face it: Michael Jordan and Nolan Ryan are not in this book. True, they are currently sports heroes, but they are not yet legends. Here we'll be reading about the years before sports became a national obsession, when boxing and the ball sports were largely recreational outlets for blue-collar America. Most of the figures here were organizers of teams or innovators of strategy. And very few were born to privilege.

George Halas was a famous football player and coach who helped start the league now known as the NFL. In 1920 he assembled his first team from workers at the grain company where he was employed in northern Illinois.

Six-foot, five-inch Joe Lapchick had the idea in 1929 to put together a basketball team and take it on the road.

Want to talk strategy? Read about Knute Rockne and football's first forward pass.

Who were about the first players to become famous for causing panic and dread among their opponents—the old-fashioned war of nerves? An odd couple if there ever was one—tough man Ty Cobb on the baseball diamond, and dapper Walter Hagen on the golf course! You can also dig out other parallels to modern-day sports stories. In the late 1920s, Red Grange in football and Babe Ruth in baseball were being paid close to $100,000 a year. They were frank about the reason, too: they filled the stadiums. People were climbing the fences to see them play. And believe me, big-money players today use the same argument.

There is irony: basketball coach Adolph Rupp is perhaps more famous for one of his team's losses than any string of victories he posted. There is poignancy: the touching stories of Christy Mathewson, Jim Thorpe, Maureen Connolly and others who became ill, died young, or suffered prejudice. But then you'll smile too, because all these people had a turn on the field, and did they make the most of it!

There is the ghost of a fifty-first legend roaming through these pages—sports journalist Grantland Rice, who is quoted time and again. Widely read in mid-century America, he was responsible for nicknames like The Galloping Ghost and the Four Horsemen of Notre Dame. He also wrote these lines: "When the one Great Scorer comes to write against your name, He marks not that you won or lost, but how you played the game."

Discover just how these legends played their games in *The New York Times Book of Sports Legends.*

—Mark Anderson

A Newbery Christmas   Grades 3-8
By Martin H. Greenberg and Charles G. Waugh, sels.

For years Rufus had asked Santa Claus for a pony along with his other requests, but to no avail. So last year he asked for just one thing . . . the pony. He got a stuffed one on wheels! This year he's going to ask for a *live* pony!

But Mama said not to ask for too much, because there was a war going on, and Santa needed extra money for the poor children in Europe.

Although Rufus doesn't get his live pony, Christmas turns out to be a day he will never forget, with wonderful surprises and mysterious happenings, bringing the family closer together and reminding us all of the true meaning of Christmas.

This is only one of the wonderful Christmas stories you'll find in *A Newbery Christmas*. Perhaps you could share your favorite one with your family on Christmas Eve.

—*Carol Kappelmann*

The Night the Bells Rang   Grades 5-6
By Natalie Kinsey-Warnock

Have you ever had to deal with a bully? I mean a *big* bully, a kid a lot older than you, who singled you out and never missed a chance to be mean to you, just for the sheer joy of making you miserable. Well, Mason knew what that was like.

It was the winter of 1918. War was raging in Europe, and in Vermont the winter was the coldest anyone could remember. And high schooler Aden Cutler was coming over to the elementary school every day just to torment Mason. He stole Mason's new mittens. He filled Mason's hat with snow and jammed it onto his head so hard the cold made tears come to his eyes. He threw Mason's boots out into the pasture, so Mason had to walk through the snow in his stocking feet to get them. It was a long winter.

Finally, in the spring, things changed. Something happened that let Mason see another side to Aden. Read *The Night the Bells Rang* to find out what Mason learned about Aden, and about himself.

—*Patricia Willingham*

Nightfall   Grade 9-Adult
By Isaac Asimov and Robert Silverberg

On July 26, 1991, there was a total eclipse of the sun. Thousands of tourists and scientists flocked to Hawaii and Mexico to watch night fall in the middle of the day. It was an exciting time, fun, even, but not completely unusual. Here on earth we are subject to periods of darkness every twenty-four hours. For us the dark holds little fear.

Now try to imagine a world that knows only perpetual day, a world with six suns to keep it always bathed in light. And try to imagine what a total eclipse would do to the inhabitants of that world. There, a group of stunned scientists have just realized that darkness is coming. According to their latest astronomical calculations, total eclipses occur every 2049 years, and the next eclipse of the suns is only months away. Worse, archeological evidence has been found showing layers of past civilizations, and each was about 2050 years old when it was destroyed—apparently by fire. And psychological research has shown that even a fifteen-minute amusement ride through a dark tunnel will leave most of the participants seriously deranged or dead from fright.

The darkness is coming. The madness is beginning. Will it mean that civilization is ending yet again?

—Linda Olson

Object Lessons   Grade 9–Adult
By Anna Quindlen

Maggie Scanlan's world was falling apart. In one summer everything and everybody that had been steady and unmoving for all of her thirteen years began to shift and change.

First, her long-time best friend Debbie deserted her and began hanging out with a crowd that Maggie didn't like. These kids were into dangerous pranks and sexual games that frightened Maggie. But Debbie's unspoken message came through loud and clear: either Maggie joined this group too or their friendship was over.

And Debbie wasn't the only person who was changing. Maggie hardly knew what to expect from her mother anymore. Ever since her parents began fighting over whether to move into the new house grandfather Scanlan had bought for them, her mom had been acting strange. For one thing, she was hardly ever home. She would disappear for hours at a time, and no one knew where she was or what she was doing. And when she *was* home, she seemed to always be talking to the foreman of the construction crew that was working on the new housing development in their neighborhood. He was an old friend from her mom's high school days, and Maggie had the feeling that her mom felt more comfortable around him than around any of the Scanlans— including Maggie's dad.

And then there was her grandfather Scanlan. For as long as Maggie could remember, he had dominated her life and everyone else's. She knew that he controlled almost everything in the family, and she also knew that he hadn't wanted her dad to marry her mom. That was one reason her mom refused to move into the house he had bought for them. But now he was dying, and Maggie couldn't imagine what the world was going to be like without him.

Maggie had always taken certain things for granted, things that would never change. Her parents would always stay together, Debbie would always be her best friend, and her grandfather would always preside over the Scanlan clan. Now she was afraid that nothing would stay the same. Not even her.

—Margie Reitsma

Of Swans, Sugarplums, Grades 3-8
and Satin Slippers: Ballet Stories for Children
By Violette Verdy

Remember seeing the ballet "The Nutcracker" at Christmastime? Its strong feeling of mystery and celebration and its fantastic music by Peter Tchaikovsky have made it a dance favorite. "The Nutcracker" is only one of the many ballets the author, Violette Verdy, has danced in the course of a distinguished career. In this charming book she retells the stories of six dance favorites in a lively, romantic style. These stories are full of magic: life-sized clockwork dolls, bewitched princesses, and even a firebird. Classical ballet can seem magical, enchanting—or sometimes just plain silly, depending on your mood. Swans, sugarplums, and satin slippers—open your imagination to these fantastical adventures, and see if the magic works for you.

—Anna Biagioni Hart

The Ogre Downstairs Grades 3-8
By Diana Wynne Jones

Just imagine using something you found in a home chemistry kit and having it make taffy candybars come alive. You might have to feed them, but what do you feed a candy bar? Or suppose it was your pencils, or building blocks, or even your stepfather's pipe that came alive and went running around the house? What then? Especially if your nickname for your stepfather was The Ogre!

Casper and Johnny had plenty to deal with before they started fooling around with the chemistry set—but then they made their sister Gwinny float in thin air, things started to come alive, and the fun really began. What *do* you feed a candy bar? Read *The Ogre Downstairs*, and find out.

—Sarah M. Thrash and J. R. B.

Old Blue Tilley   Grades 5-6
By Robbie Branscum

Hey hi, Hey hi ho,
Old Blue Tilley's a-gonna save some soul.
Preach 'bout hell, preach 'bout fire,
Preach 'bout women who bob thar hair.

That was the song of Old Blue Tilley, the travelin' preacher. As soon as I heard that song I knew Old Blue was comin' home for a spell. Bein' it was springtime, I also knew we'd soon be settin' out together for Old Blue's annual revival meetin'.

It's been quite awhile since Old Blue found me half starved along the road. He's taught me lots of things, like how to read the Bible, do my sums, and how to cook and hunt. When Old Blue's away, I tend to his place and take care of his animals.

Each year in the spring we set out to make "the circuit"—visitin' folks we haven't seen since the previous year. We stay with folks all along the way, eatin', huntin', campin' out, and we've heard many tales by the time we reach the campgrounds where the revival is always held.

But this year promises to be different. There's talk of war with Germany, and there's sure to be a confrontation between Old Blue and that devil Oxalee, who totes his whiskey jug right into the prayer meetin'. Will the revival hold other surprises? I do believe it may.

—Paulette Nelson

The Old Coot   Grades 3-6
By Peggy Christian

Bad medicine—that's what everyone says about the Old Coot who lives in the hills. They say he's meaner than a rattlesnake with its rattle caught in a door, and when the Old Coot comes to town, people stay out of his way.

He used to prospect for gold, way back when he was a young man. But they say he met up with a coyote who showed him another kind of gold: stories. That coyote filled him up with stories of every kind! Some of those stories were "frightful scary, some desperate sad, and some knee-slapping funny." The Old Coot made his living telling them.

Those stories even got him out of trouble a few times, like the time he met up with a cattle rustler. See, what happened was . . . but maybe you'd better let the Old Coot tell you himself. After all, it's *his* story!

—Donna L. Scanlon

On the Far Side of the Mountain   Grades 3-8
By Jean Craighead George

It's been two years since I moved into the forest to live, up on the mountain, far away from everyone else. The first year I was here, all I had was a tree, a bed, and a fireplace. Now I have a pond, a millhouse, a table, a lounging chair, a root cellar—and friends. My sister Alice lives here too; she didn't like living in my tree, though, so I built her a treehouse. But even though many things have changed, one thing hasn't—Frightful is still with me, my falcon, my friend, and my hunting companion. I don't know what I would do without her—and I thought I would never have to find out.

Life on the mountain has changed in the two years since I arrived, and I have learned to change with it and adapt. But I never expected my life to fall apart, to be destroyed in one short moment. But it was—a conservation officer walked into the clearing one morning, and when he walked out five minutes later, he had Frightful with him. He said she was an endangered species, and it was illegal for me to have her. Nothing I could say or do made any difference. She was gone, and for the first time in a long while I felt truly deserted and alone. I didn't want to tell anyone what had happened, not even Alice. But when I decided to go to Delhi and talk to the sheriff, to see if there was anything he could do to get Frightful back, I knew I had to leave Alice a note, letting her know where I was going and why. I knew she was around somewhere, since she'd left me a note in the hinges of the door to the root cellar: "I'm thinking waterfalls." That was all—Alice wasn't one to waste words, and she liked being mysterious.

But when I got to Delhi, I discovered that the conservation officer was genuine—Frightful hadn't been kidnapped—and I had to face life without her. I felt so rotten about it that I just wanted to be alone, so it took me a couple of days to get back home. And when I got there, I discovered that Alice was gone too. She'd taken some of our supplies, our water-carrier, her clothes, a Swiss army knife, and gloves. It didn't look like she'd be back soon. She had also left another note: "Dear Sam, I'm leaving you. Don't worry about me. I'll be just fine, thanks for all you have taught me. Love, Alice."

I knew I shouldn't worry—after all, I'd done more or less the same thing—but Alice was two years younger than I was, and she was always getting into trouble she couldn't get out of. I decided to follow her, just to see where she was going, so I'd be there to help her if she needed me. Besides, I didn't want to sit around my meadow all by myself every day, trying to figure how to survive without Frightful to help me hunt and keep me company. Even tracking Alice sounded like more fun.

Little did I know where that trail would lead me, or how much I would be changed by the journey and by Alice's new project and adventure. What lies on the far side of the mountain? Follow my trail and find out.

—*J.R.B.*

On the Third Ward   Grades 7–12
By T. Degens

Shortly after she arrived on the third floor, the kids in Wanda's room asked Wanda to stay with Albert and watch him die. They figured she needed to learn right away what life was about in the Hessian State Hospital for Children with Tuberculosis. Life was about death; Wanda knew that already, and she knew that she too was expected to die.

It was the sixth winter after the end of World War II when Wanda entered the hospital. Outside, fog and snow blanketed everything, making the world look eerie and not-quite-real. Inside, reality was shots and pills, tests and x-rays, and death—hovering, waiting to strike. Inside were the kids—the up kids, the down kids, the birds, and the screamers, all of whom fantasized about escaping to the outside.

P.B., a down kid in a plaster body-cast from neck to foot, was a master paper-cutter. She cut the shapes of whatever the other kids wanted to take with them on their escape from the hospital. Carla's world was filled with boys and men in love with her. She had hundreds of letters and magazine pictures and photographs of men and boys of all shapes, ages, and sizes. Sometimes one even came to visit her on the third floor! Then there was the Empress of China with her long, dark braid, her special yellow brocade robe, and her magical stories. Her stories wove an exotic spell so vivid and wondrous, Wanda soon had trouble knowing what was real and what wasn't. So when Wanda and P.B. actually managed a chance escape to the outside, it wasn't the snow-covered world they sought, but the world of the Empress of China.

—*Sue Padilla*

The Other Victims: **Grades 5–12**
First-Person Stories of Non-Jews Persecuted by the Nazis
Ina R. Friedman, comp.

Elisabeth Kusserow knew only too well what it was like to be persecuted. Since she and her family were Jehovah's Witnesses and did not believe in Hitler or in war, they were frequently harrassed by the Nazis. As a teenager living in Germany, she felt the day-to-day terror of persecution: " . . . the situation in school became more and more painful. Every day, the teacher reprimanded me for not saluting the Nazi flag. The big swastika on the red banner flew over the schoolhouse and hung on a pole in every classroom. My stomach churned as I tried to think of how I could avoid saluting it or saying 'Heil Hitler!'" Eventually, the Nazis put Elisabeth and two of her brothers into corrective training schools for six years, while others in her family were sent to concentration camps. Finally, after the Nazis had been defeated, Elisabeth ran back to her old home: "As soon as I walked into the kitchen, I started to cry. Silence filled a room that had resounded with talk and laughter." Later, her parents and some of her family returned, but not, sadly, two of her brothers. They had been killed by the Nazis because they had refused to serve in the army.

Can you imagine being punished and separated from your family for years the way Elisabeth was, and not having any recourse? Under the Nazis, people could be picked up, imprisoned, and killed not for anything they had done but simply because of what they were—the wrong race, religion, or nationality. And because they were the wrong sort of people, they could be treated with savage cruelty. This is what happened to Bubili, a gypsy teenager, who tells how he arrived at a concentration camp: "We waited locked in the airless boxcar for about three-quarters of an hour. Then we heard a shout as thirty or forty young SS men unlocked the bolts and threw open the doors. 'Austrian pigheads,' they screamed. . . . Their whips fell on us, killing two men as we ran toward the gates of Dachau." Once inside the camp, every effort was made to strip the prisoners of their individuality: "I cried when the prison barber clipped my hair and threw the locks into my lap. . . . Without my hair, I was no longer Bubili. I was a piece of wood. . . . We were trash, something to be thrown away."

For six long years, Bubili was moved from camp to camp as a laborer: " . . . everything had to be done on the run. '*Schnell, schnell* (faster, faster),' the guards shouted as we struggled to haul trees or dig trenches. Blows fell on our backs and necks. . . . Every night I fell asleep with a pain in my heart. I kept saying to myself, 'I am Bubili.

I will outlive those bastards! I will one day give testimony.'"

The Jews were not the only victims of the Holocaust—many different kinds of people were persecuted. Some died but others survived. You can share their stories in *The Other Victims*.

—*Mary Harn Liu*

Otto from Otherwhere   Grades 5-8
By Peni R. Griffin

Paula knew the minute she met Ahto that he had come from another dimension. When he explained how his peoples' ceremonial singing on Midwinter Eve had caused the gate between their worlds to open, she had no trouble believing him. It wasn't just the fact that he had openings in his skin where his nose and ears should be, or that he had three-fingered hands. After all, those could have been birth defects. No, it wasn't the way he looked so much as the way he acted—the birdlike noises he made at first, the speed with which he learned to speak English, and above all, his incredibly perfect singing voice. Ahto was special. Paula couldn't wait to introduce him to her fifth-grade class as her "cousin from Brazil."   —*Kim Carter Sands*

Our Sixth-Grade Sugar Baby Blues   Grades 3-6
By Eve Bunting

It's the most embarrassing and humiliating thing that any teacher could have done! For a whole week everyone in our entire class, even the boys, has to carry five-pound sacks of sugar around to help us learn responsibility—and we can't even choose whether it's a boy sugar baby or a girl sugar baby. Mrs. Oda, our teacher, says that in real life you don't get to choose, so she made everyone draw lots. Tina Fisher even got *twins*! She has to lug *two* sacks of sugar around! And we have to treat them just like real babies, too, and take them everywhere with us unless we can find someone in class who can babysit for us! Gross!

But that isn't the worst of it—the worst is that the most gorgeous boy in the world has just moved in across the street from me, and he has to be in at least the seventh grade! What am I going to do if he sees me carrying this dumb sugar baby? He'll think *I'm* the baby, and I'll *die*! Surely there's some way for me to figure out how to get him to notice me—without my stupid sugar baby!

To find out what happens to me, to my best friend Ellie, to Thunk (the gorgeous hunk), to my neighbor Mr. Ambrose, and to our sugar babies, Babe and Sweet Sam, you'll have to read *Our Sixth-Grade Sugar Baby Blues*.

—*J. R. B.*

Out of the Ordinary   Grades 7-12
By Annie Dalton

Molly Gurney: fifteen years old, sensible face, frizzy red hair, big feet. Hates gym, chemistry, and math. Perfectly ordinary, you might think. Molly thinks so too, until three mysterious visitors teach her otherwise. The first one asks, "Do you know there are some people who can travel between the worlds?" The second one speaks of an imperiled child: "He must be kept safe . . . you must cherish him for us." And the third visitor warns her of danger. Each one mysteriously vanishes, leaving Molly to cope with her everyday, boring life, a life that soon becomes far from ordinary when the promised child arrives. Suddenly she must protect Floris, a silent, possibly bewitched little boy, from an unknown enemy. Now Molly senses danger everywhere. Where did the child come from? Who are his enemies? When will they attempt to seize him? How can she protect this foundling from the hidden, evil forces of another world?

—*Sister M. Anna Falbo, CSSF*

An Owl in the House   Grade 5-Adult
By Bernd Heinrich

It was the thrill of my life when I found the tiny great-horned owlet. I knew it was too young to survive the harsh New England winter. The question was, could I raise it successfully and yet prepare it to return to the wild? Even with my training and experience as a zoologist and naturalist, I was not certain that such a feat was possible.

I kept a journal so that I could record my remarkable two years with "Bubo," the joys and frustrations of keeping house with a great horned owl.

My cabin in the Maine woods became his territory, and visitors were *not* warmly welcomed. I remember the day a newspaper reporter came to interview me about my experiences. Bubo had been with me for about fourteen months by then, and he was full grown in every sense.

As soon as he heard the reporter's call of greeting he reacted: his body became horizontal, his tail rose, the feathers on his head were sleeked back, and his ear tufts extended straight up. And then he hooted at full volume!

When he rushed at the reporter, we had to adjourn to the outdoors for the interview, while Bubo made a shambles of the cabin in his frustration at missing his kill.

As time passed, I found that I would have to make a choice—Bubo or my family and friends. Could Bubo survive the wilds of Maine on his own? The question haunts me still.

—Carol Kappelmann

Paradise Cafe and Other Stories   Grades 7-12
By Martha Brooks

"He was one of the handsomest boys I'd ever seen. Somebody said he was part Indian, and with his powerful, dark good looks and eyes blue and brooding as thunderclouds, I thought of him as some kind of bird-god in disguise. He had money, or at least his family did. On those cool summer evenings in that resort town on the only mountain (or what prairie people like to call a mountain) within a thousand miles, he wore white sweaters that looked like they cost the earth, and he didn't rent those metal skates the skinny key boys would fit, then clamp, to your runners. He wore his own boot skates made of richly glowing leather, and he was King of the Rink.

"We skated around the edges of the outdoor rink with the sunken concrete floor and the floodlights and, above, the black pine-scented sky that seemed somehow less real than the loudspeakers that blared 'Wake Up, Little Suzie' and 'Teen Angel' as we clung to each other and shrieked with desperate laughter, hoping Karl the King would notice us."

Seeking, winning, and losing love is what this collection of short stories is all about. You'll meet Marty and Elizabeth, Karl and Sheila-Rae, Johnny, Naomi, Deirdre, Alphonse the dog, and many others. Some will seek and find love, some will lose it, and others will learn hard lessons about love and life. If you like romance or stories about relationships, this is the book for you!

—Anne Sushko

Phantom   Adult
By Susan Kay

Many people have written about me, but I have never told my own story—until now. I have many different names. I am the Face of Death, the Angel of Music, the Phantom of the Opera. I am, simply, Erik.

I have spent my life hiding my face and hoping my accomplishments would change people's perceptions of me. But it was not to be. I fled the Gypsy camps because I hated being put on display as a freak. I deserted my adoptive father, Giovanni, because his selfish beautiful daughter forced me to remove my mask. Once humans have seen my face, they can never look me in the eyes again. At the court of the Shah of Persia, I was regarded with favor for my talents. I built palaces, designed death chambers, and performed odd bits of magic and medicine. I grew weary of these aimless pursuits. None of these people was ever able to give me what I craved, what I lived for—until I returned to Paris to help design and construct the Paris Opera House.

As the Opera Ghost, I was content and secure, living inside my own creation. It could even have been said that I was growing tolerant of people's thoughtless and inhumane behavior.

And then I heard her sing. A mere chorus girl. Christine. Her voice held such promise that I believed she could become my finest creation, and my final satisfaction. I was wrong. Teaching her was not enough. Having her touch me was not enough. I needed from her what I had always lacked. I needed her to love me.

This is my story. The true story of the *Phantom*.

—Kaite Mediatore

Piper's Ferry   Grades 5–8
By G. Clifton Wisler

Tim Piper is too small, at age thirteen, to be considered a man—but in the 1830s, thirteen-year-old boys are expected to choose a career and start supporting themselves. His first choice is to sail the open seas on the *Bahamas Queen* as a mess boy with his kindly stepfather, Captain Tom. But that idea is quickly discarded as Tim heaves his guts out over the rail for the entire trip.

Back home in New Orleans, Tim finds that nobody wants to hire a 4-foot 11-inch, 80-pound boy. Finally, in desperation, his mother writes to all Tim's father's relatives and gets back one offer: Tim can help run the ferry across the Brazos River in Texas and live with his father's cousin, J. C. Piper.

Although Tim's mother is anxious about sending him off alone into the wilds of Texas, Tim is excited at the prospect. On the trip down, he meets Zach Merkins and begins a friendship that changes his life forever. Zach is involved with the struggle for Texas independence, a struggle that leads straight to the Alamo.

If you like books about ordinary boys who are thrust into action and adventure, you'll love *Piper's Ferry*.

—*Susan R. Farber*

The Place My Words Are Looking For: Grades 3–8
What Poets Say About and Through Their Work
By Paul B. Janeczko, comp.

Where do poets find their poems? Where do they come from? How do they get the idea for a poem? We don't need to travel somewhere glamorous or far away to find and imagine wonderful things—we can just look at everyday things closely and use our imaginations.

Jack Prelutsky has gotten several ideas while soaking in the bathtub. When the idea of "The Underwater Wibbles" came to him, he was taking a soak while nibbling on cheese. Some fell in the water, and while he was fishing it out, an idea hit! What would it be like if there were bizarre underwater creatures who lived on a strict diet of cheese? What kinds of cheese would they eat? Would it be served on soggy crusts of bread?

Maxine Kumin tells us a poem is portable—you can carry it around with you in your head for several days while you work on it in secret. Eve Merriam says she can spend weeks searching for the right word. Rhyming words can be lots of fun—rhymes can lead you to a whole different idea than what you started with. X. J. Kennedy remembers how he started writing a poem about a poodle—but that led to noodle and strudel, and he ended up writing about food instead!

Writing poetry is fun; it's like working out a puzzle. The ways a poem can unfold give us something to think about and choices to make— different ways to remember special people and special times. We can learn how to feel, and how to say what we mean. It's not just what a poem is saying, how is it being said? Does the poem sound like a loud-mouth, or does it whisper its best stuff?

We hear so many voices every day, swirling around us, that it's nice to slow down and listen to a few things we have really heard deep inside. Take a few minutes to see how these poets discover their poems, and get some ideas about how to discover some poems of your own.

—*Maggie Carey*

A Place to Claim as Home   Grades 5–8
By Patricia Willis

Thirteen-year-old Henry Compton arrives at Sarah Morrison's farm in the summer of 1943, taken on to do a man's work because most of the men of the county are off fighting the war. Henry can see that there's a lot of work to be done. There won't be time for anything else, that's for sure. Sarah herself seems oddly hostile, with her unsmiling, expressionless face and her icy stares. Henry figures she probably prefers girls to boys. She's always nice to Mary Beth, the young girl from a neighboring farm.

Then Henry meets Evan, Mary Beth's older brother and the resident local bully. Henry finds it very easy to dislike Evan, especially after he tells Henry an unsettling story about Sarah Morrison's past. Is this the reason for her unforgiving attitude? Evan's story sets Henry to thinking about his own past as an orphan and foster child, never feeling he really belongs anywhere. Can Sarah's past be linked in some way to his own?

—Cara A. Waits

Poems for Grandmothers   Grade 5–Adult
Myra Cohn Livingston, sel.

"Grandmother." "Grandma." "Granny." "Baboo." Words that create pictures of softly wrinkled faces lovingly poised over trays of freshly baked chocolate-chip cookies, and voices that croon, "What, full already? But you've only had six!" Some grandmothers *are* like that. But other grandmothers work in high-rise office buildings:

> Between her trips she picks up the phone
> and calls from her office. She asks can I guess
> what she bought me, and won't I come
> over tomorrow for lunch
>   unless
> she has to go off to Chicago again.
> But never mind, she loves me a lot. . . .

Some grandmothers are familiar faces in their grandchildren's lives. Others are known mostly through letters, long-distance telephone calls and once-a-year visits.

Who is your grandmother? Find her and her sisters in *Poems for Grandmothers.*

—*Nancy L. Chu*

The Practical Joke War   Grades 3–4
By Alane Ferguson

It looks like a perfectly ordinary, run-of-the-mill summer for the Dillon kids. They'll be in charge of themselves and the cat, Furball, during the day while their parents are at work. There should be plenty of time for *constructive* activities . . . but when twelve-year-old Russell dresses up like a mummy to scare his sister Taffy, the Practical Joke War has begun. How humiliating for Taffy! Especially when she's been set up for the joke by a smart-alecky younger brother named Eddie. Of course a sister can't just let her obnoxious brothers get away with the trick of the century, so a brilliant pay-back joke is planned and executed—a sinister "eyeball" floats through the darkness to scare the stuffing out of Russell! Revenge is sweet, until the jokes escalate into colossal messes; exasperated parents punish all three children by grounding them. This should put an end to their shenanigans, but now these three vengeful house-captives have lost all sight of reason, especially when Taffy's new best friend Susan sneaks into the house and plays some tricks of her own. Things finally spin out of control, and innocent Furball becomes the victim. Will Furball ever come back, after being doused with ice-water and dusted with feathers? Will Taffy realize that "friends" don't tell lies? Will the Practical Joke War alienate these siblings forever?

Be sure to find out how this war ends before starting one of your own!

—*Mary MacNeil*

The Praying Flute   Grade 7–Adult
By Tony Shearer

This is the story of a boy, a boy all alone in a wild place. He has escaped from Big Smoke City. Free—but untaught in the ways of the wild.

This is the story of a Native American five-hole flute. It is the voice of the earth, the voice of the streams, the voice of the birds, the voice of the sacred.

The boy knelt beside the cascading waters. Listening. Receiving the thoughts of the earth, clear and free of fear; receiving the voice of the flute.

This is the story of Old Quanah, the oldest man ever known. His home was a tepee planted in a small grove of aspens on the western slope of Spirit Mountain. He would load up his pipe, pour a cup of pitch-black coffee, and mosey to his Memory Tree.

"This is a story about a place back East. Back beyond the Sacramento River, beyond the wide Missouri, even beyond the Mississippi and the Ohio. Back to a place where one of The People was called Little Girl.

"Little Girl learned her path. How it crossed the meadow. How the old trees bent over the path. How it ended at a big ancient tree. And yet she went beyond the path to a cave. To a very dark and very wet cave, into a dark hole, where she had to think with her heart. She had been chosen for a very special job. And she had been given a flute. A praying flute for the earth."

What is the power of the praying flute? Can it pray for the earth in a world that cannot hear the spirit of the earth? This is the job of the little girl and her praying flute, the job of every human being. This is a job for Old Quanah and the boy and you.

—Lesley S. J. Farmer

Professor Popkin's Prodigious Polish   Grades 3-6
By Bill Brittain

There was more than met the eye to the New England village of Coven Tree. And fifteen-year-old Luther Gilpin was about to discover what it was.

Luther lived with his ma and pa and little brother Bertram on a farm outside Coven Tree. Luther worked hard helping his pa run the farm, but that wasn't enough for Luther. He wanted more than just a living from the soil; he wanted to be rich.

"And just how will you go about getting rich, Mr. Luther Gilpin?" asked Dorcas Taney, his ma's hired girl. Luther replied that he was going to become a traveling salesman and make pots of money. That was too much for Dorcas (who was sweet on Luther just the way he was). In disgust she stomped back into the house and slammed the door.

As Luther sat alone, he thought about how silly girls were: "They just don't understand the dreams of a man, and being rich!" Suddenly the wind blew something white from the woods. Luther watched as it circled around and landed on his foot. It was a piece of paper. He grabbed it, crumpled it up, and threw it away. The wind blew from another direction, lifted and unwrapped the paper, and plastered it against Luther's chest. This time he looked at it. Printed on one side were the words: "SALESMEN WANTED! Wealth, Travel, Excitement. . . . These can all be yours. . . . All our salesmen need do is demonstrate the wonders of Professor Popkin's Prodigious Polish and customers will want to *buy*! Within weeks you can be rich. Your life will be changed forever!" Here was Luther's answer, and now he'd show that silly Dorcas Taney!

Before long, however, Luther and everyone else would wish they'd never heard of Professor Popkin's Prodigious Polish, and they'd wish they lived *anywhere* besides Coven Tree!

—Marvia Boettcher

R-T, Margaret and the Rats of NIMH   Grades 3-8
By Jane Leslie Conly

Margaret was disgusted. The last thing she wanted to do was go camping with her family. Now she had no one but her brother Artie to play with, and he couldn't (or wouldn't) even talk! It had been her dad's big idea—something about "family togetherness." What a waste of summer!

When her dad went into town for more supplies, Margaret was left behind to help her mom at the camp. Now, with her mom taking a nap, Margaret was in charge of Artie. As if it wasn't bad enough to be camping, she had to babysit too! Someday she wouldn't have to take orders from grown-ups: "Do this." "Do that." "Don't do this." "Don't do that." When Margaret decided they'd go for a walk, even Artie seemed to think it was a good idea. He silently put his small hand in hers, and they started out on the trail.

Well, you guessed it. They got lost, but before it got dark they found a safe place to sleep—in a cave beside a bent pine tree, growing out a crack in the rock.

Now without realizing it, Margaret's family had camped in Thorn Valley, where a superintelligent colony of rats had a secret community. Oh, not that you could tell by just looking—the nest was well hidden to ensure their survival. And today two young rats—Rasco and Christopher—decided to go on a picnic hike after they finished their chores. Like other youngsters, they sometimes quarreled, but they were friends today—that is, until Rasco grabbed more than his fair share of the picnic lunch and Christopher stomped off to sulk in his secret hideout—beside a bent pine tree growing out of a crack in the rock. As Christopher's eyes slowly adjusted to the darkness of the cave, he saw a horrible sight—another pair of eyes staring directly into his, eyes surrounded by a huge, pale face, with a mouth below that opened and closed as if it were trying to squeak but could not. Christopher had never seen a human before. He was trapped in the dark with an unknown monster—could he get away? Would he betray the secret of the hidden community?

—*Wanda McAdams*

Rachel Chance   Grades 5-8
By Jean Thesman

Fifteen-year-old Rachel Chance knew her family was made up of refugees and misfits, well acquainted with untidy predicaments. She knew the Chance family was always giving the good folks of Rider's Dock something to talk about, and she had never deluded herself into thinking that her family was widely respected.

Rachel's stubborn, hard-drinking grandpa had been left disabled after the railroad accident that killed his brother. Jonah, grandpa's brother's boy, was retarded and disfigured, and lived with them on grandpa's farm.

Rachel's widowed mother had lost her job as church secretary when Pastor Woodie discovered she was pregnant. It had taken Rachel's mother five months after Rider was born to find a job at the ten-cent store in town.

Rachel knew and understood these things.

She also knew who her illegitimate brother's father was, even if she didn't understand why her mother would never name him or even say where he was. But most importantly, Rachel knew love—the love of her family.

What Rachel didn't know and couldn't understand was how the latest disaster could come about. How could anyone steal her two-year-old brother? And why wouldn't the "good" people of Rider's Dock help, and go after the ones who had kidnapped him?

—*Olivia Jacobs*

Randall's Wall   Grades 5-6
By Carol Fenner

"He never takes a bath," whispered Tiffany Spizinski. "I wouldn't touch him with a ten foot pole." "He sleeps in his clothes and then comes to school," hissed Lynda Percherman. "He stinks," said Paul Lunde. "He simply stinks."

Randall Lord was avoided by his classmates. To avoid them, he had built a wall around himself. It was a wall that allowed him to shut out the world and fill his time with daydreams and drawings.

Although Randall spent most of his time at school alone, one morning he found himself rescuing Jean Worth Neary from two boys who were tormenting her. Randall soon realized that he had made a friend—and Jean decided that her mission in life was to clean up Randall Lord.

Randall, whose lice-infested hair had been shaved off, lived in a house with no running water. His abusive father would go off for months at a time, leaving the family with virtually no money for food or clothes. His mother was physically and mentally unable to cope with the responsibilities of caring for the children.

But none of that fazed Jean, now that she'd decided to take on Randall as a friend. Her first task would be to see to it that he took a bath and put on some clean clothes. "We have this enormous bathroom," she told him as they walked into the empty Neary house. She escorted Randall into the beautiful, sparkling-clean bathroom and started running the water in the tub. Then she poured in a long stream of bubble bath. A lovely smell began to fill the room. "Okay, into the tub," commanded Jean.

When Randall hesitated, Jean assured him that he didn't have to take off his clothes. He could get into the tub fully dressed and scrub himself *and* his clothes at once. To prove it could be done, she climbed into the tub herself, fully dressed, and demonstrated.

After a soaking wet Jean climbed out of the tub, Randall stepped into the hot bubble bath completely dressed and began to wash himself and his clothes. Jean went to put on some dry clothes herself and returned to the bathroom with a clean, dry outfit for Randall. But as he stepped out of the tub, they heard a car pull into the driveway. Jean's mother was home! *Now* what? Would Mrs. Neary let Jean help Randall, or was Jean's mission in life already over?

—Susan Wolfe

Reluctantly Alice   Grades 5–8
By Phyllis Reynolds Naylor

Sixth grade is the best. You're finally at the top of the ladder. You can be on the safety patrol; you can help out in the office, rule the playground, and even go on overnight field trips with your teachers. Now I'm in seventh grade, and *it stinks*. In fact, I can think of seven things that stink about the seventh grade. Dad said, "Try to think of one nice thing about seventh grade, Alice." That sounds like something Mom would have said, if she were here. Mom died when I was five, so I can't really remember her; but I *know* that's something she would say. OK, I'll think of one nice thing—classes are over at 2:30 instead of 3:00. Well, there are also my friends, Pamela and Elizabeth. We have vowed to share our innermost secrets and stay friends forever. Patrick's my friend too. He kissed me once last summer—but *not* like the eighth- and ninth-graders do! Sometimes they're so close together you'd think they were a grilled cheese sandwich!

So I guess there *are* some good things about the seventh grade. Maybe I'll even be able to think of seven by the end of the year. And maybe I'll even get through this year without making a single enemy. It just might work . . . except that Denise "Mack-Truck" Whitlock has already decided that *I* am her Public Enemy Number 1! She pokes me, trips me, throws food at me, and goes out of her way to embarrass me—"Aw, Poor Widdle Awice doesn't have a mama. . . . Is she gonna cwy?" Once when she was taunting me my big brother Lester came to my rescue, and the next day my locker was stuffed with wet, dirty toilet paper . . . yuck! And now Miss Summers, the language arts teacher, has assigned partners to write biographies about each other. Know who my partner is? That's right, Denise Mack-Truck! Oh boy, this could be my chance to get even with her . . . or should I?

—Marvia Boettcher

Remember Who You Are: Grades 9–Adult
Stories About Being Jewish
By Esther Hautzig

Eddy's story makes Jonah's trip in the belly of the fish sound like a vacation.

Eddy was Jewish, incarcerated with his family in the ghetto of Kovno, Lithuania, in 1941. The people in his neighborhood built false walls behind which they hid their children during Gestapo raids. The youngest were often given potent sleeping pills to keep them silent. Eventually the soldiers got suspicious and started shooting right through walls, killing many children in their sleep. Eddy remembers these nightmare raids like they were yesterday.

But Eddy got a break. His parents had enough money hidden away to bribe his way out of the ghetto.

One day Eddy's parents slipped him a strong sleeping pill. While he was unconscious, he was placed inside a large bag of dried peas. The bag was hidden among others on a truck bound for the countryside, and somewhere along the truck's route, it was tossed into the arms of a waiting farm couple. So Eddy made his escape.

When he woke up, Eddy was devastated. But after a while, he adjusted to living on this farm with his "uncle" and "auntie." In his new home Eddy was raised pretty much as a Gentile—in fact, he began carrying a small cross, a gift from his new family.

And then, when the war was over, Eddy's father miraculously appeared at the farm. He had survived the death camp of Dachau, and had come to reclaim his son. Eddy still remembers the horrible words he said to his father on that day. His father did not press him to leave the farm, but patiently continued to visit Eddy every day.

It was not until the second miracle happened, several months later, that Eddy was ready to accept his father. Somehow, his mother had also survived. She found her son, right where she knew he'd be. Eddy's ties to his mother broke down the barriers that remained. His family was truly reunited.

Not all of these stories have endings as happy as Eddy's. But each story shows how important it can be to *Remember Who You Are.*

—*Bernice D. Crouse*

Ride a Cockhorse   Adult
By Raymond Kennedy

Women's magazines like *Cosmopolitan* or *Glamour* will often run feature stories in which a make-up artist chooses several very plain Janes and transforms them into sophisticated, beautifully coiffed and painted ladies who look as though they'd stepped off a Hollywood set. Mrs. Frankie Fitzgibbons was transformed practically overnight too. She was forty-five, a modest, kind widow devoted to her job as home loan officer at a large New England bank, when she took the first step in her madcap metamorphosis and seduced the seventeen-year-old drum major who high-stepped it past her house every Saturday. But her true rise to notoriety and fortune occurred within the bank. Frankie discovered that she had a golden tongue—she could convince or cow people into doing almost anything, no matter how outlandish—like demoting her boss and giving *her* his position, or convincing the president of their chief competitor to sign over his bank and all its assets!

Once she realized her powers, Frankie took the modest amount of authority that she had been granted at the bank and embarked on a course of empire, enforcing her will on all the other employees. She fired at random and promoted at whim; she barked orders and reaped praise and glory. She even appointed herself Chief Executive Officer! And she did all of this with flair—and with the assistance of a small band of groupies. Among those cohorts were Bruce, the gay hairdresser who did her physical make-over and who truly adored her; his lover Matthew, who became her chauffeur; Emily, the dowdy bank employee who became her own personal SS, and Julie, the secretary whom she had promoted and mesmerized. Even Frankie's loony sexual sycophant of a son-in-law joined her band of devotees.

As Mrs. Fitzgibbons climbs higher and higher on the banking industry ladder, her footing begins to slip. Her descent is inevitable, but like everything else she does, she crashes with flamboyance. One person, however, stands by her through it all and is truly her saviour from insanity. Which one of her cohorts could it be? Bruce? Matthew? Emily? Julie? Her son-son-law, or perhaps even her daughter? Which one of these unlikely characters could even begin to hold a candle to the outlandish, outrageous, zany Mrs. Fitzgibbons?

—Susan Weaver

The River   Grades 5–12
By Gary Paulsen

"We want you to do it again."

Brian just stared at the three men standing on his front porch. He couldn't believe his ears—last year he'd survived for almost two months on his own in the wilderness, and now these three men were asking him to do it *again?* "Why?" he asked. He'd learned something about survival, they told him, something that they couldn't teach in the survival courses they ran, something that had changed him forever. That much was true, Brian knew. He *was* different, in ways he couldn't explain and no one else could understand. That was what Derek, the psychologist who would go with him into the woods, wanted to study. What had made the difference? Why had Brian survived where so many others hadn't? Could he communicate this mysterious advantage to Derek, and could others learn it too? "If I could make a difference in someone's life," Brian decided, "then I should go."

So once again Brian got into a bush plane and landed on a lake. He and Derek were left alone with only their knives, a radio, and the contents of their pockets. Brian refused to let Derek unload supplies or provisions. If Derek was to learn the lessons that the wilderness could teach him, then he must do it just as Brian had, without any of civilization's trappings or comforts. And within hours, Derek admitted that Brian had been right—now they'd be forced to survive on their own.

But neither Brian nor Derek could guess what was to come. A freak lightning storm knocked out their radio and left Derek unconscious—still breathing, but in a deep coma.

Brian knows how to survive on his own, but now he has a helpless partner, who will certainly die if Brian abandons him. Can Brian save himself *and* Derek? Or will he lose everything, including his life?

—J. R. B.

Robin on His Own   Grades 3–6
By Johnniece Marshall Wilson

Robin has finally realized that his mother will never come back; she left him when she died three months ago.

Aunt Belle came to live with them soon after his mother got sick, but she too will be leaving him soon—she's going to marry Monroe in a few weeks and move to another city.

Yes, his father loves him, but now more than ever he leaves Robin with sitters and goes on the road with his band.

And the band, they're like part of his family too. Yet lately he hears his father saying that the band will be breaking up soon, so they will be leaving him also.

The only things that seem to want to stay with him are Watusi and Pollymae, his cat and dog. But they are not people, and the people he loves most seem to all be leaving him, in one way or another. Is there anyone who will stay with him, or is he now truly alone, really out on his own?

—Faye A. Powell

Roger Caras' Treasury   Grade 10–Adult
of Great Horse Stories
By Roger Caras, ed.

There are a lot of things about this book that might make you *not* want to pick it up. First, there's the title—descriptive, but definitely boring. There's the size—at almost 500 pages, definitely formidable. The cover is not what I would call a grabber, or even interesting. And finally there's the idea of reading a lot of stories about just one thing—horses. A lot of us got over our fascination with them about the time we became teenagers. If you didn't, then there's no need for you to hear this booktalk: you're already a customer. But what I want to do now is talk to those of you who aren't into horses, and who may be looking at this book with just a bit of skepticism. Frankly, that's where I was when I picked it up. But Caras had the good sense to make sure that the first few stories are among the best, just to guarantee that the reader get well and truly hooked right away. And I did, with the first lines of Mark Twain's "A Horse's Tale": "I am Buffalo Bill's horse . . . I am his favorite horse, out of dozens. Big as he is, I have carried him eighty-one miles between nightfall and sunrise on the scout; and I am good for fifty, day in and day out. . . . I am not large, but I am built on a business basis. . . . I am the best-educated horse outside of the hippodrome, . . . and the best mannered. . . . Buffalo Bill taught me the most of what I know, my mother taught me much, and I taught myself the rest.

"But my story isn't just about me," Soldier continues, "it's about Cathy, the sweetest child ever to walk the face of the earth, an orphan who was sent to live at the fort while I was there with Buffalo Bill. She absolutely took over the fort the very first day she was here—and I quite lost my heart to her. Then, about four or five weeks after she arrived, the day she won the children's steeplechase, Buffalo Bill gave me to her—and I could not have been happier. She invented a bugle call just for me, and told me that it says 'It is I, Soldier—come!' And for her, I *would* come, no matter how far—even from death itself."

In Larry Niven's "The Flight of the Horse," Svetz travels back in time looking for a horse. They are unknown in his time, and the scientists at the Institute have only a few pictures in an old salvaged children's book to show him. But the one Svetz found was not quite like the pictures—for one thing, it was larger, and was pure white, not brown, with a long flowing mane and tail. But the most disturbing thing was that long pointed horn right in the middle of its forehead!

And be sure you don't miss Rudyard Kipling's "The Maltese Cat," about a cagey polo pony who plays with his head as well as his feet, a Past Pluperfect Prestissimo Player of the Game. You'll also meet "The Doctor's Horse," and "The Old Jim Horse" who served the men of Engine Thirty-Three of the New York Fire Department for eighteen long years, and "The Black Roan of 265," another New York fire-horse. And not all the memorable characters in these stories are horses—there's Champ Carter, "The Man Who Could Not Lose"; John Shadow, a drifter who has a way with animals, who hunts the great white stallion Diablo in "Shadow's Quest"; and Canady, a gambler, outlaw, and thief, who uses an old broomtail stud to try to escape from "The Trap."

So ignore this book's size, the bland cover, and the boring title, because inside you'll find some of the most loyal, intelligent, hardworking, strong, canny, and loving creatures you'll ever meet—horses. Let them carry you into the past, the future, the possible, and the seemingly impossible, in these stories of fact, fantasy, and fiction.

—J. R. B.

Rosemary's Witch   Grades 5-6
By Ann Turner

It was *not* a dark and stormy night. In fact, it was a beautiful sunny day—if anything, too sunny and too hot—when Rosemary and her family moved into their new home. They'd found a dream house in a dream place: an old farmhouse with charm and history in a small New England town. And Rosemary's father the history professor loved it, and her mom the dancer loved it, and her little brother the computer whiz loved it too. But Rosemary loved it most of all, because everyone else in her family had something of their own, except Rosemary—until now. But Rosemary didn't really know what she had—more than she ever dreamed, imagined, or feared.

It was a dark and stormy night when Mathilda found the house. "Home," she said when she saw it. "Things," she said as she looked around in the emptiness. "Rotten," she said, as she remembered how—long, long, long ago—the children had tormented her, and how she had suffered, and how *they* would suffer now. She didn't say the word, but she certainly must have thought it: "Revenge!"

It was a strange, cold summer. It was a summer when things disappeared from the town: tools and bikes and cats. It was a summer when rumors grew hot as the season turned cold, so cold. And rain fell from the sky, and then toads fell from the sky, worse than you ever dreamed, imagined, or feared. Rosemary's parents had everything, but Rosemary had only Mathilda. And Mathilda had Rosemary, because she was *Rosemary's Witch.*

—*Patrick Jones*

Rotten Egg Paterson to the Rescue   Grades 3–6
By Colin Thiele

Danny looked down and gasped. A large, angry, goanna lizard stood at his feet, its body held high in displeasure. It raised its head menacingly.

Desperately Danny searched for sticks to defend himself against the poisonous reptile. Where had it come from? Why was it so angry? He didn't understand until he saw the nest of emu eggs—obviously he had interrupted the lizard's lunch. Only one egg was still intact.

If he could drive off the lizard, he might be able to save the last egg. But then what? Could he really take home a two-pound egg and hatch out a baby emu? Emus are very large birds, a lot like ostriches. Danny's parents might not be thrilled. But he *couldn't* pass up a chance like this!

To find out if the egg ever hatched, and to see how Danny outsmarted the school bully, who *lived* to destroy emu eggs, read *Rotten Egg Paterson to the Rescue.*

—*Suzi Smith*

Round the Bend   Grades 7–8
By Mitzi Dale

Difficult. Emotionally disturbed. Mentally unbalanced. Wacko! Insane! Round the bend! Crazy! That's what they called Deirdre, and if you hear those things long enough I guess you start to believe them. If you daydream too much because school is just too boring, that doesn't mean you're crazy, does it? And if your health-food-nut mother is always reading magazine articles about surviving the trauma of adolescence and it just makes you scream—*makes you scream!*—that couldn't mean you're crazy, could it?

And when Mrs. Johnson gave Deirdre the look in class—you know, the look when the teacher asks the stupid question and she's waiting on you to answer and she stands there [mimic] and stares at you [mimic] and taps her foot [mimic] and sighs [mimic]—well, Deirdre looked her right in the eye and said, "You know, Mrs. Johnson, I have no idea."

And the kids in class laughed, which Mrs. Johnson didn't like because teachers don't like you to laugh in class unless it's at one of their own goofy jokes. And it *was* funny the first time. But every time and every day after that, Deirdre just replied, "You know, Mrs. Johnson, I have no idea." But that shouldn't give you the idea that Deirdre is crazy, should it?

And if you are thirteen and tired of teachers and parents and principals and all these adults who say they want to help you but nothing really helps because you are thirteen and you want to be an adult yourself now—like, *right now*—but you know life doesn't work that way, that doesn't make you crazy, does it? not just that. And if you take a match [mimic] and strike the match [mimic] and toss the match [mimic] onto your bed—that doesn't make you crazy, does it? Maybe Deirdre's not crazy at all; maybe she's just gone *Round the Bend.*

—Patrick Jones

The Rowan   Grade 9–Adult
By Anne McCaffrey

She was only three years old, but when she was in danger, every telepath on the planet Altair knew it. Her psychic scream of terror was impossible to ignore, even coming, as it did, from where she lay buried under mountains of mud. They called her the Rowan, because that was all they knew about her; that, and the prophecy from Yegrani, the clairvoyant who showed the rescue teams where to dig. Yegrani said, "Guard this one well. She has a long and lonely road to go before she travels. But she alone will be the focus that will save us from a far greater disaster than the one she has escaped. Especially guard the guardian." That was all, and there was no way to know just what Yegrani had meant.

The galaxy that Rowan was to grow up in was vastly different from the one we live in today. Because of the evolution of major psionic Talents, it had become possible to span the immense distances of the galaxy and keep the network of planets and star-systems linked together. The Talents were usually either telepaths, who could provide reliable and instantaneous communication between Earth and its colonies, or telekinetics, who could transport people and cargo by force of mind. But the most gifted of the Talents combined both abilities, and could act as double links between Earth and their own planets. They were called Primes—and there was little doubt in anyone's mind that little Rowan was Altair's newest Prime.

But one doesn't automatically become a trained Prime, and Rowan had long years of schooling ahead of her. It left little time for play or for fun, or even for love, until she met Jeff Raven, a Talent almost as strong as she was, the man who would help her begin to fulfill the prophecy that Yegrani had made so long ago. Rowan was not just one of the most powerful Talents ever born; she was also the only one who could save her world, her galaxy, from the greatest danger it would ever face.

—*J. R. B.*

Saturnalia   Grades 7–12
By Paul Fleischman

For six years now, Weetasket (or William, as the white men call him) has been roaming Boston's streets after curfew, searching for his twin. On a small bone flute he plays a restful tune that only another Narraganset Indian would recognize. He searches the windows of the houses he passes, hoping Cancasset will hear him and appear. As he walks along, he thinks back to the winter day when the English attacked his island village, killing many of his kinsmen, taking others captive, and burning their homes. He and his brother had managed to escape and evade the enemy for a week, but finally they too were captured and taken to Plymouth, where they were separated. William was taken to Boston and apprenticed to the printer Mr. Currie. Some of the other captives William knows are beaten regularly, starved, and scorned as godless heathens. But William is lucky: Mr. Currie is a good master, who treats his new apprentice like family. Mr. Currie even celebrates Saturnalia, the ancient Roman festival where master and servants exchange places for a day. Besides teaching William the printer's trade, Mr. Currie instructs him in Latin, Greek, and the Bible, and William is a bright student who learns quickly. Now, as he wanders through the darkened streets, he can't help wondering whether his clan would be proud of his success in the world of the English or scornful.

There is one Englishman, though, who despises William's intelligence. It's Mr. Baggot, the tithingman, who drills William and the Currie children on their knowledge of the Bible. Mr. Baggot vows that one day he will see the dark-skinned scholar suffer. "I want you to know that my eye is upon you. Like the spider's eye upon the fly," he tells William. "And that one day soon—I'll snare you!" Mr. Baggot has the power to have William publicly whipped, put in the stocks, or branded. All he has to do is catch William with one foot outside the law. Though breaking curfew is risky, William can't give up his search, and after he finds his cousin and uncle, he begins to sneak out every night. He smuggles food to them from the Currie kitchen, and in exchange his uncle teaches him how to heal the sick, bring rain, and see into the future. But then his uncle's master is murdered, and William is accused of the crime. Not only must he defend himself against this false accusation, but he must also decide whether to remain among the English or escape with his uncle back to his own people.

—Kathy Ann Miller

Saving Lenny
By Margaret Willey
Grades 9–12

Jesse and Kay are seniors, and best friends until the day Jesse sees Lenny at a football game. She's instantly attracted to this mysterious new boy, feeling he's going to change her whole life—and he does. For the first time, pretty, popular Jesse becomes tongue-tied. So Kay urges her lovesick friend to write Lenny a note suggesting a date.

It works. Lenny and Jesse fall in love immediately. They want to be together all the time. Lenny constantly tells Jesse how much he needs her. He only feels happy, strong, when he's with her. Quitting the tennis team, letting homework slide, he convinces Jesse to join him skipping school. Now she has less and less time to spend with Kay and her own parents.

Jesse soon shares Lenny's dark secret. An over-achiever, he's been suffering from deep depression, and he has given up everything but her.

To Kay's horror, Jesse decides to forego her long-awaited freshman year at college and move to a lakeside cottage with Lenny. Alone in the middle of nowhere, they will lead an idyllic life together, just the two of them. But once they are there, Jesse's romantic dreams slowly fall apart. She begins to wonder if Lenny's sickness is making her sick too. He's so possessive it's suffocating. But he needs her so much—how can she pull back now?

—Susan Rosenkoetter

School's Out
By Johanna Hurwitz
Grades 3–4

School's out, school's out!
Teacher let the monkeys out.

One jumped in, one jumped out,
One jumped in the teacher's mouth!

No more pencils, no more books.
No more teacher's dirty looks!

You've probably heard these rhymes. You've probably recited them yourself on the last day of school. Right? Well, Lucas Cott was a boy very much like most of you. He was glad when the last day of school arrived; he couldn't wait for summer vacation—no more homework, no teachers, no rules, *freedom*! You can imagine how he felt when his mother told him she'd hired a college girl named Genevieve to help her take care of Lucas and his two younger brothers for the summer. *Just* what he needed—another adult checking up on him. He was sure it would be worse than having a teacher living right in his own house *all* summer long. Some vacation!

But when Lucas discovered that Genevieve was from France and didn't know much about America, he saw a way to have a wonderful vacation—teaching her his *own* version of how things are done here!

One time he convinced her that ice cream should be the main course for supper. Another time he taught her how to pop popcorn in a pan—without a lid! (you can imagine the popcorn blizzard in the kitchen). And that was only the beginning. Read *School's Out* and find out just how much fun a boy can have during summer vacation—even with an extra adult around.

—*Sandra Carpenter*

Scotch on the Rocks   Grade 9–Adult
By Howard Browne

The Dawsons were desperate people. On a hot, dusty road in Texas they stared at the bullet-riddled body in the front seat of the abandoned Diamond-T truck. In the bed of the truck were about 600 bottles of high-grade, top dollar, bootleg whiskey.

These were desperate times. Like many other families during the Depression, the Dawsons had been thrown off their farm when the bank foreclosed on the mortgage. All they now owned were the clothes on their backs and whatever they had been able to stuff into their rickety Ford station wagon.

But desperate times call for desperate measures. So Emily, her son Ambrose, and his wife Ruby decided to adopt the abandoned truck. In a fit of morality, Ambrose says they should turn over the vehicle and the whiskey to the authorities. In a fit of practicality, Ruby convinces him to drive the truck to Kansas City and sell the whiskey.

Enter Lee Vance: smart, talented, good-looking, and spoiled. He's a card shark and part-time con man with connections in Kansas City. He'll introduce the Dawsons—for a nominal fee, of course.

And so begins this strange odyssey of would-be bootleggers who are almost too moral to break the law. Emily, a devout Christian, confesses to everything at a revival meeting. Ambrose foils a bank robbery in a small town, and the grateful townsfolk want to know what brings a Texas boy all the way to Oklahoma. Double-crossing Lee tries to fend off the irresistible advances of the equally double-crossing Ruby and discovers he is not quite the slick hustler he thought he was.

There must be an easier way to make a dishonest living. But if there is, the Dawsons haven't found it. Read *Scotch on the Rocks* and follow this band of reluctant outlaws into a comical life of crime.

—Kaite Mediatore

Secret Anniversaries   Adult
By Scott Spencer

People have their own secret anniversaries, days they remember for the rest of their lives. Your driver's license, your first kiss, the day you met the person who became your best friend—we all have anniversaries that we secretly celebrate. Caitlin Van Fleet is no different. As she begins adulthood on her own, she doesn't realize that these last few days before the Second World War are going to be filled with events that she will never forget.

Her first anniversary, for example, commemorates the day she gained her freedom from her childhood home, leaving behind a flurry of scandal. She became a congressional aide in Washington.

Her second anniversary marks her first adult love affair—with the only true love of her life, a colleague in the congressman's office. The birth of her son is a third anniversary. The boy's father was a dear friend who helped her understand herself during the troubled times of the war. In particular, he was able to show her that the congressman she revered was virtually a Fascist puppet. This anniversary has plagued her entire life. But there are others as well.

What are those other secret anniversaries that Caitlin celebrates? Discover them here, in *Secret Anniversaries*.

—*C. Allen Nichols*

The Secret Keeper   Grades 7–12
By Gloria Whelan

Wow! Only the rich can live like this! The Beaches is a select summer haven for the wealthiest families I have ever met. You know, the ones with yachts and money to burn. What is Annie, from the other side of the tracks, doing here then?, you ask. I'm just a "keeper," or babysitter, for a ten-year-old named Matt. I wouldn't be here if I hadn't started babysitting for the Larimers, Matt's grandparents, back in Colonial Gardens. I'm awed by the huge "cabins" and the glitter of the sun on Lake Michigan. But there is more to this playground of the idle rich than meets the eye.

A man stood on the shore watching Matt and me.

"You look like you've seen the devil," he said. I probably did, because I guessed in a moment who he was. Matt's eagerness to reach him gave it away. This was Bryce, his father, the person the Larimers had warned me about.

Bryce wasn't just attractive, he was reassuring, disarming. I thought of making Matt come back, but that seemed overly dramatic. After all, who could deny a child the right to see his father? Bryce was so friendly, I began to relax a little.

"I'll leave notes for you to give Matt, and you can leave a note or two for me. . . . That's all I ask. If you say yes, I'll be on my way," promised Bryce. Matt was startled by my nod of consent. I think I was too.

If only Matt's grandparents had told me the whole truth from the beginning. Instead I just had to learn the hard way. By the time the secrets began to unfold, I had already stuck my neck out too far to pull it back. Worse yet, Matt's life could depend on my good judgment.

"Think about Matt. What kind of life do you want him to have?" asked Dr. Bradford.

"What kind of life will he have if it's based on lies?"

"If he knew the truth? It would be a horror."

"But suppose Bryce comes back."

"He won't."

But he has, and I'm the only one besides Matt who knows. Should I tell someone, or is this elite bunch of snobs just trying to keep an ordinary man separated from his only son?

Believe me, the evil is only beginning to come to the surface. Can Matt be saved?

—Bernice D. Crouse

The Secret Life of Hubie Hartzel   Grades 3-6
By Susan Rowan Masters

What would *you* do if Marruci, the class bully, were out to get you? And your dad wanted to put Fred Ferkle, your pet cat, to sleep? And you got a 39 on your math test? And you got teased because of your weight? Fifth-grader Hubie Hartzel daydreams and doodles to escape all these problems. In his imagination he can beat Marruci and be a champion. He can be rock star. In his imagination.

In real life, though, Hubie is getting to be a dynamite doodler, and maybe he could even be an artist, if he just didn't have to spend most of his energy dealing with all the things that happen to his family, teachers, and friends—including his good friend Frank. Now he and Frank have devised a master plan to get even with Marruci. Can they do it? Read *The Secret Life of Hubie Hartzel* and find out.

—Monica Carollo

Seymour, the Formerly Fearful   Grades 3-6
By Eve B. Feldman

Have you ever been really afraid of something? So that your hands were sweating and you got this terrible feeling in the pit of your stomach? Well, that's how it is for Seymour, except that he's not just afraid of one thing, he's afraid of everything. His friends and family aren't aware of his problem (he hopes) because he is really good at covering up his fears. If his friend Ted asks him to go to the beach, he says he has a sprained ankle or a sore tendon instead of telling him that he's afraid of water. Or if Ted wants to ride bikes, he simply says he has a flat. And instead of going to a summer sleep-away sports camp with Ted, he chooses a safer computer day camp to attend. No matter what the occasion, Seymour has a ready excuse. Things change, however, when Seymour's older cousin, fresh out of the army, visits him from Israel. Pessach is tough—not only won't he believe Seymour's excuses, he won't take no for an answer. But with Pessach's encouragement, Seymour learns that he can overcome his fears and start to be a brave *mensch*, instead of a *pachdan* chicken.

—Kathy Ann Miller

The Shadow Brothers   Grades 7–12
By A. E. Cannon

Sometimes in my mind I can still see him running, late at night when he loved to run. Even if I never see him again, that's one of the ways I'll always remember him, running alone, just as he described it in one of his poems—"I weave through the night, run patterns in air, with the moon in my eyes and the stars in my hair."

You may say that's not the way for a guy to talk about his brother, especially a sixteen-year-old guy, but I remember when Henry came to live with us. We were both seven, and he was the son of my father's best friend. His mother had just died, and his dad asked if Henry could come live with us because he didn't think the reservation schools would be good enough for him—Henry's so smart, he's almost a genius. Oh yeah, I guess I didn't mention that—Henry's a Navajo. At first that made him different—the color of his skin and the way he almost sang his words when he talked. But now that doesn't really make any difference to me or to anyone else. He's just a guy—a leader, a great runner, and good-looking to boot. My brother. Or so I thought.

All that changed last year. Henry started dating Celia, the major fox at school, and Frank moved to town—another Indian, one who could run even better than Henry. And after that Henry changed. He wasn't the same old Henry that I'd been living with for years—he was angry and tense, and wouldn't talk about what was bothering him. I guess I didn't really want to hear it anyway. I didn't want anything to change—I wanted the same old Henry back—I wanted things the way they had been, when he led the way and I always had somewhere to go and something to do and someone to do it with. Suddenly Henry was always off with Celia, and I was on my own most of the time—and when he *was* around, he was mighty hard to live with. But just the same, things went along pretty much as they had until that day at the track meet, when Henry and Frank had a fight and I tried to pull them apart. I pulled Henry off, but then he turned around and decked me, right in the face. Broke my nose. That's when I called it quits—no bro of mine is going to bust me in the chops, say "So sorry, pal, my fist slipped," and forget it.

What happened after that? Well, I think I'll just let you find that out yourself—about Lazarus, about Sutton and DeeDee, about Celia, and about what happened to Henry, and what happened to me.

—J. R. B.

Shadows   Grades 3-4
By Dennis Haseley

Jamie was staying with his aunt and uncle while his mother went to look for a new job up north. He wasn't very comfortable around Aunt Elena and Uncle Edward—he was sure they thought he was different somehow. Why did they stare at him in such a funny way? Why did they think he looked so much like his father? There was a secret about his dead father that no one wanted to tell him. Why was it such a mystery?

Then one day an older man turned up at his aunt and uncle's house—he said he was Jamie's grandfather. Jamie could tell his aunt didn't approve of Grandpa and wished he would stay away. But Jamie thought his grandfather was great—he showed Jamie how to make shadow-pictures on the wall. It was amazing how Grandpa's hands could make a hawk, moving its wings as if it were soaring through a patch of sky and then swooping downward with tailfeathers spread and sharp claws out, to snare a fish for dinner. Amazing! Grandpa did lots of animals on the walls, and Jamie liked talking to him, but he didn't come to visit very often. Jamie wasn't sure why. His Aunt Elena told him that Grandpa needed to be watched.

Grandpa had tried to show Jamie how to make shadows come alive on the wall, and Jamie practiced and practiced, hoping to get it just right so that he could surprise Grandpa. But where *was* Grandpa? Was he in some kind of trouble? Could it have something to do with Jamie's father and the secret no one would tell?

—*Maggie Carey*

Shelter for a Seabird   Grades 9-12
By Terry Farish

Two months ago I had a baby and gave her up for adoption. No, I didn't keep her. How could I? My parents wouldn't even let me stay here on the island while I was pregnant—sent me off to the mainland to some home for teens in trouble. Now that I'm back, everything's . . . different. My mother acts like it never happened. My father acts like I'm some kind of slut. And my best girlfriend? We don't talk the way we used to. In fact, we barely speak.

The biggest change of all is that my parents have sold our home and the land. Our land. This land has belonged to Taggs for generations and generations, but now it's been sold to outsiders. You know, summer people. I hate summer people; I despise them. Well, maybe not all of them. Swede Stuhr's parents are building a house next door to us, and even though we've only just met, I can tell that Swede's not like the others. Somehow we can connect, because we're on the same wavelength. Sometimes we don't even have to talk. We're good for each other. I can't explain it. I think I love him—seriously!

—*Mary Ann Capan*

Shiva Accused: Grades 5–8
An Adventure of the Ice Age
By J. H. Brennan

Shiva of the Shingu Tribe stood before the purple-faced elders of the Barradik Tribe. She stood outwardly calm, though inwardly shaking with fear—she would not give these people the satisfaction of knowing how terribly afraid she was. Shiva was on trial, and the charge was murder. She was accused by the Barradik tribe of murdering the Hag, spiritual leader of the Cro-Magnon tribes. The trial was for show only— Shiva knew that the sentence had already been decided.

It had all started a few days ago. Shiva had discovered the body in the pool where she often bathed. This day the smell of lion was in the air, so she had approached the pool cautiously. From her vantage point downwind, she saw the lionesses drinking and a human body floating in the pool. She wondered about the body, whose it was, and why it was there. In her mind (for she had the ability to see the unknown) a horrible picture began to form. She saw a heavy wooden club come crashing down on someone's head. The person floating in the pool had been murdered. After the lions left, Shiva pulled the body—that of an old woman—from the water. She knew that the Shingu elders would have to decide what to do next, but until she could get help, the dead person had to be hidden in a place safe from predators. It was while hiding the body that she had been captured by the Barradik tribe.

Now she was on trial, the sentence already decided. For among the tribes of that long-ago Ice Age time, the penalty for murder was death. It would take a miracle from the spirit world to save her now. *Shiva Accused: An Adventure of the Ice Age.*

—*Linda Olson*

Note: This book is the second in a series. It can stand alone, but you may wish to present the first title (*Shiva*, Lippincott 1990) as well.

The Sierra Club Book   **Grades 5–8**
of Weatherwisdom
By Vicki McVey

Do you know what I like most about *The Sierra Club Book of Weatherwisdom*? The experiments. Of course, that's not all that's in this book—it has stories of weatherwise kids and it explains all about stuff like fronts and highs and westerlies. (Guess what. All that mumbo-jumbo from the weather report on TV actually makes sense! Who knew?)

But what made me take *Weatherwisdom* home was the experiments. Assembling a weather station. Building a weathervane. And that's just the beginning. This isn't a sit-down-and-read book; it's a take-home-and-do book. My favorite experiments are the hygrometer and the greenhouse.

A hygrometer is a weather instrument that measures humidity. You'll never guess what they use to find out how much moisture is in the air. [Allow students time to guess.] Give up? To measure moisture in the air, they use three strands of human hair! Can you believe it?

Then there's the miniature greenhouse. You use a gallon jar. First fill it with gravel and dirt and plants and ants. Then—get this—you seal it up, and it makes its own oxygen. That's fascinating, but do you know what? You can even make it rain inside the jar! No kidding, I promise! This book actually tells you how to make it rain inside a jar. It's right here in *Weatherwisdom*. You gotta try it!

—Tracy Revel

Silver Light   **Grade 9–Adult**
By David Thomson

What do a hard-nosed, eighty-year-old female photographer, a museum researcher, Wyatt Earp, Billy the Kid, Willa Cather, Liberty Valance, John Wayne, and Bark Blaylock have in common? Answer: You'll get to know them all in *Silver Light*.

The wild-spirited Susan Garth grew up during the frontier years and became intrigued with a new process that used wet collodion plates to create pictures. She had a younger male friend named Bark, who was reportedly the son of Bat Masterson . . . or maybe the son of Bill Bro-cius . . . or maybe the son of Wyatt Earp. (Susan said Earp was a "downright tedious man" and that the children used to chant, "Earp burps!")

Bark, like Susan, led an adventurous life. When he was only six he made a trip west, swam the Pecos River on a horse, and was sleeping on the saloon porch when Pat Garrett shot Billy the Kid. He went on to write stories of the Wild West and even produced one of the very early silent movies—a Western, of course. But always, through the years, he remained Susan's best friend and best enemy. Susan put it this way: "You might have reckoned Bark and I would end up falling in love. Maybe we did, every day, with time to fall out again before sup-per. . . . But in silence, Bark and I loved each other. If we'd never met, we'd have been the happiest of couples."

In 1950, Susan and her photographs are discovered by Nora Stod-dard and James Averill. Nora is an art historian who is certain that Su-san will be famous once the world sees just a few of her thousands of photographs. James is the man who can make it possible with his wealth. As they dig into Susan's past, the story of Susan and Bark un-folds like a movie on the screen, winding here and there, rubbing el-bows with outlaws and celebrities, separating and coming back together, exploding with the color and wonder of the Old West.

Get acquainted with Susan and Bark and the rest. You may never be their best friend, but you'll surely never forget them!

—*Susan Weaver*

Sisters Long Ago   Grades 5-9
By Peg Kehret

The first time it happened was on my thirteenth birthday. Gretchen and I had gone to the lake for a picnic, and while I was swimming, I got a cramp. I couldn't scream; I couldn't even stay on top of the water long enough to breathe. Suddenly I knew I was drowning. And then it happened. While I was still struggling and trying to get back to the surface, I saw my grandmother. She was holding a yellow and red card that I had made, and my grandfather was standing near her, and I could feel how very much they loved me. But then they were gone, and instead I saw a girl on a small raft piled high with grain. She was dressed in a long white dress and her name was Kalos, and I realized that I was watching myself in another body, in another time. Then suddenly the raft ran into a crocodile, turned over, and Kalos was caught in the reeds of the river and pulled under the surface of the water, drowning just as I was drowning. But another girl managed to pull her out—a girl named Tiy, Kalos' sister. And I was pulled out too, and when I looked at the girl who had saved me, I recognized Tiy—in another body, in this lifetime. She had saved my life twice, once as Kalos, once as Willow.

And it didn't end there. I began to have dreams about Kalos and her world, her lifetime. And I began to wonder: Is it true? Can we live more than one life? Because, you see, my sister Sarah has leukemia—if she dies, will she have a chance to come back again? Will we ever have the chance to be sisters for more than just a few short years? Somehow, I have to find out, I have to find out for Sarah, and I have to find out for me.

—*J. R. B.*

Sixties People   Grade 9–Adult
By Jane and Michael Stern

Take this simple test. Find out if you're Sixties people! Even if you weren't even born in 1959, you might have what it takes to be in the Sixties groove.

Do you wear your hair in cute flips? Do you draw big smiley faces at the bottom of your letters? Is your favorite color cheery yellow? Do you love life? Do you think positively? Can you shake up your friends with some devastating remark just when they think you've curled up to do a little quiet thinking? Then you're a Perky Girl.

Do you dream of knife-creases, no-cuff, no-belt, low-rise, pipe-leg, perma-press Life O' Ease trousers? Do you slap on palmfuls of Hai Karate Oriental Lime cologne? Do you stride through the world searching for sophistication? Are you into the Good Life: jet set tours, erotic European movies, satin smoking jackets? Is your philosophy "work hard and play hard"—with the best? Then you might be a closet Playboy.

Is your look hoodlum-baroque? Do you combine a city-tough attitude with a formal hairdo? Do you sport shades, dramatic make-up, and a transistor? Do you dream of American Bandstand, Murray the K, or the Ronettes? You may be a Young Vulgarian.

Do you like to escape with a keg of brew, blasting "Louie, Louie" on the stereo, lying out in the sun, and dancing till your backbone cries for mercy? Do you believe that riding waves equals freedom? Can you define "The Hully Gully" and "The Watusi?" Do you wish Spring Break lasted all year? Hi, there, Party Animal!

Haven't found yourself yet? Don't worry, there are plenty of other options—Folkniks, the English (Beatles forever!), Hippies, Rebels, and Mr. and Mrs. Average. They're all *Sixties People*. Yours for the reading and dreaming.

—Lesley S. J. Farmer

Sleepers, Awake   Grades 5–8
By Paul Samuel Jacobs

Dody was watching every minute today. He tried to write to his friends back home to pass the time. "Dear Alan and Tony," he wrote, in large cursive looping letters. Maybe one day they would get all his letters.

He logged on to Mickey, the Master In-Craft Computer. He typed in the necessary code for his Wednesday morning pancakes. Dody was tired of endless solitary, predictable breakfasts, but he couldn't change the computer's routine.

Today, though, Dody's routine would change. After being in space for 107 years, 57 of those in hibernation, today Dody would welcome all the other space passengers on the ship as they woke up one by one. Finally he'd have people to talk to and play with; he'd see his parents and his older brothers and sisters.

Suddenly he heard his mother murmuring in her sleep. To Dody, there was no more beautiful sound in the universe. He moved so close to her that he could smell the chemicals, sharp and stinging. Her eyes blinked open.

"Father!" she exclaimed. "Oh, Papa!" She threw her arms around Dody's head. "But you're not supposed to be here, Father. We left you behind!"

"I'm not your father," Dody said very softly. "I'm your son."

Dody has been awake for fifty years, so he has grown fifty years older while everyone in hibernation has stayed the age they were. But though he's grown older physically, Dody hasn't grown up; fifty years of isolation have preserved the thoughts and attitudes of a ten-year-old. And now Dody and his family will have to figure out how to deal with a gray-haired boy who is older than his parents.

—Lesley S. J. Farmer

Smart Rats   Grades 7–12
By Thomas Baird

Laddie smelled a rat. Ever since the Progeny Reduction and Relocation Program had been announced by NORSAC, he'd been suspicious of the motives behind it. The announced purpose of the program was to reduce overcrowding on Earth's remaining habitable lands by removing one child from every two-sibling household and relocating all those children to underpopulated sectors elsewhere. But now, after watching the first load of progeny being taken away, Laddie was sure that something was terribly wrong.

One of that first group had been George, a friend of Laddie's and a member of his club, the Smart Rats, named after the bands of intelligent rodents that prowled outside the sector's protective fences, waiting to prey on runaways. The corpsmen who took George had stamped him on the forehead and cheek with indelible ink and then put him into a caged van—supposedly to take him to the relocation center. To Laddie it looked more like the disposal of the condemned.

When Laddie's turn came, he learned the horrible truth behind the Progeny Program . . . and he also learned the depths to which he could sink in the name of survival.

—Jeff Blair

Someday I'll Laugh About This   Grades 5–8
By Linda Crew

Changes, changes, changes! Nothing stays the same. This summer, when Shelley is twelve, she learns just how very true that is!

The annual vacation with her cousins at Sea Haven begins with the discovery that her favorite cousin Kirsten (who's thirteen) has gone boy- and mascara-crazy. The summer goes downhill from there. The uncle she worships announces that he's bringing his new fiancee to meet the family. And a greedy developer, Max Dymond, is threatening to decorate the landscape with condominiums and parking lots.

Will Shelby be able to live through a "Kirsten make-up makeover," really mean it when she welcomes her uncle's sweetheart into the family, and maybe even help stop Dymond's plans for "progress"?

Read *Someday I'll Laugh About This* and find out!

—Judy Thomas

Someone's Mother Is Missing   Grades 7-12
By Harry Mazer

Until recently, Sam Green had always believed his cousin Lisa Allen was one of those stuck-up beautiful girls he could never talk to. Her family had money and all that money could provide: a plane, a boat, a pool, private tennis lessons, the works.

But Lisa's world of comfort and protection was turned upside down when her father died in a plane crash. First her mother, who had never even discussed business with her father, had to practically live on the phone with the accountant and the lawyer talking about money: money owed, money promised, money still to come. Then came the days when her mother didn't get out of bed, or the afternoons when Lisa returned from school to find her mother sitting in the same place she'd left her in the morning. For a day or two after that, her mother would seem okay and things would get done. But then it would be the same all over again.

It got so that Lisa could never be sure *what* her mother would say or do. She seemed so confused! But since Lisa's family was never one to let private things hang out like clothes on a line for all the world to see, neither Lisa nor her mother shared any of this with anyone.

Then, three months after her father's death, Lisa came home from school to find her mother gone—not just out for a walk or visiting relatives or working at the restaurant, but gone, missing.

—*Olivia D. Jacobs*

Song of the Gargoyle   Grades 5-8
By Zilpha Keatley Snyder

Undoubtedly Tymmon would never have heard the song of the gargoyle had it not been for that strange night. He woke to the sound of intruders and heard his father being questioned by unknown men. Tymmon didn't know why, but the men were taking his father away, and they were looking for *him* as well. He hid deeper in the shadows and heard his father tell the intruders that his son had left in the quiet of the night through the postern gate. As the men hauled his father away, Tymmon knew he had been given instructions for saving his own life, instructions to quietly leave his home and all that he knew, instructions not to return until it was safe to do so.

Tymmon took the route his father had described and escaped the city, but his problems were far from over. The whole countryside was on the lookout for him, and he needed a place to hide. It was frightening, it was dangerous, but there was no other choice—he would have to spend the night in the deepest, darkest and most feared forest in the North Country, the Sombrous. He had heard all the stories about the creatures who lived there and the fate of those who dared to enter it after dark. But with pursuers on his trail, Tymmon knew the Sombrous was the only place that offered any hope of safety. But there was no safety there either, for suddenly, staring at him from across the dying fire, was a hideous, inhuman face, the stuff of nightmares—a gargoyle!

Tymmon is on the run in a fight for his own life and his father's. Will his fight be ended quickly and violently with the *Song of the Gargoyle*?
                                                          —*Helen Schlichting*

Stay Tuned   Grades 7–8
By Barbara Corcoran

"You're listening to FM station WILD, folks, your favorite spot on the dial. News coming up after this word from our sponsor. Stay tuned." [Change to a smooth, oily voice.] "Folks, I want to ask you a *very* personal question. Ladies and gentlemen, how is your love life? Is it drab? Monotonous? Has the glitz gone out of it? My friends, what *you* need is our brand-new product, Love Me Toothpaste. You'll be the life of the party, the toast of the ball! Friends, Love Me Toothpaste is made from tasty fresh cornflakes mashed up with glue and boiled to a fragrant, yummy mixture. As you know, most toothpastes are made with paste, but *we* use *glue*, and that's the secret. . . . Your teeth will shine like piano keys! [Bare your teeth for a moment; then go on talking as though your jaws were glued together.] So schlep on down to your favorite drugstore and get your Love Me Toothpaste. Guaranteed to please, or your money back! . . . And now, back to Jeremiah for the news. Stay tuned!"

Needless to say, this is *not* a real commercial. It's just Eddie's way of cheering up his friends. They're all homeless for one reason or another—Eddie and Fern because their mother left them in a welfare hotel, Stevie because her train ticket was stolen, and Alex because his dad threw him out of the house. But at least Alex can drive and knows of an abandoned camp in the woods where they can probably stay for a while. So here they all are, three kids and a teenager who's beginning to feel as though he'd been kidnapped by dwarves. Will they ever go back to civilization? Or can they make a home of their own in the wilds? Stay tuned!

—*Mary Hedge and J. R. B.*

Stolen Away   Grade 9–Adult
By Max Allan Collins

Remember Nate Heller? Yeah, yeah, he's a private eye now, but back a few years he was a Chicago cop. Well, one day he was working the train station, plainclothes, pickpocket detail. Off the train from New York came a suspicious-looking dame. He thought he had the Lindbergh kidnapper. So it goes, but the kid she had with her wasn't kidnapped from the Lindberghs; he'd been snatched from some kind of crime boss.

Just the same, it all ties back into the Lindbergh case. Seems that after Lindy heard about Nate's finding that one kidnapped kid, he thought this cop had to be an expert or something, so he borrowed him from the Chicago PD to work on finding his own kid. There were plenty of suspects: the pretty Scottish nanny, the prim British maid, a Scandinavian sailor, Al Capone, and just about anyone else who had ever crossed the Lindberghs' path. Why, maybe even the butler did it! The cops already on the case didn't help, either. The head of the state police, Colonel Schwarzkopf, was in charge of the investigation, but he was no "Stormin' Norman."

Lindy was kind of off-the-wall too (though who wouldn't be if his kid was snatched). He was willing to listen to anyone and try anything, even if it did mess up good police procedure. There were psychics practically coming out of the woodwork, volunteering to help find the kid, but the information they had was way off the mark—or was it? Edgar Cayce seemed sincere enough, but his directions didn't really make sense . . . or maybe they just weren't interpreted right.

Read *Stolen Away* and find out if Heller really unraveled the mystery of the Lindbergh kidnapping.

—*Di Herald*

Stolen Season   Grade 9–Adult
By David Lamb

In minor-league baseball there is a beautiful relationship between the players and the fans. The players play hard, hoping to do well enough someday to get a chance in the majors. Or, if they know they will never get that chance, they just play hard to make a living—low pay, lots of travel (by bus!), and terrible hours. And the fans love these guys—local heroes they can talk to, cheer for, bake cookies for—because fans in minor-league towns know that a night at the ball park is going to be some great summertime entertainment.

In *Stolen Season*, David Lamb tells us about his travels across America, about the dozens of games he saw in some of the neatest old-fashioned parks in the country. He talked to players and learned of their dreams, to team employees who had watched hundreds of those dreams either come true or die. He found former major-league stars who had decided to take jobs back in the minors, to work with the young players, teaching them and dreaming right along with them.

It takes a special kind of team owner, too, to make sure that the games are fun—with mascots roaming the stands, product give-aways, between-inning contests, and always a P.A. announcer who keeps the crowd noisy and involved in the game. It's really like a neighborhood party—and baseball nut David Lamb captures it all.

This book is a good look at America—its places and personalities—and at a game that keeps us coming back for more. So whether it's Birmingham, Bluefield, or Elmira; Wichita, El Paso, Stockton, or any of 150 towns across America, there's probably a minor-league club near you. Go there, yell your lungs out! It's great!

—*Mark Anderson*

Stonewords   Grades 5–8
By Pam Conrad

Zoe's best friend is a ghost. And her name is Zoe too—Zoe Louise, to be exact. Zoe Louise died in 1870 when she was eleven years old, but by using the kitchen stairs in Zoe's house, she can come and go as she pleases from 1870 to 1990. And remember, Zoe Louise is a ghost, so no one can see her, except Zoe.

But one day Zoe Louise gets tired of always going to Zoe's house. She wants Zoe to come back to her house, down the kitchen stairs, back to 1870. Zoe is scared. If she goes with Zoe Louise back to 1870, will she become a ghost too? And will she ever be able to return to 1990, to Grandma, PopPop, and her dog Oscar? But if Zoe doesn't go back with Zoe Louise, she'll lose her friend. And if Zoe does go back, maybe she can help Zoe Louise on her eleventh birthday, the day that Zoe Louise died.

Does Zoe go back in time to become a ghost and help her best friend? Read *Stonewords* and find out. —*Kaite Mediatore*

Straight Talk with Kids: Adult
Improving Communication, Building Trust,
and Keeping Your Children Drug-Free
By The Scott Newman Center

Picture yourself in the following situations:

1. You are sitting at the dinner table when your fifteen-year-old daughter breaks down in tears and announces that she is pregnant.

2. You are at work and you receive a phone call from school. Your child is about to be suspended for drinking.

3. It is the middle of the night, and you are awakened by a ringing phone. It is the police, telling you that your child has been arrested for stealing.

4. You discover that your son, the star athlete in the family, is ruining his health by taking steroids—a direct result of the competitive spirit you have been pushing into his head ever since he was a baby.

5. You find crack cocaine in your daughter's bedroom. Then you discover that she is selling the drug at school to support her habit.

How would you deal with situations like these? Even more important, how can you keep them from occurring in the first place? Parenting is one of the most difficult jobs in the world, even under ordinary circumstances. How can we, as adults, help kids face pressures and temptations that most of us never had to cope with when we were growing up? Today children are bombarded with conflicting, confusing, and often seductive messages from the media, from public figures, and from their peers. To help children deal with these conflicting messages, parents have to build trust and keep the lines of communication open. We need to work with our children on developing positive self-esteem, on handling peer pressure and parties and teenage sexuality, on recognizing the threat of AIDS and the menace of drugs. We know that an ounce of prevention is worth a pound of cure, but what if you discover that your child is already using drugs? Now you must try to intervene. Ask yourself, how did you miss the signs, the behavioral changes? How are you going to handle the confrontation and your own feelings of anger, guilt, and disappointment? And where are you going to turn for help? For a great starting point, try *Straight Talk with Kids.*

—Barbara Bahm

The Strange Case   **Grades 5-6**
of the Reluctant Partners
By Mark Geller

Did you ever wonder why people seem to go out of their way to make your life difficult? You're happy, things are okay . . . and then it happens—class assignment. Bad enough, right? But to make it worse, your teacher says that you'll be working with a partner. You quickly look around the room and pick out the people you'd like to work with. Probably your best friend, or maybe the boy or girl that you've been wanting to talk to for weeks but never had the nerve to approach. Now's your chance! But wait . . . your teacher says that *she* is going to choose the partners. You look around the class and pick out the people you *don't* want to work with. You cross your fingers and toes and look up and pray that none of these people gets tagged as your partner. You're almost afraid to listen as the teacher gets to your name and . . . life can be so cruel!

Thomas Trible can't understand it. He thinks that he's been a pretty good kid. He's no angel, but he's not *that* bad. So why would his teacher do this to him? He's paired with Elaine Moore. Elaine Moore never talks, never smiles. She's weird. No one in his class likes her. Why does he have to be *her* partner? This means they'll have to spend time together. His friends think that's hilarious. Poor old Thomas. Oh, life can be so cruel.

It's a cruelty joke, that's what it is. His teacher has a rotten sense of humor. He's supposed to write Elaine's biography. He's supposed to really get to know her, see what she's really like. Fine. He'll do it. He'll spend time with her. Go to her house. Meet her parents. Stay for dinner. He'll write a great biography. The best one in his class. Even if it kills him.

So if this is his teacher's idea of a joke, Thomas isn't laughing. You see, in spite of everything, Thomas is falling for the most unpopular girl in his class.

—Paula Paolucci

Summer　　　　　　　Grade 10–Adult
By Alice Gordon and Vincent Virga, eds.

When someone says "Summer!" what do you think of? The first day of summer when you were a kid and September seemed years away? Watermelon? Swimming pools and the sting of chlorine in your eyes? Mowing the yard and the clean smell of the cut grass? Fireworks on the Fourth of July? Baseball—Little League and big league? When I think of summer, somehow I always think of myself as a child, when summer was really significant, and the library put out all the mystery series again and I could renew my acquaintance with Nancy Drew, Jack Bolton, the Dana Girls and the Hardy Boys. If I walked slowly, I could usually finish the first book in my tall, just barely balanced stack before I got home.

Everyone has their own special memories of summer, for many of us our favorite time of year. This book records thirty-seven memories from some of America's finest writers—essays, stories and poems in honor of summer. For Calvin Trillin, it's chiggers; for Alice Adams, romance. Summer means endless baseball to Daniel Okrent, and gardens, both successful and unsuccessful, to Louise Erdrich. Phyllis McGinley remembers sand; Meg Wolitzer, the summer reading club and the mountains of books she checked out; and John Updike, the Fourth of July. Summer is amusement parks, a late afternoon breeze that momentarily relieves the blanketing heat, a summer job, fishing, card games, open-air concerts, family trips, sunbathing until you were dark brown with stark white tan lines, sudden thunderstorms, long twilights and playing till the fireflies danced, summer camps, and summer beaches.

Let these writers take you back to the summers of your youth. Let them bring the light, the colors, the smells, the sounds of summer back to you, and make even a winter day seem, just for a moment, as sunlit as June, as free as July, or as hot as August.

—J. R. B.

Susanna Siegelbaum Gives Up Guys　　Grades 5–6
By June Foley

Susanna Siegelbaum give up guys? *Never!* Not possible! Why, she had boyfriends even before kindergarten. Way back in nursery school, when Charles Milton slipped her a handful of Cheerios, she put one on her finger and told him they were married.

Flirting was as natural to Susanna as breathing. She couldn't walk down the street without seeing at least one guy she had dated sometime or other. Once, when she and Annie Cassidy were walking by Central High, they saw some teenage boys playing a pickup basketball game. Naturally Susanna checked them out—and realized she'd gone out with the entire team. (One by one, of course, not all at the same time.)

So what dire turn of events would cause Susanna Siegelbaum, age fifteen, to give up guys for three long months? Not just dating guys or kissing them, but flirting with them and even talking to them? How could she do it? To all who knew her, it seemed a bet she was destined to lose. But could she win? Read *Susanna Siegelbaum Gives Up Guys* and find out.

—Marianne Tait Pridemore

Take a Chance, Gramps!   Grades 5–8
By Jean Davis Okimoto

Jane and her best and only friend Alicia do everything together and think they always will—until the horrible news comes: Alicia is moving away. Now Jane is left to start seventh grade in a new school all alone. She can't decide which is worse, riding the bus by herself or having no one to eat lunch with. But Jane isn't the only one who's alone. Her grandfather just sits in his room upstairs since Gramma died. He doesn't even bother to put his teeth in! Then one day Jane's mother decides Jane should take Gramps to Seattle Centre. There they discover a seniors' dance, a cute boy with a skateboard, and lots of nice ladies who (Jane is sure) would love to dance with Gramps if he would just put his teeth in and ask!

Even though Gramps won't talk to any of the ladies (yet), he has some good advice for Jane on making new friends—just say "Hi!" Jane isn't so sure about this idea, but she gives it a try. And people start saying "Hi" back! Jane is thrilled to have her new friend Carly save her a seat on the bus and to have some people to eat lunch with. Then, Saturday night, Jane and Gramps go to another seniors' dance; this time they agree to say Hi to the cute boy with the skateboard and his lovely grandmother. Things turn out better than Jane ever expected, and everybody has a great time. But the following Saturday brings an awful surprise for Jane and Gramps. Together they learn that sometimes no matter *how* old you are, you just have to take a chance.

—Colleen Smith

A Tale of Antarctica
Grade 3–Adult
By Ulco Glimmerveen

A blue and white blanket of snow and ice glistens as spring arrives in Antarctica. Spring is an unsettled time, full of promise and hope for the hundreds of penguins that inhabit this vast wilderness. Spring also brings a surprise—strangers come to the rocky shore. Their gentle voices reassure the penguins; these visitors mean no harm.

And so the penguins continue to enjoy their frozen, undisturbed homeland. They are happy swimming, fishing, exploring, and napping in the sun until one day they wake up to find their snowy land covered with oil drums, boxes, roaring machines, and garbage. The blue and white blanket of safety has been torn away by an invader. An invader who forgets that all living things share the earth. An invader who ignores the leaking oil that makes the fish taste strange and the feathers clump together. An invader who litters the nesting sites with garbage.

Human beings have invaded the majestic, icy-blue homeland of the penguins. Catch a glimpse of the consequences in Ulco Glimmerveen's beautifully illustrated *Tale of Antarctica*.

—Susan Wolfe

Tales of the Early World
Grades 3–8
By Ted Hughes

Did you ever stop to think just how or why earthworms came to be? I mean, what purpose do they really serve, except as bait for fishing? Well, Ted Hughes has his own story about that.

It was back at the dawn of creation, and God had been making an elephant out of great hunks of elephant clay. It was such a big job that He was very tired when He finally got finished. He threw Himself down in His chair with a sigh and poured a cup of tea. Absentmindedly, He began to scrape the last of the elephant clay out from under His fingernails, and when He finished He had a little ball. He began to play with it, rolling it back and forth on His palm. He was thinking of the elephant He had just made, particularly its trunk. He was very proud of that trunk because He'd never made one before—it was a brand new invention. So just as an experiment, He began to make a miniature trunk out of the tiny piece of clay. He put it up to His lips to blow nostrils into it and without thinking accidently blew life into it instead. The little trunk squirmed in His hand and yelled at Him in a tiny little voice. And what it said was, "Finish me! Where's the rest of me? Finish me!"

And now God was in a predicament, because He had no more elephant clay. He'd used it all up—that's why the elephant had turned out so big. And to make matters worse, elephant clay was rare and precious stuff, very difficult to find. The tiny trunk was most upset to hear this and began to cry. It was meant to be an elephant, it said; it had elephant thoughts and feelings, and it felt horrible wiggling around with no elephant body or head or legs. It wanted God to start looking for some more clay immediately! But God was tired. So He gently laid the little trunk down on the ground and told it to start digging. As soon as it came up with the right sort of clay, He would finish it. The tiny trunk began to dig. And dig. And dig. But none of the clay it brought back was right, and God sent it out again to keep looking. So the days passed. And the weeks, and the months, years, centuries . . . and the little trunk is still digging today, looking for the elephant clay that will finally make it whole.

And that is the story of how the earthworm was created. Except now we know the earthworm isn't really an earthworm, is it? And if that's how the elephant and the earthworm came to be, what about the horse, the parrot, and the cat? Discover their stories in *Tales of the Early World.*

—Susan Dunn

Teenage Wasteland: Grade 9–Adult
Suburbia's Dead End Kids
By Donna Gaines

What compels teenagers to take their own lives?

For most of us, teenage suicide is hard to imagine, let alone understand, and suicide pacts or multiple suicides seem almost unthinkable. Following an epidemic of suicides and suicide attempts among high school students in suburban New Jersey, Donna Gaines, a journalist and certified social worker, decided to explore the world of these troubled kids.

She gained entry and gradually won acceptance into their world, hanging out with friends of the dead teens. As her circle of contacts expanded, she discovered that many troubled teens are just barely getting by in school or have dropped out altogether. Drugs and alcohol are in common use. Home life for some is practically nonexistent—their parents are absent or preoccupied—while for others it's something to escape—their parents are abusive. These kids, known as "burnouts," are often viewed as losers by their parents, their teachers, and the communities in which they live.

Like many teens, the burnouts feel trapped between childhood and adulthood. In American society their age labels them as children, but their experiences thrust them into adulthood. They don't fit into any of the molds that society offers. Some have adult responsibilities and resent the fact that they are barred from adult rights and freedoms. Most feel they are constantly and unfairly harassed for their dress, hair, language, and music.

To escape their feelings of hopelessness and powerlessness, they party. They party hard, long, and loud. Music blares, and the lyrics of their favorite songs are bluntly expressive. No topic is taboo. Friends and friendship are a special priority for many of the burnouts, offering a chance to love and be loved unconditionally—and making it likely that one suicide will be followed by other, "copycat" attempts.

Gaines doesn't give us reasons why teens commit suicide, but she does provide a window into their world. She doesn't presume to speak for these kids, but she lets them express their thoughts and feelings in their own, uncensored language.

Look into an alien world, under the bland suburban surface, and see if you recognize the *Teenage Wasteland.*

—Cynthia Lopuszynski

A Telling of Tales   Grades 3–8; Adults
By William J. Brooke

I'll bet you think you know all about the story of Cinderella and her prince and how they lived happily ever after, don't you? Well, what would have happened if Cinderella had refused to try on the slipper when the Prince arrived? Or what if he got tired of going from house to house, watching all those women try to shove their big feet into that tiny slipper, and decided to find his bride some other way? Would the story still be magic? Would there still be a happy ending?

Or maybe you remember the story of Sleeping Beauty. What do you think she thought when she woke up? Well, what would *you* do if a strange man suddenly appeared in your bedroom, saying you'd been asleep for a hundred years and that he'd just fought his way through a forest of thorns to wake you up with a kiss—especially if he didn't even look like a prince! Maybe ask him for some identification? That's exactly what Sleeping Beauty did! And being the Prince, he'd never had anyone ask him that before, and so of course he didn't have any. So she had the guards arrest him, right on the spot. Hard for there to be a happy ending after that!

And what do you think were the real tales of Jack and the Beanstalk, John Henry, Paul Bunyan, and Johnny Appleseed? You think you know the truth? Think all those books of fairy tales and legends gave you the real scoop? Think again—*this* is where you'll find the *real* truth!
—*J. R. B.*

Thin Air   Grades 3–6
By David Getz

Why couldn't anyone treat him like a normal person? Just because he had asthma, it didn't give everybody the right to feel sorry for him or act as if he were some kind of special case. He wanted to be part of a regular class at school, be chosen first for the roller-hockey teams, and be accepted for what he *was*, not what he had. The only problem sixth-grader Jacob Katz had was convincing everyone *else* of that fact.
—*Barbara Bahm*

This Is the Life   Grade 9–Adult
By Joseph O'Neill

I always thought that when I grew up I'd be a schoolteacher. I'd be a teacher like Mrs. Conklin, my sophomore English professor—wise and kind, knowledgeable and demanding. The students would love me. It never occurred to me that I might become a teacher like my chemistry instructor, whose classes were dull, routine, and downright boring. We all have dreams of what we will become, and in those dreams we're always the best in the field. Who would dream of being the mediocre doctor, or the architect who designs boring little boxes, or the cop who writes out parking tickets?

James Jones always wanted to be a lawyer, and not just any lawyer. He wanted to be like Michael Donovan, the brilliant, insightful, inspirational, international attorney who was his idol. But things don't always work out the way we think they will, and Jones became, instead, a member of a small firm that handled domestic cases and minor municipal disputes. For ten years or so he led a quiet existence. He did the same thing every day; he went to the office, he dodged complaining clients, he ate "prawn and mayonnaise and tuna and mozzarella sandwiches" for lunch, he dodged more complaining clients and then went home to his apartment. Occasionally he would spend an evening with his girlfriend, Susan. A quiet, predictable existence—but Jones still dreamed of what he might have been.

Finally Jones is given his big chance. Imagine his surprise when he sees Donovan's name on his list of messages. Donovan is seeking *Jones'* help in fighting a turbulent divorce action. Jones spends the next year looking for brilliant solutions, not only to Donovan's problems but to his own. Once again, he is dazzled by the powerful Donovan and envious of all that he stands for. Once again, he shuffles through the dreams of all he might have been and the reality of what he has become. Maybe there *are* no "second chances" or "happily ever after" endings. Maybe there is just the life there is. Maybe *This Is the Life* of James Jones, warts and all.

—Stacey M. Weaver

Thunderwith   Grades 7-10
By Libby Hathorn

Lara Ritchie's world has been turned upside down. Her mother has died, and her dad, whom she hasn't seen in over twelve years, is coming to pick her up. From now on, Lara will be living in a different part of Australia. Her new home will be in a rain forest where her dad and his wife and their four kids are starting a palm tree farm.

It sounds like a new beginning, but right from the start Lara feels unwelcome. Her stepsister Pearl doesn't want an older sister, and her stepmother, Gladwyn, resents having a reminder of the first marriage around. Lara's dad must leave the farm for long periods of time to look for work, and Lara feels alone in an unfriendly house. At school, Gowd Gadrey, the local bully, takes an instant dislike to her and makes her life hell. He ridicules Lara every chance he gets, and when no one is looking he twists her arm or pinches her.

Lara's memories of her mom help her through these hard times, and she keeps an American silver dollar her mom gave her close to her bed. One afternoon while on a walk, Lara "finds" a dog. It looks like a dingo, a wild Australian dog. At the very moment she sees the animal, thunder crashes around her, so she names the dog Thunderwith. Lara believes her mom sent her the dog to comfort her. Whenever she can, Lara escapes to the mountain to be with Thunderwith.

And just as life seems to be getting a bit better, Gowd Gadrey forces Pearl to tell him about Lara's silver dollar. He demands that Lara give *him* the dollar and threatens her when she refuses. Then Lara overhears Gladwyn telling someone that Lara will be with them only for "a period of time." What does she mean? Lara feels as though her life is falling apart all over again, and runs to the mountain to be with Thunderwith.

But while she is sitting there, Gowd Gadrey approaches with a rifle. He's been hunting, but when he sees Lara, he remembers that silver dollar. He threatens her. Lara jumps to her feet and starts running. She calls to Thunderwith, and together they run up the mountain. Gowd is furious. Out of control, he raises the rifle—and shoots.

—Paula Eads

The Tiger in the Well   Grade 7–Adult
By Philip Pullman

Sally Lockhart, the feisty main character from Philip Pullman's two earlier novels, *Ruby in the Smoke* and *The Shadow in the North* is being divorced by a man she's never even heard of. But he's obviously heard of her, and he must have been watching her for years—he seems to know everything about her. The legal document in which he filed for divorce lists all the significant dates and details of her life: her age, occupation, bank account, present address, and even the birth date of her daughter Harriet.

But all these true details are twisted to support a monstrous lie! Because Mr. Parrish, this perfect stranger who claims to have married Sally almost three years ago, isn't just taking her to court for a divorce, he's also filing for legal custody of Harriet. He claims that Sally is a drunkard and an unfit mother, and that Harriet will be better off with him, her father. Harriet's real father is dead. Sally knows that, but she can't prove it. Oh, she can prove that Frederick is dead, of course, but she can't prove that Frederick was Harriet's real father, because Frederick was killed before Harriet was born—and also before he and Sally could get married. And that fact not only puts Sally in a very weak position in the London of 1881, but also means that there is no legal record of any real marriage to disprove this imaginary one. To make matters worse, there *is* a legal record of the imaginary marriage, even though it never took place. Sally has seen it with her own eyes.

Sally can't believe what's happening to her. Mr. Parrish has twisted her past and threatens to destroy her future. If he can prove in court that she *was* his wife—and how is she going to explain away that entry in the church register?—the laws of England will not only give him control of her business and all her possessions but of Harriet as well.

Why is Parrish doing this, and what is he really after? Searching for the answer, Sally finds herself immersed in the underworld of London, a world she never knew existed. And she discovers that she isn't the only one whose life has been destroyed by Mr. Parrish and his boss, a sinister figure called the Tzaddik, which means "the saint" in Hebrew. But this Tzaddik is a saint of evil, the power behind a massive plot to cheat and persecute the poor Jewish immigrants who are flooding into London from Eastern Europe.

Sally still can't see the connection between what's happening to her and this plot to fleece the immigrants; but she decides to act anyway. She has thought of a way to save herself and help all the other people this monster Tzaddik has persecuted as well. And once she's thought up her plan, she's determined to carry it out. Sally's not afraid to fight. But if she knew who the Tzaddik really was, maybe she would be. Even tigers can be trapped.

—*Margie Reitsma*

The Time and Space of Uncle Albert   Grades 3-6
By Russell Stannard

I have a problem. We have to do research science projects for school, and I'd really like to do a good one, one that will please (and impress) old Turnip—actually Mr. Turner, the science teacher. I don't want to do something stupid like volcanoes or dinosaurs. Turnip suggested "Energy in the Home," but that's so dumb. I want to do something really special, something creative, that no one else has ever done before. Maybe Uncle Albert can help me. He always has great ideas.

After school I stopped by his house, hoping that two heads would be better than one. Now, you have to understand that Uncle Albert isn't your average, run-of-the-mill uncle. Some people might call him odd— or even eccentric. But life is never dull around Uncle Albert!

That afternoon we got to talking about stars and space and the speed of light. And do you know what Uncle Albert suggested? He asked me if I wanted to go chase a beam of starlight. He wasn't kidding—he actually wants me to chase a beam of light . . . in a spacecraft!

As we walked into his study I saw something hovering over one of his chairs, something resembling a giant soap-bubble. Uncle Albert said it was a thought-bubble. When he thinks hard enough, his thoughts appear in the thought-bubble.

Guess what! That's what he's going to do. He's going to think up a spacecraft, a spacecraft with me inside, and I'm going to chase a light beam for him. Wow!!! Now that's a *really* impressive science project! Say—why don't you come along too? Who *knows* what we'll find!

—*Carol Kappelmann*

Time Is the Longest Distance: Grade 5–Adult
An Anthology of Poems
By Ruth Gordon, sel.

Do you ever think about time, or about how time passes? How does it move—steadily onward, never stopping, never hurrying? Always at the same pace? Or does it speed up, slow down, or just slip away unnoticed?

Have you ever wondered what time is like for mosquitoes and flies—those little pests you'd like to swat? They seem to

> . . . fill the world.
> So many, should you fight them all?
> And yet, how short a time they live.
> While they last, give in and let them bite you.
> October, and a cold wind wipes them out.
> You don't remember then they ever were.

Did time pass?
    When you go out to dinner, what happens?

> Customers flood the Inn's restaurant
> at dinner. We have to wait for a table.
> In the sitting room
> a large fish tank's bubbling
> but there are no fish.
> We take in the view of the Russian River.
> Eight-thirty and it's still sunny.

What makes time pass; what mades it drag?
    Ever stop to think about time and light? In early March,

> . . . I open the kitchen door:
> someone left the light on.
> No, for the first time this year the sun's
> reflecting off the brick wall
> outside the window.
> At the end of the afternoon
> I walk into my room
> and step on a fire. I jerk

my foot away, but it isn't burnt.
I guess for the next few months
I'll be finding these chips of reddish light
on the wood floor
just before nightfall.

You can almost see time passing as the days begin to get longer like this.
Discover that *Time Is the Longest Distance*—or perhaps, in some of these poems, the shortest.

—Maggie Carey

To the Moon and Back: Grades 3–8
A Collection of Poems
Nancy Larrick, comp.

To the Moon and Back is a collection of poems that will take you to wondrous places—as high as the moon, as far as the wind, and as down-to-earth as the city dump. Some tell a story, like this one called "About the Teeth of a Shark," by John Ciardi:

The thing about a shark is—teeth,
one row above, one row beneath.
Now take a close look. Do you find
It has another row behind?
Still closer—here, I'll hold your hat;
Has it a third row behind that?
Now look in and . . . Look out! Oh my,
I'll never know now! Well, goodbye.

Still others stir up word-songs in our heads. Imagine the Sia Indians chanting and dancing the "Rain Song":

White floating clouds,
clouds like the plains,
come and water the earth.
Sun, embrace the earth
to make her fruitful.
Moon,
lion of the north,
bear of the west,

wolf of the east,
shrew of the earth,
speak to the cloud people for us,
so that they may water the earth.

You are sure to find at least one poem here that sings your song, expresses your feelings, or tickles your funny-bone and sends you *To the Moon and Back*, again and again.

—*Diane L. Deuel*

Tom Loves Anna Loves Tom   Grades 7–12
By Bruce Clements

Have you ever thought about falling in love? What it would be like the very first time? Sixteen-year-old Tom Post wasn't expecting to fall in love. He was in the hardware store looking for a bargain when he first saw Anna Milton. He didn't even see her face, just her back, but he knew right away he had to meet her.

He followed her home from the hardware store, keeping his distance, not knowing how to introduce himself (after all, he had always told his little sister that if she ever saw anyone following her she should call the police). When he found out where Anna lived he went back later and left a jar of wildflowers on her front step. But now that he's fallen in love with a perfect stranger, how can he arrange to meet her?

—*Marianne Tait Pridemore*

Tomorrow's Crimes   Adult
By Donald E. Westlake

Of all times for the elevator to break down! This has *never* happened to Edmund before, never in his whole life. But today has just been one of those days. You know, when positively everything goes wrong.

He'd been thinking that a proposal to Linda would turn the whole day around, but not at this rate. Linda is a stickler for punctuality, and Edmund is going to be very, very late for their date.

Edmund tries calling her but can't get through. Next he calls the receptionist. Unbelievable! There is a spy in the elevator! The spy hid there to escape being caught by the Army. Every time someone enters the shaft to get him out, the spy aims the elevator at him like a missile.

Edmund lives on the one hundred fifty-third floor of the Project. The Project is one of the many self-sufficient apartment buildings that became nations just before the Third World War. This building survived the atomic war with the aid of force screens that deflected the radioactive particles. Each surviving project distrusts all other projects and is armed against them. Between the fear of people from other projects and the fear of radiation, Edmund has never been outside his own building.

Well, the spy in the elevator is just too much for Edmund to handle. There's no other option—he'll have to brave the thirteen flights of stairs down to Linda's apartment. Edmund vaguely remembers playing on the stairs as a child. Who knows how long it's been since anyone set foot on them?

He steps out onto the dusty landing and begins his descent. One floor, two floors.

What's this? A tiny door between floors 150 and 149 with some barely readable lettering: "Emergency Entrance, Elevator Shaft, Authorized Personnel Only, Keep Locked."

Just as Edmund passes, the doorknob turns, and out steps a man waving a gun—the spy!

At gunpoint, the spy escorts Edmund back to his apartment and forces him to listen to a most unbelievable story. The man claims he's not a spy, but an atomic engineer. Back home in his own project, he began to wonder if the radiation outside was decreasing. He wanted to test his theory, but the Project Commission wouldn't hear of it. So he went outside on his own, knowing he would be shot if he returned. He has lived safely outdoors for five months before appearing in Edmund's building.

At this point in his story the spy becomes quite agitated and forces Edmund to look out the window. Yes, there may be just a trace of green below. "Plants," claims the spy. But, oh, the horror of the outdoors! It just can't be safe! The very thought nauseates Edmund.

In the excitement, he has just a moment to disarm the spy. Edmund fells him forever with a karate chop to the neck.

The Project gives Edmund a medal. They've been saved from a dangerous spy—or have they been trapped by their own ignorance?

For more suspenseful stories of science-fiction crime and mystery, try *Tomorrow's Crimes*, by Donald E. Westlake.

—Bernice D. Crouse

The Torment of Mr. Gully: Grades 7–12
Stories of the Supernatural
By Judith Clarke

The thing that always impresses me about [name of school] is how much the students here love their teachers. How much they . . . [mock surprise] what, did I say something wrong? Are you telling me that you *don't* love all your teachers? That there are actually teachers you dislike? Even a few you hate? Right now I want you each to think about one teacher you really hate—and all the reasons why. Don't yell out names, but get that person locked in your mind. But let me tell you this: no one, and I mean no one, could be as bad as Mr. Gully.

He was the science teacher for the kids in Room 1D, and they *loathed* him! Why? Because he was so weird, and *so boring*. His long-winded lectures on physics droned on, class after class, day after day. Nobody listened anymore—the kids would pass notes and talk or do crossword puzzles. Another teacher would have made them stop, but Mr. Gully just went on and on in his monotone monologue about physics. So he bored them, and that's why they hated him. And they hated him because he was gross—the way he dressed and the way he smelled. And when he talked he spat, so you needed a raincoat if you wanted to sit in the front row. And sometimes he burped, and legend has it he once actually threw up in a school drinking fountain. But most of all the kids hated him because he didn't even notice.

The kids in 1D were the smartest, and they were used to having attention paid, but nothing they did seemed to register with Mr. Gully. Not stealing his chalk or dumping water on his desk. Nothing bothered Mr. Gully, so they hated him. And they challenged him. And so it was war. The first casualty was the rat they killed and stuffed into his desk. Who would be next? Mr. Gully himself, or maybe all the kids of Room 1D? And that's *just* the beginning.

—Patrick Jones

A Tribe for Lexi   Grades 5–8
By C. S. Adler

Twelve-year-old Lexi has long looked forward to coming to stay with her cousins for the summer. These people are family, and she knows that they will accept her and welcome her just because of their blood ties. Lots of people think Lexi's strange—but she's not really, it's just that her life has been so unusual it's hard for people to relate to her. Lexi's dad is a construction manager who builds things all over the world. She's just come from West Africa, and before that they lived in Brazil. Lexi can speak the common words in five different languages and knows what to do for snakebite and bee sting, but she finds it a lot harder to fit in with American kids her own age.

When things got too dangerous in West Africa, Lexi's parents sent her off to boarding school in the States. Lexi hated it—she wanted to be with her parents, and besides, everyone at school thought she was weird. When summer came her parents wanted to ship her off to camp, but Lexi had a better idea—she asked to stay with her aunt and uncle and cousins in upstate New York instead. She'd been there once before for Christmas and had a really good time. She figured her relatives, at least, would accept her—after all, she *is* blood kin.

Unfortunately, it doesn't work that way. Her two girl cousins think she's odd because she can't cook or sew and likes to fish, and two of her three boy cousins aren't interested in anything but baseball. The only one Lexi can relate to is her middle cousin, Jeb. Like Lexi, Jeb is an outcast in the family. He spends most of his time staying out of everybody's way so he won't get picked on.

Jeb is very interested in Indians—he's read all the books about them he can find and made a bow and arrows to practice with. He tells Lexi that he wishes he'd been born into an Indian family. Long ago, tribes of Indians lived in the very area of New York where Jeb's family have their house. Jeb thinks that maybe, somewhere back in the wilderness where no white man has ever been, some of those Indians are still there. And Jeb hopes that maybe, if he can find them, they'll take him in and adopt him as one of their own.

So together Jeb and Lexi build a raft and float down the river into the woods in search of Indians. Since neither of them fits in with their own people, maybe somewhere out there they can find a home in a different culture. *A Tribe for Lexi* is the story of the sad, funny, and scary things that happen to Jeb and Lexi on their wilderness journey.

—*Susan Dunn*

Truce: Ending the Sibling War Grades 9–12
By Janet Bode

Have you ever watched a family sitcom and come away wondering why *your* family isn't like that? If you have, you're not alone! There are probably very few real-life families that can measure up to the model versions shown on TV, the kind of nearly-perfect families where the parents and children always manage to resolve their problems before the last commercial.

Well, maintaining peaceful family relationships usually isn't that easy, especially for teenage siblings. When research author Janet Bode started to interview teenagers about how they got along with their sisters and brothers, she was expecting to hear about routine aggravations, like borrowing stuff without asking or fighting about whose turn it is to set the table. And in most cases, that *was* the extent of the problems. But for about 25% of the students interviewed, the problems were a lot more serious. Take this one, for example:

"My brother Darnell—he's thirteen—he cursed at me, called me a female dog. I got real mad. So I hit him and made his nose bleed. I fought him and fought him," says fifteen-year-old Cherisse.

"Yeah, she was beating me up bad," Darnell agrees. "So I went to the kitchen and picked up a big knife. I threw it at her. She ducked. There it was, sticking in the wall."

The sibling war: verbal assaults, physical violence, theft, and sometimes even sexual abuse. If conflicts like these are a part of your life with your brothers or sisters, then *Truce: Ending the Sibling War* is for you.

—*Sister M. Anna Falbo, CSSF*

Tug of War   Grades 5–8
By Joan Lingard

"Don't lose sight of the one in front of you," their father had stressed, "not even for a second." A second was long enough to lose someone in the middle of the milling crowd.

It was 1944, and the Russians were invading. Fourteen-year-old Hugo and his family were fleeing their home in Latvia. While awaiting a train to freedom among hundreds of people, Hugo's glasses were knocked off, and he bent down to pick them up. Those few seconds were all it took for Hugo to become virtually blind and alone among a sea of strangers. Hugo missed the train that carried away his family to their hoped-for freedom.

Hugo's journey began when he boarded another train, took a different path, and became entangled in the lives of another family. Meanwhile, his own family traveled along the intended route desperately searching for any sign of him, but for four long years all their inquiries were in vain. Would Hugo meet his family again? Would he marry Bet-tina, who had helped nurse him back to health? In what direction would Hugo travel in this *Tug of War?*

—*Lisa Broadhead*

Twelve-Year-Old Vows Revenge!   Grades 5-8
After Being Dumped by Extraterrestrial on First Date
By Stephen Roos

Summer vacation has arrived, at last.

Claire Van Kemp is set to spend the summer at her uncle's hardware store, continuing as manager of the video games area. Customers, however, have dwindled since the spring weather started, and when her uncle is suddenly given the chance to get some extra lawn furniture, a sure-fire seller if he has room for it, Claire is shocked to find herself out of work—unless she agrees to help clean the store and sell the hardware, plus the new lawn furniture he's put in the video games area!

Meanwhile, Shirley Garfield doesn't have any summer plans—except to get back at Claire for humiliating her on the last day of school. But when classmates Warren and Gaylord decided to start a newspaper just for kids, they ask Shirley to be their reporter because she wrote such entertaining stories for English class. Sidetracked for a while from her plan, Shirley joins the *Bugle* team, but the only stories she can find in their little town are a potholder contest and some old stuff found in a cellar. However, Shirley manages to make even these "small potatoes" sound like big scoops. And then she discovers a genuine scoop—one that she can use to get back at Claire, too. And the feud is on! Who can come up with something the other one can't top? Who will find the ultimate big scoop?

—*Carolyn M. Johnson*

Twenty Pageants Later   Grades 5-8
By Caroline B. Cooney

I was always second best. Scottie-Anne McKane, younger sister to Dane McKane, the sixteen-year-old professional beauty queen. Since age two, Dane has entered sixty pageants, and she's won nineteen. Her absolute goal in life is to be Miss Teenage America.

These pageants are actually big business! Dane has her gowns designed for her by a team of pros called Micharde-Miquelle; she has a coach who analyzes the pageants and decides what Dane should wear and say; and she studies ballet, jazz, tap, ballroom, and modern dance to compete in the talent section of the contest. Our family's had to purchase a custom-made van, with hanging space for the gowns, mirrors for Dane, and a special lock-up cabinet for Dad's video equipment. It seems like every weekend we're at a Hyatt or a Sheraton or a Plaza Hotel, waiting, waiting, waiting. If there were an award for patience, I think *I* would win that!

Don't get me wrong. I love Dane (usually) and I'm proud of her success. That's why I told Mrs. Gold that I thought Lillie *should* enter the fund-raiser beauty pageant that our school is holding. "She will gain poise, self-confidence, and stage ability," I said. Boy, did that backfire on me! See what happens when you try to help out your best friend? Mrs. Gold gave her permission, with one condition: I had to enter too. And when I filled out that form, I was surprised at just how much *I* wanted to win!

—Susan R. Farber

Twenty Ways to Lose Your Best Friend   Grades 3-4
By Marilyn Singer

It's rotten not having a best friend. It's more alone than being alone. When you have a best friend and you're alone, you always know you'll see her soon and then you won't be alone anymore. But when you *don't* have a best friend and you're alone, you feel you're going to be alone forever! And that's how Emma feels now. Her best friend Sandy is furious with her. She won't have anything to do with Emma anymore— just because Emma wouldn't vote for her as the best person for a part in the school play. Emma didn't feel Sandy *was* the best person—and hadn't her mother told her once not to vote for somebody just because that person was a friend? She said to vote for the person who would do the job best, and that's just what Emma had done! And now she's in a mess, with no best friend! Sandy won't eat lunch with her; she won't choose her to be on her team; she even laughed when mean Bobby Deacon tripped Emma as she was walking past him. Things just keep getting worse, and Emma's miserable! Read *Twenty Ways to Lose Your Best Friend* and find out how *really* rotten things get for Emma and Sandy.

—Maggie Carey

The Two Faces of Adam   Grades 9–12
By Carolyn Meyer

Getting involved with the school's crisis hotline was a way Lan could help kids in trouble—not that he didn't have troubles of his own. When he wasn't on the hotline after school, he was working, tutoring people in music, trying to earn the money that would get his sister and her child away from his angry, violent brother-in-law. It seemed as though there'd never be enough money. But Lan's problems were small compared with those of the people he listened to, especially the kid who called himself "Ninja." The Ninja's brother was an addict *and* a pusher, and the Ninja was the only one in his family who had figured that out.

Lan has never swayed from his anti-drug stand, but gradually the Ninja has become a friend. Can he refuse to help just because he doesn't approve of the problem?

—Barbara Bahm

Up in the Mountains   Grade 5–Adult
and Other Poems of Long Ago
By Claudia Lewis

Memories of a time long past wait for you here. Hot chocolate sending rich aromas through the evening air. A comb of pine trees rising along a hillside signaling a favorite picnic spot. The eerie creaks of floorboards in the dead of night silenced by the comforting tread of a parent who peeks through the bedroom doorway. Comfortable memories of a time gone by, of childhood remembered.

Some memories are not so sweet. The jovial principal who kept a paddle up his sleeve and who used it just often enough to keep everyone careful. The cruel taunts leveled at a classmate whose dress was just a little too different to be accepted by the popular girls. Angry, quarreling words filtering sharply through a closed door, and then a slam as Mother leaves the house.

But most of all the memories are fond ones, and those that are remembered with a touch of sadness only make the good ones better. Like faded, brownish photos in an old family album, these poems remind us of a past that can never be relived, only remembered. *Up in the Mountains and Other Poems of Long Ago*, by Claudia Lewis.

—Nancy L. Chu

Upchuck Summer's Revenge   Grades 5–6
By Joel L. Schwartz

Richie had had such a terrible summer last year, he just knew this summer had to be better. He'd learned something, of course—he knew he'd have to keep a distance from Chuck, the one person at camp who could turn a good day into a disaster simply by being around.

But when Richie got to camp and met Lisa, the most gorgeous girl he'd ever seen, he knew that Chuck wouldn't be his only problem that year. Because Richie wasn't the only one who'd fallen in love with Lisa—another counselor, Jerry, had too.

Somehow, whenever Lisa was around, Richie found himself doing the craziest things. When she was giving a tour of the camp, he just happened to be trimming trees above her, wearing a zombie mask to keep the poison ivy off. When he sneaked into the girls' dormitory and ducked into the shower to avoid getting caught, Lisa was there to see him.

Richie was grounded, confined to his dorm; he hated Jerry; he was stuck with Chuck; his team was composed of the world's worst football players; things just couldn't get any worse. But they did. Jerry dared Richie to a football game between his team of campers and Richie's. The winner would get the loser as his slave for a week.

To see how Richie survived his summer and how Lisa helped him, read *Upchuck Summer's Revenge.*

—Sharon O'Connell

Vampires   Grades 7–8
By Jane Yolen and Martin H. Greenberg, eds.

As far as I can see, the problem is, you have absolutely the wrong idea about vampires. I mean, you've read Bram Stoker or seen the old Dracula movies, and now you think a vampire is some stuffy, middle-aged guy who lives in a castle in Transylvania. *If* you believe in him at all.

But suppose a vampire is a guy who caught the virus just before he was killed in an auto accident. The cleaning lady at the funeral home has kicked him out—she's really tired of corpses rising up! He can't go home—his parents have fits when he breaks curfew; they're *really* not going to like his being undead. And as if tonight weren't bad enough, tomorrow's funeral will be worse: his weird Uncle Marko always carries a stake and mallet to funerals, just in case!

Or suppose a vampire is a girl who's going to fix the babysitter who tried to molest her little sister. Or a lonely boy hanging out at the mall, looking for a girlfriend. What if everything you think you know about vampires is wrong? Middle-aged? Not if he died young. Black tuxedo? Why not a black t-shirt? Want to scare him off with a cross? What if he's Jewish? Can't go out by day? She can with today's sunblocks. Allergic to garlic? So don't put it on the pizza! As a matter of fact, a vampire could look like anyone at all. Or be any place at all. I'd keep an eye on that kid sitting next to you. . . .

—*Rene Mandel*

Voices on the Wind   Grades 3–6
By David Booth, comp.

Have you ever enjoyed a season so much that you wished it would never end? Or that you could time-travel back and forth into any season of the year whenever you wanted? Well, seasons don't last forever, and time-travel is out of the question for most of us. However, there *is* a way for you to experience the joy of any season any time you want! *Voices on the Wind* is a collection of poems about all of the seasons. It lets you savor the suddenness of spring splashing in your eyes, to recall the excitement of planting seeds and watching for their growth. Then,

> If you try very hard,
> Can you remember that time
> When you played outside all day
> And you came home for dinner
> And had to take a bath right away
> Right away?
> It took you a long time to pull
> Your shirt over your head.
> Do you remember smelling the sunshine?
> That was summer.
>
> (Marci Ridlon)

Perhaps you prefer fall, bringing the crunch of leaves beneath your feet, or winter with its biting winds and chill. Whatever your favorite season may be,

Sing a song of seasons!
Something bright in all!
                    (Robert Louis Stevenson)

Let them speak to you at any time through *Voices on the Wind.*
                              —*Sister Mary Anna Falbo, CSSF*

Walker of Worlds   Grade 9–Adult
By Tom DeHaven

If you met a man who told you that he was from a different universe
(which he called Lostwithal) and that he could learn everything about
you simply by having his pet wasp sting you, would you believe him?
Or would you think he was crazy? This really happened to Geebo, and
at first he did think the man was crazy. But Geebo was no stranger to
unusual happenings. To start with, he had lost his memory—he just
woke up one morning with nothing on his mind but the word "Geebo,"
which he took for his name. Since that day he had been living in a
cardboard box and washing windshields for small change. But now
Jack, who claimed to come from a different universe, had come along
to put some real excitement into Geebo's world.

Jack was fleeing from the Mage of Four, Mage of Luck. This Mage
had evil plans that would put an end to all the universes. Jack and his
master, Squintik, had dodged the Mage's wrath by escaping to our
world. But they had to get back to Lostwithal to inform their King of
the Mage's scheme of destruction. The great King Agel was the only one
who could defeat the Mage and preserve the worlds.

While hiding out on our planet, Jack and Squintik managed to stir
up a lot of excitement. The Mage sent a Finder and four Claws to track
them down and destroy them. The Finder was disguised as an ordinary
man, and the Claws were vicious little creatures trained to kill. A
bloody battle in a hospital pitted Jack, Geebo, a bag lady, a beautiful
college student, and Herb the chauffeur against the Finder and the
Claws. Thanks to some sorcery (including a hand that operated without
a body and a room that froze over), Jack and company were the victors.
But the war had just begun. Would Jack, his master, and his human
friends be able to reach Lostwithal and warn the great King? Or would
the wicked Mage destroy them first?

                              —*Susan Weaver*

Wanted . . . Mud Blossom   Grades 3-4
By Betsy Byars

Ralphie was in love with Maggie—had been for ages, ever since he'd heard her tell the story of how she had busted *into* the city jail. But the feeling wasn't mutual, and Ralphie had to realize that. He just wouldn't: he hung around her a lot; couldn't she see how much he liked her? Maybe, just maybe, he could change her mind.

On their way home from school one day, Maggie and Ralphie found the old sack that the Bag Lady always carried. It had a possum inside, a dead possum! Ralphie wanted to pitch the sack right then—it really stank! But Maggie wanted to show it to the police—she was convinced that old Mad Mary had been kidnapped. The Bag Lady carried that sack everywhere. She must have been ready to cook the possum for her dinner when somebody, or something, stopped her. But why had the bag been left lying on the ground? Mad Mary would *never* have left it, even for a minute. Maggie suspected a kidnapping, but Ralphie wondered. Who would *want* to kidnap an old lady who hadn't had a bath for fifteen years?

Know where the Bag Lady is now? She's lying on an old, cold floor, and a monster is after her—the same monster that's been chasing her ever since she was a little girl. Will she be able to escape? Will Ralphie and Maggie and the police be able to reach her in time?

—Maggie Carey

War Boy: Grade 5-Adult
A Country Childhood
By Michael Foreman

The war came to our home with the force of a bomb. It *was* a bomb, actually. It crashed through the roof, flew by my bed, bounced over my mother's bed, smashed the mirror, and exploded up the chimney. It was an incendiary, a fire bomb. That was as close as the Germans ever got to me personally, but they and the rest of the war effort had a huge effect on my life. Our village was located on the coast of England near an air base, which made it a prime gathering-place for Allied servicemen as well as a target for all sorts of Nazi deviltry. From the time I could walk until I'd almost finished grade school, my life was saturated with war. We played on abandoned jeeps, drilled with the King's Own Scottish Borderers, spent long nights in bomb shelters, enjoyed showers of gum from passing Americans, and watched barrage balloons go up like circus tents.

Through it all, everyday life went on for me and the rest of the kids in the village. We learned to cope with living on a military target, and we accepted the prospect of an exploding chimney as just another one of the normal surprises of growing up.

What's daily life like for a *War Boy*? Come with me and I'll show you.

—Jeff Blair

The Warnings   Grades 5–8
By Margaret Buffie

Suppose you could see things *before* they happened, important things like fires or drownings. You could warn people of danger (that is, if they'd listen to you). But you'd probably feel like a freak—which is how Rachel felt. She knew she was different; still, she had friends, until her mother left the farm and Dad had to go on the road to support them. He felt he had no choice but to dump her on her great aunt in an old house in the city. That meant a new school and *no* friends, and feeling more different than ever. On top of that, the house was filled with retired circus people—"fossils," Rachel called them. And as if *that* weren't enough, Rachel sensed a threatening ghost in her attic room. Her premonitions hadn't warned her about that. Nor had she foreseen that her lockermate at school would be the boy next door (a total dweeb!). Then she felt the ghost getting anxious, and she realized that there was more than one spirit—and they were fighting over *her*. Share Rachel's fears as she finds out what is going on, why she is there, and whether her powers will be strong enough to fight back the evil hovering over the old house.

—Sarah M. Thrash

A Wave in Her Pocket: Grades 3–6
Stories from Trinidad
By Lynn Joseph, retel.

Almost every family in Trinidad has a Tantie. A Tantie is usually a great-aunt, and she always has a story—a story to teach her nieces and nephews a lesson, or to make them laugh, or to give them a good shiver. Amber and her four cousins love and respect their Tantie because no matter what, Tantie can tell a story. Tantie has stories about strange creatures like the soucouyant and the ligahoo, and scary creatures like the jumbies. As a matter of fact, the jumbies are practically her neighbors. Tantie lives on a lonesome street. At one end of the street is a forgotten graveyard, at the other is Tantie's house, and in between there's nothing except grass and left-over pieces of houses that used to be there. Many years ago, the jumbies, the spirits of the graveyard, forced the people to move out of their homes and broke the houses to pieces.

When Tantie invites Amber and her cousins to her house for a sleepover party, the children are frightened about spending the night so close to the haunted graveyard. They're afraid that the jumbies will come into Tantie's house when it's dark. But Tantie tells them not to worry, the jumbies won't come into *her* home. Then, in the middle of their party, the lights go out! Is it the jumbies? Yes, it is! But Tantie makes the children feel better by telling them a story that explains why the jumbies will never come inside—and also why they knock the lights out from time to time. This story is one of six that will captivate you just as surely as they captivated Amber and her cousins.

—Maureen Whalen

Weasel
By Cynthia DeFelice
Grades 5–8

Weasel's dead, it's true, but in some ways I don't think he'll ever die. There's those of us who'll never be the same because of knowing him. And even if Weasel's not around, there's likely to be someone else like him, or some other kind of meanness and sorrow and sadness. But there's plowing and planting, and kinfolk and Kansas, and whistling and fiddling, too. That's what Ezra wanted to tell me, I think. And I reckon if he can let go of hating Weasel, I can too.

Nathan, not yet twelve, and his younger sister Molly follow a speechless stranger to their father, who has been severely wounded and left to die by Weasel, the renegade killer. That's when Nathan decides to track Weasel down and kill him, to get even for this horrible crime. But Nathan discovers that the mission of revenge doesn't always make you feel good inside.

—Betty A. Holtzen

Whatever Became of Aunt Margaret?   Grades 5–9
By Gene DeWeese

Everyone says my Aunt Margaret died last Sunday. I don't believe it, and neither does my twin sister Julie. Because we know the truth about Aunt Margaret—we've known it for the past ten years, ever since we saved Aunt Margaret, saved her from creatures from another time and place who were trying to take her away.

When Aunt Margaret showed up one Sunday and offered to take Julie and me for a ride in her Studebaker, we hoped we'd end up at Dairy Queen for ice cream. Instead, we ended up traveling into another dimension, fighting off evil beings right out of a science-fiction movie, and throwing water into innocent people's faces! And I wound up having my mind put into another person's body.

The really weird part was that we thought we were doing this for Aunt Margaret—only she wasn't really Aunt Margaret at all, but something completely different. And you know what? It didn't bother us one little bit!

—Nancy A. Weitendorf

When Grandfather's Parrot   Grades 3–4
Inherited Kennington Court
By Linda Allen

When Grandfather Kennington's will was read, all the greedy relatives waiting to get their hands on his fortune were shocked and horrified. Carey, his pet parrot, was the sole beneficiary of the entire English manor estate. All the relatives could continue to use the house as long as Carey remained in good health, but when the parrot died, everything would go to charity. There was only one possible exception built into the will: if anyone found the key to a small box that was kept in the lawyer's office, that person would inherit the entire fortune.

The relatives were more than happy to accept young Miranda's offer to look after Carey. That would give the child something to do and keep her out of their way while they rummaged through the closets and tore up the rugs, hunting for the key.

That's how it all began, on the day *When Grandfather's Parrot Inherited Kennington Court.* How will it all end? Will Carey remain the world's wealthiest parrot, or will somebody find that key?

—Frances W. Levin

When I Dance   Grades 9–Adult
By James Berry

Take a rural Jamaican imagination, transport it to inner-city England, and watch the language dance!

There's Granny: "Toothless, she kisses with fleshly lips rounded, like mouth of a bottle, all wet. She bruises your face almost, with two loving tree-root hands."

There's a letter, signed Your One Baby-Person. "I say 'GA, GA,' and you know I say, 'Go-Ahead, Go-Ahead. Make funny faces, talk, sing, tickle. Please. Make me chuckle this time, next time, every time.'"

There's a question: "Girls, Can We Educate We Dads?"

> Listn the male chauvinist is mi dad—
> A girl walkin night street mus be bad.
> He dohn say, the world's a free place
> For a girl to keep her unmolested space.
> Instead he say—a girl is a girl.

There's a Barkday party for Runabout and his six dog friends.

There's a Sunny Market Song for everyone to try.

There're Jamaican proverbs like, "De tick wha flog de black dog wi whip de white one." (The same stick that flogs the black dog will also whip the white one.)

There're riddles like,

> Riddle my this, riddle my that—
> guess my riddle, or perhaps not.
> Little pools cluster in my father's yard,
> A speck in one and it overflows—what is it?
> (Somebody's eye with dust in it.)

Berry says, "What do we do with a difference? Do we communicate to it, let application acknowledge it for barriers to fall down?" Lord, they tumble down here!

—Lesley S. J. Farmer

When Kids Drive Kids Crazy: Grades 5–8
How to Get Along with Your Friends and Enemies
By Eda LeShan

The other day Sylvia was talking to the school counselor: "Last week
I was in the girls' bathroom giving myself my shot of insulin when I
heard a sound. I looked up and there were two girls from my class
peeking over at me. I wanted to crawl away and hide. When I went out
for recess they were whispering and looking over at me. I just knew they
were talking about me. It's not fair! Why do I have to be different? Why
do I have to be the one with diabetes?"

Melissa screamed at her mother, "I'll kill myself if you throw out
those jeans!" She was talking about her favorite jeans . . . the ones
with the big hole in the knee, just like everyone else wears.

Jonathan, an A and B student in sixth grade, began bringing home
Cs and even a D on his report card. His parents were shocked and concerned about this sudden change. Jonathan's teacher gave them a clue
when she told them that it wasn't cool to be smart. The popular boys
were the jocks, interested only in sports.

Have you ever felt left out? Alone? Different? When you care about
being accepted, it's *not* cool to be different. It's *not* cool to have diabetes, to wear stiff new jeans, or to be too smart. What can you do about
it? Maybe this book can give you some ideas.

—Carol Kappelmann

Where Rag Dolls   Grade 10–Adult
Hide Their Faces
By Lesley Koplow

I think Rafael puzzled me the most. When I went to observe him in
his class, I couldn't find him at first. He was crouched under an easel,
looking fierce, despite his precarious position. He looked like a statue
on a shaky pedestal ready to collapse at any moment. I didn't dare
come too close and risk startling him. Instead, I introduced myself from
a distance and said, "I'm going to come and visit you every day. When
you feel safe with me, we'll go and play in my special room."

I am Lesley Koplow. I work with troubled children at a Headstart
center in New York City. Rafael is one of them. He lives just a few
blocks from the school, so I was able to schedule a home visit immediately; I needed to get some kind of handle on Rafael's fears. Our
student intern went along too.

Rafael's mother, Digna, welcomed us into the apartment. It was clean and neat, in contrast to the building hallways. Rafael was crouched behind a chair in his usual statue-like pose, but did seem to look at us with recognition. Digna took Rafael into the bedroom to play while we talked. He immersed himself in a box filled with Leggos, Gobots, robots, and Transformers. This conglomeration of pieces attracted his undivided attention.

"Tell me, when did Rafael start to be quiet the way he is now?" I asked in Spanish. Digna spoke in a low voice, relating a mysterious event in Rafael's early life. One evening when Rafael was two he suddenly began screaming. He was alone in the living room at the time, but both parents immediately rushed to his aid, only to find nothing apparently wrong. Rafael kept screaming for the better part of two hours, until he exhausted himself and fell asleep. He awoke the next morning silent and distant, and has been in his own little world ever since.

Rafael's behavior is scary. He seems oblivious to everything and everyone most of the time. The only exception is when disaster strikes. If a toy breaks, a tower of blocks crashes to the floor, or a classmate gets hurt, he dissolves into laughter. Rafael's only source of amusement is destruction. He is also extremely attached to one toy, a Gobot. There has to be more to Rafael's withdrawal than a single screaming episode as a toddler. His fascination with the robot toys and destruction have to be the keys. If I could just find the locks they fit.

Rafael is only one of the special four-year-olds I work with. Shirin is a sweet shy girl still in diapers, who sweeps through the playroom buzzing like a fly. Louie is intelligent beyond his years, able to read the printing on billboards and toys, but unable to share his thoughts or his feelings. Robin, intelligent as he is, has no concept of fun, thanks to a father who restricts his every movement, seeing Robin only as a bad boy.

How much can I help these beautiful children in just one year? Share their stories and mine in *Where Rag Dolls Hide Their Faces*.

—*Bernice D. Crouse*

Where'd You Get the Gun, Billy?   Grades 7–12
By Fran Arrick

Murder! A word seldom heard in the small town of Crestview. An event that was never supposed to happen in that protected community. Lisa is dead—a high school girl, shot by her own boyfriend.

Lisa's best friends—Liz Goldman, Ellen Holly, and Andrea Mc-Bride—are looking for answers. So is David Fuller, even though he was only an acquaintance. He can't get the murder off his mind.

Why would anybody shoot someone like Lisa? What was going on in the killer's head when he pulled the trigger? And where did he get that gun?

Police Lieutenant Wisnewski tries to help David and Liz find the answers, but he has to be honest with them, even when it hurts.

Do David and Liz find the answers? Can they make sense of a meaningless act of violence?

—*Mary Cosper*

White Hare's Horses   Grades 5–12
By Penina Keen Spinka

White Hare is a Chumash Indian, living in the hills near the Pacific Ocean in what is now California. A gentle and peaceful people, the Chumash lead a quiet life, tending to their everyday affairs.

Quiet, that is, until the day the strangers from the south arrive. These strangers call themselves "Aztecs," and with them are four powerful animals, such as the Chumash have never seen. The Aztecs call these animals "horses," and the Chumash are terrified of them.

Willingly, however, the Chumash give welcome to the strangers. White Hare grows especially close to the Aztecs, teaching them her language and learning theirs.

A friendship develops, until the day when the Aztec warriors reveal their true purpose for being in the Chumash lands, a purpose that will mean the death of many Chumash.

On his deathbed, White Hare's grandfather told her that one day she would need to draw upon her courage to save her people from destruction. Now it seems that the prophecies of that wise man have come true. His spirit has shown White Hare what she must do, but will she be able to do it? Can one young girl really make the difference between life and death for an entire village?

Though it may mean her own death, it's a risk White Hare has to take. She's the only chance the Chumash have of living safely once again.

—*Melinda D. Waugh*

Why the Whales Came   Grades 5–8
By Michael Morpurgo

Hi, my name is Gracie. I live on Bryher Island, just off the coast of England. I remember the year I was ten. It was the year of the boats, of Birdman the hermit, of the curse, and the beginning of World War One. It was the year the whales came, and it all began with a pair of swans.

Every summer my best friend Daniel and I would work on our collection of boats. Daniel would carve them and I would make the sails. We had quite a fleet of blue and white boats that we would sail on a quiet pool. Only that summer when I was ten a pair of swans decided that the pool was theirs and we were no longer welcome. We tried some of the bays around the island, but they were either too rough or too public. It was Daniel who decided we should try Rushy Bay. I didn't want to, because that was where the Birdman lived. Nobody understood the old hermit, and children were warned to stay away from him. But Rushy Bay was perfect for sailing our boats, and before long Daniel and I got to know the Birdman.

It was Daniel who knew the Birdman best, for they both loved to carve. It was Daniel who first learned about the curse on Samson Island, across from Rushy Bay. The Birdman had been a boy when it happened. Narwhales had beached themselves on Samson. When the people found out, they killed the whales for their ivory tusks. All the men then loaded a ship to take the ivory to the market. The ship capsized, and all hands were lost. On the island the crops failed, the wells dried up, and the people had to leave. Samson Island was cursed.

But as we were getting to know the Birdman, life on our own island began to change—for the worse. Father had joined the navy and had gone off to war. People started accusing the Birdman of lighting signal fires on Samson, to help enemy boats. Then word came that Father was missing in action. And now the whales had come again, to Bryher Island this time. Had the curse of Samson Island reached Bryher? Read *Why the Whales Came* to find out.

—Linda Olson

Windcatcher   Grades 5–8
By Avi

Quartermaster Littlejohn was rudely awoken by the frightened cry—"All hands! All hands!"—and the sounds of breaking wood, shattering crockery, and a shrieking wind. His first thought was that the *Swallow* had come under Rebel attack, but when another great blow shook the ship he knew they were caught in a terrible storm. As the ship rolled, the iron chest he guarded with his life careened against the farthest wall, cracking it. Water poured in. Littlejohn struggled toward the cabin door. As he pulled it open, a wall of water rolled in, pushing him back into the flooded room, almost drowning him.

Tony used the $300 he had made delivering papers to buy a small sailboat named the *Snark*. Sailing it would be the perfect way to spend his summer vacation at his Grandma's house on Long Island Sound. He started sailing lessons on his second day in Swallows Bay, and he loved them. What really kept Tony at it, though, was the legend of the Swallows Bay treasure. He began his search for the sunken treasure with these clues:

—At the end of Haycock Point was a statue of Captain Ezra Littlejohn, the founder of Swallows Bay.

—Tony had an antique ship model his grandfather had bought at a yard sale.

—Every day a mysterious couple left Swallows Bay in a speedboat with digging equipment displayed prominently—shovels and picks which had never been used.

Will Tony find the treasure, or will the couple in the speedboat find it first? Read *Windcatcher* to find out.

—Diantha McCauley

Window   Grade 3–Adult
By Jeannie Baker

We see the world around us every day—from the windows of our houses, from the schools and offices where we work, from the parks where we play. These are views we are so used to that perhaps we don't really see them any more, or notice changes. But there *are* changes—and the world looks very different from the way it did a generation ago. (I am reminded of that whenever I look out my kitchen windows—ugly, hastily constructed houses are marching across what used to be my view of the beautiful mountains.)

Look out a bedroom window and watch the view change, as the child grows up to be a man and the man, in his turn, becomes the father of a child. This may be only one window, but . . . is the view you see here the one you want for your own children?

—*J. R. B.*

Wings   Grades 3–6
By Bill Brittain

My friend Ian Carras grew *wings* the year we were in seventh grade. At first, when he didn't come to school, we thought he must be sick or have a broken leg. But once the truth was out, Ian's dad decided he might as well send him back to school. That first day, most of the class didn't say much about the wings, but I knew what Ian was feeling. See, I'd been considered the class freak before, because of the six fingers on my left hand. But things got worse after school: the ninth graders were waiting for Ian, and when he got home reporters had his house surrounded.

Mama and I decided to take him home with us. There nobody could pester him except his parents—they'd found a doctor to cut his wings off. Well, Ian had a decision to make, but I'll let him tell you the whole story when you read *Wings*, by Bill Brittain.

—*Melanie L. Witulski*

Winning Scheherazade   Grades 5–8
By Judith Gorog

Talk about adventure! I'm a storyteller, and that's what I do—talk about adventure. But tonight I could scarcely believe my ears. This caravan is supposed to be taking us out of the desert to safety, but I overheard the leaders planning their dinner menu—with *me* as main dish! My stories have saved my life before, but I don't think these ruffians—these cannibals—are going to listen. My companion and I will have to escape.

Talk about adventure! It was just a few nights ago that I started out to visit relatives—and since then I've been accused of murder, lost my horse, and had to join up with a scruffy, mysterious stranger. Now we face walking miles across the desert without food or water.

My name is Scheherazade. For my storytelling skills, the Sultan of my land rewarded me with a palace, and for a while my life was easy and peaceful. But now, besides getting out of *this* mess alive, I have two other mysteries to solve. Who is this man I'm walking beside? And who is the flutist at my palace who plays such haunting tunes, but hides whenever we wish to thank him?

—*Willa Jean Harner*

Winter-Broken   Grades 5-8
By Marya Smith

Dawn had learned early in life that the only way to insure that she would not say the wrong thing was to say nothing at all. That way her father wouldn't slap her around, her mother wouldn't yell at her, and her sister wouldn't taunt her. She had to keep the family secret; the prying eyes of classmates, teachers, and social workers must be averted. No one must know that her father was a hard-drinking man who abused his wife and children. Keeping quiet was one of the things Dawn was good at. She was glad of it. Now she had her own secret, and no one knew it. No one could take it away.

Wildfire was the best part of the secret. Oh, his name wasn't really Wildfire; that was just what she called the beautiful horse pastured in the meadow behind their house because it seemed to be the perfect name for him. Eleroy Everly, the old farmer who was the horse's care-taker, was the nicest adult Dawn had ever met. He didn't ask questions she had to answer. And he let her help take care of Wildfire and even let her ride him. Never before had Dawn felt such joy. Never had she been so happy. But it couldn't last; it just could not last. Not all secrets end up staying secrets.

—*Maureen Whalen*

Wish on a Unicorn   Grades 5-6
By Karen Hesse

"Wishes don't ever come true, Hannie. Especially not wishes made on a broken-down old unicorn. Believe me."

That's what Mags says to her seven-year-old sister, Hannie, when Hannie discovers a dirty stuffed unicorn in Newell's field. It's not that Mags doesn't *want* to believe in magic and wishes. She'd like to wish away Hannie's brain damage or keep her little brother Moochie out of trouble. But Mags has learned that the usual answer to a wish is disap-pointment.

But now the wishes do seem to be coming true! Mags suddenly has friends in her sixth-grade class, and pretty clothes to wear. She begins to believe in the unicorn's magic, until trouble strikes, and the only person who can help her is—Mags herself.

—*Donna L. Scanlon*

Witch Baby Grades 7–12
By Francesca Lia Block

Witch Baby didn't feel like part of her family. She watched them from the outside, and none of the pictures she took of them included herself. She didn't know who she was or where she belonged. She wasn't like her sister Cherokee, or her almost-mother Weetzie Bat, or her almost-father, My Secret Agent Lover Man. Weetzie and My Secret had each other, Dirk had Duck, Cherokee had Raphael, and Valentine had Ping. Only Witch Baby was alone. And she was unhappy. So she made sure that everyone else was unhappy too—she screamed, and teased, and she did exactly the things that would make everyone else in her family unhappy. She cut off Cherokee's hair, she ran away, she told Duck's mother that he was gay, she stole Coyote's special Joshua tree seeds, and she took pictures of everyone when they were feeling and looking their worst. She made just as much trouble as she could, And all the time she was crying inside, but she never told anyone, because Witch Babies don't cry, so no one knew how much she was hurting and how alone she felt.

It wasn't until she'd met the angel-boy of her dreams and then lost him, had gone to find her real mother and found her, that Witch Baby began to understand that when you get to know who you are, you find out where you belong, too.

There was a "Once upon a time" for Witch Baby, but will there ever be a "happily ever after"?

—*J. R. B.*

The Witch House Grades 5–8
By Norma Tadlock Johnson

Ginny is the practical one in her family, so when she discovers that there may be a ghost in the house they have inherited from Great Aunt Maybelle, she has a hard time believing it. But now she's convinced, now that she and her brother and sister and even her friend Tom have all felt the rush of cold air from Maybelle's bedroom, and found other rooms in the house ransacked. Then one night Ginny and the others actually see Maybelle's ghost and read her cryptic message: "Go! My house is not for you!"

But what does *that* mean? After all, Ginny and her family were Maybelle's closest relatives, so maybe it *isn't* really Maybelle's ghost that's doing the haunting, but someone trying to scare them out of the house. Maybe someone from the Historical Society! Those ladies claim that Maybelle wanted *them* to have the house after she died.

Who's really haunting Maybelle's house, her ghost or some trickster? What was Maybelle's last wish about her house—the place everyone calls *The Witch House*?

—Anne Liebst

Witch Weed   Grades 3-6
By Phyllis Reynolds Naylor

Considering all the crazy things going on around her, Lynn would appear to be the sanest one in the family. Why then, she wonders, is it *she* who sits in the psychologist's office, ever closer to spilling the beans on the whole "witch thing" with each gentle coaxing of his eyes? If she tells, he'll surely think she's crazy, and then she'll have to prove she isn't. So she waits, remaining silent, but knowing that *it's* all still going on. True, Old Witch Tuggle went up in flames with her house, but what about that glass eye of hers that got hurled into the grasses? Come to think of it, there *are* those strange purple flowers with an odd, familiar scent growing in that area now; they seem to hum each time Lynn approaches. The thought that it's starting again sends a shiver of panic up Lynn's spine. Where can she turn for help? Not to Mom, who's barely been released from Witch Tuggle's spell. After all, Mom just placed a vase of those weird flowers, that "witch weed," on the dining room table! And that big book of spells and potions Lynn found under her dad's bed definitely rules *him* out. Usually Lynn's best friend Mouse would love a mystery like this, but Mouse, it seems, has been hypnotized by the neighborhood girls: Lynn can see them out in the grasses—the witch weed—reciting chants and attracting crows! How can one girl fight against the powers of a witch and all her followers?

Or is there another reason for Lynn's visits to the shrink? Let's hope so, because, if she's *not* crazy, it may be too late for her and her friends and family! Read *Witch Weed* and maybe you'll find out . . . or maybe not!

—Cynthia Cordes

The Witching Hour
By Anne Rice

Adults

Do we really have free will, or are our lives controlled by patterns we did not make? And once we have begun to walk in one of those patterns, are we forced to continue, even against our will, or are we able to break free? Are we actors following our own chosen and mutable script, or are we merely puppets, following the patterns of our lives as someone else pulls our strings? And if you say that *you* are the master of your fate, how do you know absolutely? Perhaps part of the design is your belief that you *are* in charge, when in fact you're not. Michael and Rowan believe that they are free to make their own choices, create their own futures. You will have to decide for yourself if that is true after you have heard their story, and the story of the Mayfair Witches.

First there was Suzanne, then Deborah, Charlotte, and all the rest, and now finally there is Rowan, and Michael with her. And the patterns begin to work, and the pieces fall into place. Their story together begins with a rescue at sea, as Rowan Mayfair, a brilliant neurosurgeon, pulls Michael Curry from the Pacific Ocean and brings him back to life. She has long known that she has special powers, and she has used them to tell if her patients can be saved or not. She fears these powers, though, for she knows she could use them to kill as easily as she uses them to heal. She calls on her powers to save Michael, but at first refuses to let him know who she is, even after she finds out that he acquired special powers of his own during his ordeal. Three months later they meet again and immediately fall in love, unaware of the patterns and forces that may have begun to control their lives. Rowan was an adopted child and knows nothing of her real heritage, her natural family. She knows only that her adoptive mother made her swear never to go to New Orleans or contact any of the Mayfair family who live there. She doesn't know that she is the last of a long line of witches, stretching back over three centuries, haunted, perhaps even controlled, by a powerful, dangerous, and seductive spirit. This spirit (who appears as a tall, slender, dark-haired man) can only be seen by certain members of the family, the witches who inherit the legacy in each generation—the money, the emerald pendant, the power, and the man. At least the Mayfairs believe that only family members can see the man, but Michael grew up in New Orleans and has seen him over and over, starting one Christmas Eve when he was just a child.

And what will happen when Michael takes Rowan back to New Orleans, to the huge house in the Garden District that he yearned after as a child, the house where the Mayfairs lived? Forces are coming together, forces that neither Michael nor Rowan know anything about or can control. *They* believe that they move and love and make their decisions as autonomous human beings—but do they? Or are they bound by patterns of which they are not aware, forced to walk along paths they only think they have chosen? And the story of the Mayfair Witches—will it continue to unfold in Rowan's life, as it has in the lives of all the others in her family, or can she and Michael conquer the past with the power of their love?

—*J. R. B.*

Wizard's Hall   Grades 3-6
By Jane Yolen

How did an absolutely ordinary 11-year-old boy like Henry wind up enrolled at Wizard's Hall, studying magic? It wasn't as if Henry had any special talent. As a matter of fact, Henry lacked the most basic skill of all for becoming a wizard—he was tone-deaf. In other words, he couldn't carry a tune, and if you know anything about what it takes to be a wizard, you know that magic spells have to be chanted in the right pitch, or they won't work. No one who was tone-deaf had ever been accepted as a student at Wizard's Hall. No one until Henry, that is.

So maybe Henry wasn't so ordinary after all. His teachers certainly didn't seem to think so. They changed his name from Henry, which wasn't magical enough, to Thornmallow, which meant prickly on the outside and squishy on the inside. And they kept reminding everyone that Thornmallow was the long-awaited 113th student, the one who was destined to lead them in the approaching conflict.

Thornmallow didn't know exactly what they meant, even when he heard them talking about the Quilted Beast and his evil master. Still, he was willing to try his best at whatever his teachers had in mind. He figured that was the least he could do; he might not be very talented, but he was good at trying. And that, you see, was the point. Because his teachers knew (even if Thornmallow didn't) that in the life-and-death battle ahead, the willingness to try could be the most important talent of all—as well as the most dangerous, because no awards would be given for trying, only for winning. And the penalty for losing would be death, not just for Thornmallow but for everyone at Wizard's Hall—and beyond.

—*Margie Reitsma*

Wolf   Grades 7–12
By Gillian Cross

Who's afraid of the Big Bad Wolf? Cassie is. The wolf has Grandmother Nan, and it's up to Cassie to save her. But no one will believe her—and time is running out.

It all started with the muffled tap on the door in the night. The next morning Cassie was hustled off, as always, to stay with Goldie, her mom. But this time, things were different. Nan sent her on the train alone to find Goldie in vast London. Cassie finally located her mom in an abandoned derelict house, where she was squatting with her friend Lyall and his teenage son Robert. They were supporting themselves by doing dramatic workshops in schools. Their newest, most exciting project was "Wolf."

Cassie's feelings of unease deepened. First she found strange, bright-yellow plastic gunk at the bottom of a bag of groceries Nan had sent with her—and then it disappeared. She couldn't reach Nan—not at home, not at work. So Cassie broke the rules: she sent Nan a postcard with Goldie's address. Then a man was spotted prowling around, Cassie's room was searched, and a note was discovered: "Bring back the stuff in the basket of food," it said, "or Grandmother will die." And it was signed "The Big Bad Wolf." Who *is* the Wolf? Cassie thinks she knows—and she's desperately afraid.

—Diane L. Deuel

Wolf by the Ears   Grade 9–Adult
By Ann Rinaldi

"As it is," Thomas Jefferson wrote about slavery, "we have the wolf by the ears, and we can neither hold him, nor safely let him go."

Harriet Hemings is a slave. Oh, you couldn't tell by looking at her, with her light skin and red hair, her nice clothes. You couldn't tell by the work she does, either—a few hours a day in the weaver's cottage, the rest of the time spent as she pleases. She lives in Monticello, Thomas Jefferson's plantation. Her mother, Sally Hemings, is in charge of the master's wardrobe, and according to some, she was once his mistress. Harriet considers herself black, and although she is called a servant, in her heart she knows that she, her mother, and brothers are all slaves— slaves who could be sold at the master's whim.

The master, Thomas Jefferson, may in fact be her father. There's a persistent rumor to that effect, but Jefferson has never acknowledged Harriet or her brothers as his own. He treats Harriet kindly, making sure that she's well-clothed, well-cared for, educated, and not over-worked. He treats all his "servants" kindly. But at nineteen, Harriet is beginning to wonder about her future. She knows that when she's twenty-one, the master will give her freedom if she asks, but she can't imagine living anywhere else, or being separated from her family. On the other hand, Jefferson is seventy-seven years old, and when he dies, his slaves could be sold to pay off the plantation's debts.

The decision is forced on Harriet one day when the master's son-in-law tries to rape her. Now she must make a choice about her future. Should she leave Monticello, the home and family she loves? What are her prospects as a freed slave in a white society? Harriet has always thought of herself as black, but she could probably pass for white. Should she?

—Rosemary Moran

Wolves   Grade 9–Adult
By Candace Savage

Enter the intriguing world of wolves, part fact, part folklore. Have you ever wondered why wolves are seen as ferocious, evil monsters who cannot wait to sink their fangs into their helpless victims? (Remember the sinister wolf and Little Red Riding Hood? Remember the werewolf?) And yet, at the same time, wolves are also perceived as nurturing, protective beings. According to legend, Romulus and Remus, the founders of Rome, were raised by a she-wolf who rescued them in the forest where they had been left, as babies, to die.

In fact, wolves are very much like human beings in certain basic ways: they are sociable creatures, living in families that include a mother, father, and siblings, and often uncles and aunts as well. Like people, wolves have expressive faces, capable of revealing a wide range of emotions and moods. They can communicate with each other and often co-operate in getting food. And of course they are the ancestors of our own pet dogs—and when we play with them, we are playing with wolves.

For centuries people have been fascinated by these compelling animals. Ancestral Native Americans admired wolves and performed rituals to attain their powers. Wolf cults existed in ancient Rome. In more recent times, horror movies have focused on the transformation of a man into a formidable, howling werewolf. *Wolves* uncovers a wealth of fact and folklore, and captures the splendor of these wild creatures with many stunning photographs.

—Mary Harn Liu

Woman Hollering Creek   Grades 9–Adult
By Sandra Cisneros

"It's Rachel's eleventh birthday, but she wishes she was 102 instead. Because then she would have the courage and wisdom to form and speak the words in her mind, in order to deny the ownership of the old ragged, red sweater the teacher has placed on her desk. The teacher has said it is Rachel's, and adults are always right, correct? So how is Rachel going to go against a person of authority and say, 'You are wrong. It is *not* mine!' And the teacher has already humiliated Rachel by announcing, in front of the whole class, that 'it' belonged to her! Therefore, throughout the morning, that horrible red sweater has just sat there, accusingly, on the corner of Rachel's desk. Rachel has been hating it all morning too, wanting it to disappear. She can't wait till recess, then she will dispose of it somehow or other. But just before the bell rings, the teacher tells her to stop being ridiculous and put the sweater on. And Rachel obeys. And all the time the girl who really owns the sweater is sitting and watching. Rachel's birthday is not a day old yet, but she wishes she were 102, and that eleven was many, many years behind her."

This is only one of the twenty-three *very* short stories in this collection, about the people who live on both sides of an invisible line called the Border, between the United States and Mexico. Some of the stories are narrated by children, some by teenagers, some by adults—married, single, young, old, Anglo and Mexican. These mini-stories are intense, comical, reflective, poignant, dismal and loving—they are life as their narrators have lived it. Share it with them.

—Faye A. Powell

Woman Without a Past   Grade 9–Adult
By Phyllis A. Whitney

Mystery novelist Molly Hunt had always known that she was adopted as a child, but she hadn't the least curiosity about her biological parents until the day she met Charles Landry. He startled Molly with his conviction that she was his fiancée's twin sister.

Learning that she might be a twin was amazing enough, but what really stunned Molly was that apparently she had been kidnapped when she was an infant—stolen from the aristocratic Mountfort family of Charleston, South Carolina. These revelations drew Molly from her home on Long Island down to Charleston. There she met her "real" family—her twin, Daphne; her mother, still grieving, who couldn't accept her; the suspicious family patriarch; and his psychic wife, who warned of *murder*. Molly's reappearance and her questions about the past have awakened dangerous secrets surrounding the Mountforts, stories about a man who died mysteriously on the family estate when she and Daphne were infants. Now these secrets from the past threaten to destroy the Mountfort family—and Molly too.

—Sue Padilla

A World of Ideas II   Grade 9–Adult
By Bill Moyers

Democracy as conversation is an old idea. At one point, "public" could be defined as "a group of strangers who gather to discuss the news." Bill Moyers, public conversationalist par excellence, introduces twenty-eight brilliant public opinions from twenty-eight private citizens.

Maxine Hong Kingston, the Chinese-American writer, says: "I think I teach people how to find meaning. I write about the most chaotic, tragic, hard-to-deal-with events, and these events are sometimes so violent and so horrible that they burst through bounds of form and preconceptions."

Bharati Mukherjee, a writer who came to the United States from India, asserts: "New epic themes are washing up on our shores. We are going through lives that are larger than real in many ways, we new immigrants. We're coming with so much energy and curiosity in order to make new lives for ourselves, that to me, those are big stories to tell, very dense lives to chronicle. Some of the fiction editors don't want to acknowledge the rawness and messiness out there in America."

What about entertainers, or the sports figures who are today's idols? Literary historian Leo Braudy believes "that fame is connected with democracy in a very important way. It is the way we view people, and it is, in part, the way we view ourselves."

And as for people like Johnny Carson, "They are like fairy godparents who come down and tap you and turn the normal everyday you into something special. Myth is underneath it."

If you want to savor the American spirit, if you want to relive Bill Moyer's TV interviews, then sample the ideas of these thoughtful Americans.

—Lesley S. J. Farmer

You Don't Need Words! Grades 3-6
By Ruth Belov Gross

Do you realize that people can say things to each other and be perfectly understood without using words? If you couldn't talk and didn't know how to write, you'd *have* to communicate without words. If you went to a country where no one spoke your language, or if you wanted to leave a message for somebody who couldn't read, you would have to rely on nonverbal communication. You might use gestures, sign language, facial expressions, body language, or signs and symbols to explain what you meant. You might even discover that you don't *need* words!

There are lots of nonverbal languages—Native American picture-writing, the code flags that sailing ships use, sports signals. You can even make up a nonverbal code language of your own, to use with one of your friends. Here are a few things to get you started—can you guess what this means? [End with two or three gestures from the book or show an illustration.]

—Anna Biagioni Hart

You Take the High Road Grades 7-12
By Mary K. Pershall

Samantha has *always* wanted a baby brother or sister. When her mother breaks the news that she is pregnant, it's a dream come true for Sam. She marvels at "the miracle of two cells joining, with a built-in love of chocolate cookies. . . . " She and her reluctant father are even present at the baby's birth, and Sam is awed when she holds little Nicky for the first time—"He was a thing I wished for on falling stars and birthday candles for years."

But taking care of Nicky in her new role as big sister is more challenging than Sam had imagined—babies need a lot of care. But Nicky brings new joy and love into their home, and Sam's special bond with her little brother brings an indescribable happiness to her life.

Just before Nicky's second birthday, he dies in a household accident while Sam's mother is taking a nap. Nicky's death comes as an unbearably brutal blow. Sam can barely manage to function at school, much less talk with her mother, whom she blames for Nicky's death. As her parents are torn apart by grief and guilt, Samantha questions whether there is meaning in life at all.

Can Samantha survive? Can her family?

—Susan A. Jones

Yours Till Niagara Falls: Grades 3–8
A Book of Autograph Verses
Lillian Morrison, comp.

[Note: I have my own autograph book in hand as I begin.]

> Mary had a little lamb.
> She kept it on a shelf.
> And every time it wagged its tail,
> It spanked its little self.

> When you grow up and you have twins,
> Don't come to me for safety pins.

Everyone likes to sign his or her name on something, and it is especially fun to sign a friend's autograph book. It's even *more* fun if you can write something funny. Years later, you and your friend can look back with fond memories.

I thought my friends had spent hours making up the verses they wrote in my autograph book. Whether they did or not, now we have help! In this book, *Yours Till Niagara Falls*, you will find just the right verse for that special friend of yours.

> When you grow old and have no teeth,
> Remember the candy you used to eat.

> Success and happiness run in pairs.
> If you can't find the elevator, use the stairs.

> I love you, I love you, I love you, I do.
> But don't get excited, I love monkeys too!

What do you want to say to your best friend? your worst enemy? or to that certain someone you've got a crush on? Find just the right words in *Yours Till Niagara Falls.*

—Marvia Boettcher

Zoobabies   **Grades 3–6; Adults**
By Michael O'Neill and Carolyn Fireside

In any town I've ever lived in, large or small, the birth of a new animal at the local zoo was an event to celebrate, especially if the new baby was a member of an endangered species. Newspapers and TV stations all tried to be the first to get a picture, and people would sometimes wait in line to get a glimpse of the new arrival and comment on how sweet or cute or funny or awkward or totally charming it was. In this book, Michael O'Neill has given us close-up views of zoobabies from around the country.

Some were easier to photograph than others. [Show pictures from the book as you talk.] The koala Dakin was relaxed enough to let O'Neill get very close to him, while Abrams the armadillo, as you can see, spent his time looking for an escape route—he must be very camera-shy! Bouree, one of only eighteen white, blue-eyed alligators in the world, jumped high off the floor, and Bob the orangutan wanted to take the pictures himself. Patches is a Cape hunting dog, one of a breed that can't be tamed—and looks warily at the camera, ready to protect himself. Patriot is a black-footed penguin, and when he is an adult, he will mate for life, returning to the same nesting site each year. He and his mate will be able to pick out their own chicks from a huge crowd of young birds.

But my favorite is Besar, a Sumatran tiger cub, snarling at the camera from only a foot away—there's no doubt about *his* opinion of this intrusive stranger! Find your own animal favorites in *Zoobabies.*

—J. R. B.

BIBLIOGRAPHY BY AUTHOR

Ackerman, Karen. *The Leaves in October*. Atheneum 1991. (Grades 3-6; 3P, 3Q)

Adams, Douglas and Mark Carwardine. *Last Chance to See*. Harmony 1991. (Adult; 3P, 4Q)

Adamson, Joe. *Bugs Bunny: Fifty Years and Only One Grey Hare*. Holt 1990. (All ages; 4P, 4Q)

Adler, C. S. *A Tribe for Lexi*. Macmillan 1991. (Grades 5-8; 2P, 2Q)

Allen, Linda. *When Grandfather's Parrot Inherited Kennington Court*. Little 1990. (Grades 3-4; 4P, 4Q)

Alther, Lisa. *Bedrock*. Knopf 1990. (Adult; 2P, 3Q)

Anderson, Scott and Les C. Kouba. *Distant Fires*. Pfeifer-Hamilton 1990. (Grade 9-Adult; 3P, 4Q)

Angell, Judie. *Don't Rent My Room!*. Bantam 1990. (Grades 5-8; 2P, 2Q)

Arrick, Fran. *Where'd You Get the Gun, Billy?*. Bantam 1991. (Grades 7-12; 3P, 3Q)

Arter, Jim. *Gruel and Unusual Punishment*. Delacorte 1991. (Grades 5-8; 3P, 3Q)

Asimov, Isaac and Robert Silverberg. *Nightfall*. Doubleday 1990. (Grade 9-Adult; 3P, 4Q)

Auch, Mary Jane. *Kidnapping Kevin Kowalski*. Holiday 1990. (Grades 5-8; 2P, 3Q)

Avi. *Windcatcher*. Bradbury 1991. (Grades 5-8; 3P, 3Q)

Baird, Thomas. *Smart Rats*. Harper 1990. (Grades 7-12; 3P, 3Q)

Baker, Jeannie. *Window*. Greenwillow 1991. (Grade 3-Adult; 3P, 4Q)

Baker, Sharlene. *Finding Signs*. Knopf 1990. (Adult; 3P, 4Q)

Barlowe, Wayne Douglas. *Expedition: Being an Account in Words and Artwork of the 2358 A.D. Voyage to Darwin IV*. Workman 1991. (Grade 9-Adult; 3P, 4Q)

Bausch, Robert. *Almighty Me*. Houghton 1991. (Adult; 4P, 4Q)

Beatty, Patricia and Phillip Robbins. *Eben Tyne, Powdermonkey*. Morrow 1990. (Grades 5-8; 2P, 3Q)

Benchley, Peter. *Beast*. Random 1991. (Grade 9-Adult; 3P, 3Q)

Bennett, James. *I Can Hear the Mourning Dove*. Houghton 1990. (Grades 7-12; 4P, 4Q)

Benson, Michael. *Dream Teams: Best Teams of All Time*. Little 1991. (Grade 5-Adult; 3P, 3Q)

Berry, James. *When I Dance*. Harcourt 1991. (Grade 9-Adult; 3P, 3Q)

Blackwood, Gary L. *Beyond the Door*. Atheneum 1991. (Grades 7-8; 2P, 3Q)

Block, Francesca Lia. *Witch Baby*. HarperCollins 1991. (Grades 7-12; 3P, 4Q)

Bode, Janet. *Truce: Ending the Sibling War*. Watts 1991. (Grades 9-12; 2P, 4Q)

Booth, David, comp. *Voices on the Wind*. Morrow 1990. (Grades 3-6; 2P, 4Q)

Bradbury, Ray. *A Graveyard for Lunatics*. Knopf 1990. (Grade 9-Adult; 3P, 3Q)

Branscum, Robbie. *Old Blue Tilley*. Macmillan 1991. (Grades 5-6; 2P, 3Q)

Brennan, J. H. *Shiva Accused: An Adventure of the Ice Age*. HarperCollins 1991. (Grades 5-8; 3P, 3Q)

Brittain, Bill. *Professor Popkin's Prodigious Polish*. Harper 1990. (Grades 3-6; 3P, 3Q)

———. *Wings*. HarperCollins 1991. (Grades 3-6; 3P, 3Q)

P's and Q's: Point to Remember

P (Popularity)	Q (Quality Level)
4P— The book everyone wants to read	4Q—Couldn't be better.
3p— Most people will want this after they hear about it	3Q—Some flaws, but nothing to hinder the story.
2P— Booktalking can sell this, but it may need pushing	2Q—Major flaws; worth pushing only because of its high P rating.
1P— For the special reader, or for those into the subject.	

All titles are recommended for use with the designated age group.
The rating scale is adapted from that used in *Voices of Youth Advocates*.

Brooke, William J. *A Telling of Tales.* Harper 1990. (Grades 3-8; Adults; 2P, 4Q)

Brooks, Bruce. *Everywhere.* Harper 1990. (Grades 5-8; 3P, 4Q)

Brooks, Jerome. *Naked in Winter.* Orchard 1990. (Grades 7-8; 2P, 3Q)

Brooks, Martha. *Paradise Cafe and Other Stories.* Little 1988 (U.S. 1990). (Grades 7-12; 2P, 3Q)

Browne, Howard. *Scotch on the Rocks.* St. Martin's 1991. (Grade 9-Adult; 4P, 3Q)

Buffie, Margaret. *The Warnings.* Scholastic 1991. (Grades 5-8; 3P, 3Q)

Bunting, Eve. *The Hideout.* Harcourt 1991. (Grades 5-8; 4P 3Q)

_____. *Our Sixth-Grade Sugar Baby Blues.* Lippincott 1990. (Grades 3-6; 3P, 4Q)

Busch, Frederick. *Harry and Catherine.* Knopf 1990.(Adult; 2P, 4Q)

Byars, Betsy. *Wanted . . . Mud Blossom.* Delacorte 1991. (Grades 3-4; 4P, 4Q)

Callen, Larry. *Contrary Imaginations.* Greenwillow 1991. (Grades 5-8; 2P, 3Q)

Cameron, Peter. *Leap Year.* Harper 1990. (Adult; 3P, 4Q)

Cannon, A. E. *Amazing Gracie.* Delacorte 1991. (Gra&es 7-12; 2P, 3Q)

_____. *The Shadow Brothers.* Delacorte 1990. (Grades 7-12; 3P, 4Q)

Cape, Tony. *The Last Defector.* Doubleday 1991. (Adult; 3P, 4Q)

Caraker, Mary. *The Faces of Ceti.* Houghton 1991. (Grades 7-12; 1P, 3Q)

Caras, Roger, ed. *Roger Caras' Treasury of Great Horse Stories.* Dutton 1990. (Grade 10-Adult; 2P, 4Q)

Carris, Joan. *The Greatest Idea Ever.* Lippincott 1990. (Grades 3-6; 3P, 3Q)

Carter, Peter. *Borderlands.* Farrar 1990. (Grade 7-Adult; 3P, 4Q)

Cary, Lorene. *Black Ice.* Knopf 1991. (Grade 9-Adult; 2P, 4Q)

Caseley, Judith. *Kisses.* Random 1990.(Grades 7-12; 3P, 3Q)

Castaneda, Omar S. *Among the Volcanoes.* Lodestar 1991. (Grades 7-12; 2P, 3Q)

Cates, Emily. *The Ghost in the Attic.* Bantam 1990. (Grades 5-8; 4P, 4Q)

Chandra, Deborah. *Balloons and Other Poems.* Farrar 1990. (Grades 3-4; 2P, 3Q)

Christian, Peggy. *The Old Coot.* Atheneum 1991. (Grades 3-6; 3P 3Q)

Ciardi, John. *Mummy Took Cooking Lessons and Other Poems.* Houghton 1990. (Grades 7-12; 2P, 4Q)

Cisneros, Sandra. *Woman Hollering Creek.* Random 1991. (Grades 9-Adult; 4P, 4Q)

Clarke, Judith. *The Torment of Mr. Gully: Stories of the Supernatural.* Holt 1990. (Grades 7-12; 2P, 3Q).

Clements, Bruce. *Tom Loves Anna Loves Tom.* Farrar 1990. (Grades 7-12; 2P, 3Q)

Clifford, Eth. *Harvey's Wacky Parrot Adventure.* Houghton 1990. (Grades 3-4; 4P, 4Q)

Connolly, Pat. *Coaching Evelyn: Fast, Faster, Fastest Woman In The World.* Harper Collins 1991. (Grades 5-12; 2P, 3Q)

Cohn, Livingston, Myra (sel). *Poems for Grandmothers.* Holiday 1990. (Grade 5-Adult; 2P, 4Q)

Collier, James Lincoln. *My Crooked Family.* S&S 1991. (Grades 7-12; 4P, 4Q)

Collins, Max Allan. *Stolen Away.* Bantam 1991. (Grade 9-Adult; 2P, 3Q)

Conford, Ellen. *Loving Someone Else.* Bantam 1991. (Grades 7-12; 3P, 3Q)

Conly, Jane Leslie. *R-T, Margaret and the Rats of NIMH.* Harper 1990. (Grades 3-8; 3P, 4Q)

Cooney, Caroline B. *Twenty Pageants Later.* Bantam 1991. (Grades 5-8; 3P, 3Q)

Cooper, J. California. *The Matter Is Life.* Doubleday 1991. (Adult; 2P, 4Q)

Corcoran, Barbara. *Stay Tuned.* Atheneum 1991. (Grades 7-8; 3P, 3Q)

Cormier, Robert; edited by Constance Senay Cormier. *I Have Words to Spend: Reflections of a Small-Town Editor.* Delacorte 1991. (Adult; 3P, 4Q)

Crichton, Michael. *Jurassic Park.* Knopf 1990. (Grade 9-Adult; 3P, 4Q)

Cottonwood, Joe. *The Adventures of Boone Barnaby.* Scholastic 1990. (Grades 5-7; 4P, 4Q)

Coville, Bruce. *Jeremy Thatcher, Dragon Hatcher.* Harcourt 1991. (Grades 3-6; 3P, 3Q)

_____. *Monster of the Year.* Pocket 1989. (Grades 5-8; 3P, 3Q)

Crew, Linda. *Someday I'll Laugh About This*. Delacorte 1990. (Grades 5-8; 3P 3Q)

Cross, Gillian. *Wolf*. Holiday 1991. (Grades 7-12; 3P, 3Q)

Dailey, Janet. *Masquerade*. Little 1990. (Grade 10-Adult; 4P, 3Q)

Dale, Mitzi. *Round the Bend*. Delacorte 1991. (Grades 7-8; 3P, 3Q)

Dalton, Annie. *Out of the Ordinary*. Harper 1990. (Grades 7-12; 3P, 4Q)

Danziger, Paula. *Make Like a Tree and Leave*. Delacorte 1990. (Grades 5-8; 3P, 3Q)

Deaver, Julie Reece. *First Wedding, Once Removed*. Harper 1990. (Grades 5-8; 2P, 3Q)

DeClements, Barthe. *Breaking Out*. Delacorte 1991. (Grades 5-6; 3P, 3Q)

DeFelice, Cynthia. *Weasel*. Macmillan 1990. (Grades 5-8; 4P, 4Q)

Degens, T. *On the Third Ward*. Harper 1990. (Grades 7-12: 2P, 4Q)

DeHaven, Tom. *Walker of Worlds*. Doubleday 1990. (Grade 9-Adult; 4P, 4Q)

DeWeese, Gene. *Whatever Became of Aunt Margaret?*. Putnam 1990. (Grades 5-9; P, Q)

Durell, Ann and Marilyn Sachs, eds. *The Big Book for Peace*. Dutton 1990. (Grade 3-Adult; 4P, 4Q)

Edwards, Richard. *A Mouse in My Roof*. Delacorte 1990. (Grades 3-9; 1P, 2Q)

Erdoes, Richard. *Crying for a Dream*. Bear 1990. (Grade 9-Adult; 2P, 3Q)

Farish, Terry. *Shelter for a Seabird*. Greenwillow 1990. (Grades 9-12; 2P, 4Q)

Farris, John. *Fiends*. Dark Harvest 1990. (Grade 9-Adult; 3P, 4Q)

Faulkner, Matt. *The Moon Clock*. Scholastic 1991. (Grades 3-6; 1P, 3Q)

Feinstein, John. *Forever's Team*. Villard 1990. (Grade 10-Adult; 2P, 4Q)

Feldman, Eve B. *Seymour, the Formerly Fearful*. Macmillan 1990. (Grades 3-6; 4P, 4Q)

Fenner, Carol. *Randall's Wall*. McElderry (Collier Macmillan Canada) 1991. (Grades 5-6; 4P, 4Q)

Fenton, Kate. *The Colors of Snow*. Doubleday 1990. (Adult; 3P, 3Q)

Ferguson, Alane. *Cricket and the Cracker Box Kid*. Bradbury 1990. (Grades 3-6; 3P, 4Q)
——. *The Practical Joke War*. Bradbury 1991. (Grades 3-4; 4P, 4Q)

Ferris, Jean. *Against the Grain*. Farrar 1990. (Grades 7-12; 3P, 3Q)

Ferris, Susan. *Author! Author!*. Farrar 1990. (Grades 5-6; 2P, 3Q)

Fisher, M. F. K. *The Boss Dog*. North Point 1991. (Adult; 3P, 4Q)

Fleischman, Paul. *Saturnalia*. Harper 1990. (Grades 7-12; 4P, 4Q)

Fleisher, Paul and Patricia A. Keeler. *Looking Inside: Machines and Constructions*. Atheneum 1990. (Grades 3-4; 1P, 3Q)

Foley, June. *Susanna Siegelbaum Gives Up Guys*. Scholastic 1991. (Grades 5-6; 3P, 2Q)

Foreman, Michael. *War Boy: A Country Childhood*. Arcade 1990. (Grade 5-Adult; 2P, 4Q)

Friedman, Ina R., comp. *The Other Victims: First-Person Stories of Non-Jews Persecuted by the Nazis*. Houghton 1990. (Grades 5-12; 1P, 4Q)

Gaines, Donna. *Teenage Wasteland: Suburbia's Dead End Kids*. Pantheon 1990. (Grade 9-Adult; 3P, 3Q)

Garden, Nancy. *Lark in the Morning*. Farrar 1991. (Grades 9-12; 2P, 3Q)

Geller, Mark. *The Strange Case of the Reluctant Partners*. Harper 1991. (Grades 5-6; 3P, 3Q)

George, Jean Craighead. *On the Far Side of the Mountain*. Dutton 1990. (Grades 3-8; 3P, 4Q)

Geras, Adele. *Happy Endings*. Harcourt 1991. (Grades 7-12; 3P, 3Q)

Getz, David. *Thin Air*. Holt 1990. (Grades 3-6; 3P, 4Q)

Giff, Patricia Reilly. *Matthew Jackson Meets the Wall*. Delacorte 1990. (Grades 3-6; 2P, 3Q)

Giuliano, Geoffrey. *Dark Horse: The Private Life of George Harrison*. Dutton 1990. (Grade 10-Adult; 2P, 3Q)

Glimmerveen, Ulco. *A Tale of Antarctica*. Scholastic 1990. (Grade 3-Adult; 4P, 4Q)

Gordon, Alice and Vincent Virga, eds. *Summer*. Addison-Wesley 1990. (Grade 10-Adult; 3P, 4Q)

Gordon, Ruth, sel. *Time Is the Longest Distance: An Anthology of Poems*. HarperCollins 1991. (Grade 5-Adult; 1P, 3Q)

Gorog, Judith. *Winning Scheherazade*. Atheneum 1991. (Grades 5-8; 2P, 3Q)

Graham, Alastair. *Full Moon Soup, or The Fall of the Hotel Splendide*. Dial 1991. (Grades 3-8; Adults; 2P, 4Q)

Grant, Charles L. *Fire Mask*. Bantam 1991. (Grades 5-6; 3P, 2Q)

Grant, Michael. *Line of Duty*. Doubleday 1991. (Adult; 3P, 3Q)

Greenberg, Martin H. and Waugh, Charles G., sels. *A Newbery Christmas*. Delacorte 1991. (Grades 3-8; 4P, 4Q)

Griffin, Peni R. *Otto from Otherwhere*. McElderry 1990. (Grades 5-8; 3P, 3Q)

Gripe, Maria; translated from the Swedish by Rika Lesser. *Agnes Cecilia*. Harper 1990. (Grades 5-8; 3P, 2Q)

Groening, Matt. *The Big Book of Hell*. Pantheon 1990. (Grade 9-Adult; 4P, 4Q)

Gross, Ruth Belov. *You Don't Need Words!*. Scholastic 1991. (Grades 3-6; 3P, 3Q)

Hall, Lynn. *Dagmar Schultz and the Green-Eyed Monster*. Scribners 1991. (Grades 5-8; 4P, 3Q)

———. *Halsey's Pride*. Scribners 1990. (Grades 5-6; 3P 2Q)

Haseley, Dennis. *Shadows*. Farrar 1991. (Grades 3-4; 3P, 3Q)

Hathorn, Libby. *Thunderwith*. Little 1991 (U.S.). (Grades 7-10; 3P, 3Q)

Hautzig, Esther. *Remember Who You Are: Stories About Being Jewish*. Crown 1990. (Grades 9-Adult; 3P, 3Q)

Heegaard, Marge Eaton. *Coping with Death and Grief*. Lerner 1990. (Grades 3-6; 2P, 4Q)

Heinrich, Bernd. *An Owl in the House*. Joy Street/Little 1990. (Grade 5-Adult; 1P; 4Q)

Heller, David, comp. *Dear God: What Religion Were the Dinosaurs?*. Doubleday 1990. (Adult; 2P, 4Q)

———. *Growing Up Isn't Hard To Do if You Start Out as a Kid*. Random 1991. (Adult; 3P, 3Q)

Herbst, Judith. *Animal Amazing*. Atheneum 1991. (Grade 5-Adult; 2P, 3Q)

Hersey, John. *Fling*. Knopf 1990. (Adult; 2P, 3Q)

Hersom, Kathleen. *The Half Child*. S&S 1991. (Grades 7-12; 2P, 4Q)

Herzig, Alison Cragin. *Boonsville Bombers*. Viking 1991. (Grades 3-4; 2P, 3Q)

Hesse, Karen. *Wish on a Unicorn*. Holt 1991. (Grades 5-6; 3P, 3Q)

Higa, Tomiko. *The Girl with the White Flag*. Kodansha 1991. (Grades 5-8; 3P, 4Q)

Hobbie, W. D. *Bloodroot*. Crown 1991. (Grades 5-8; 3P, 4Q)

Hobbs, Will. *Downriver*. Atheneum 1991. (Grades 7-12; 4P, 4Q)

Holland, Isabelle. *Journey Home*. Scholastic 1990. (Grades 3-6; 3P, 3Q)

———. *The House in the Woods*. Little 1991. (Grades 5-8; 2P, 3Q)

Howard, Ellen. *The Chickenhouse House*. Atheneum 1991. (Grades 3-4; 3P, 4Q)

Howe, James. *Dew Drop Dead*. Atheneum 1990. (Grades 5-12; 4P, 4Q)

Hughes, Ted. *Tales of the Early World*. Farrar 1991. (Grades 3-8; 2P, 3Q)

Hurwitz, Johanna. *School's Out*. Morrow 1991. (Grades 3-4; 3P, 4Q)

Iverson, Carol. *I Bet You Didn't Know That Fish Sleep with Their Eyes Open and Other Facts and Curiosities*. Lerner 1990. (Grades 3-6; 3P, 3Q)

———. *I Bet You Didn't Know That Hummingbirds Can Fly Backwards and Other Facts and Curiosities*. Lerner 1990. (Grades 3-6; 3P, 3Q)

———. *I Bet You Didn't Know That There Are Golf Balls on the Moon and Other Facts and Curiosities*. Lerner 1990. (Grades 3-6; 3P, 3Q)

———. *I Bet You Didn't Know That You Can't Sink in the Dead Sea and Other Facts and Curiosities*. Lerner 1990. (Grades 3-6; 3P, 3Q)

Jacobs, Paul Samuel. *Sleepers, Awake*. Scholastic 1991. (Grades 5-8; 2P, 2Q)

Janeczko, Paul B., comp. *The Place My Words Are Looking For: What Poets Say About and Through Their Work*. Bradbury 1990. (Grades 3-8; 1P, 4Q)

Jeffers, Susan (adapted from a speech by Chief Seattle). *Brother Eagle, Sister Sky*. Dial 1991. (Grades 3-12; 3P, 4Q)

Johanson, Dr. Donald C. and Kevin O'Farrell. *Journey from the Dawn: Life with the World's First Family.* Villard 1990. (Grade 9-Adult; 4P, 2Q)

Johnson, Annabel. *I Am Leaper.* Scholastic 1990. (Grades 3-6; 3P, 3Q)

Johnson, Julie Tallard. *Celebrate You!.* Lerner 1990. (Grades 7-12; 1P, 4Q)

Johnson, Norma Tadlock. *The Witch House.* Avon 1990. (Grades 5-8; 3P, 3Q)

Jolley, Elizabeth. *Cabin Fever.* Harper 1990. (Adult; 2P, 3Q)

Jones, Adrienne. *Long Time Passing.* Harper 1990. (Grade 9-Adult; 3P, 3Q)

Jones, Diana Wynne. *Castle in the Air.* Greenwillow 1991. (Grades 7-12; 2P, 4Q)

Jones, Rebecca C. *Germy Blew the Bugle.* Arcade 1990. (Grades 5-6; 3P, 4Q)

Joseph, Lynn, retel. *A Wave in Her Pocket: Stories from Trinidad.* Clarion 1991. (Grades 3-6; 2P, 4Q)

Kay, Susan. *Phantom.* Delacorte 1991. (Adult; 3P, 4Q)

Kehret, Peg. *Sisters Long Ago.* Dutton 1990. (Grades 5-9; 3P, 3Q)

Kennedy, Raymond. *Ride a Cockhorse.* Ticknor & Fields 1991. (Adult; 4P, 4Q)

Kennedy, X. J. *Fresh Brats.* McElderry 1990. (Grades 5-12; 3P, 4Q)

——. *The Kite That Braved Old Orchard Beach: Year-Round Poems for Young People.* Macmillan 1991. (Grades 5-12; 3P, 4Q)

Kilworth, Garry. *The Foxes of FirstDark.* Doubleday 1990. (Adult; 4P, 2Q)

Kinsey-Warnock, Natalie. *The Night the Bells Rang.* Cobblehill 1991. (Grades 5-6; 3P, 4Q)

Kirwan-Vogel, Anna. *The Jewel of Life.* Harcourt 1991. (Grades 7-8; 3P, 3Q)

Koertge, Ron. *The Boy in the Moon.* Little 1990. (Grades 7-12; 3P; 4Q)

Koplow, Lesley. *Where Rag Dolls Hide Their Faces.* Dutton 1990. (Grade 10-Adult; 1P, 4Q)

Korman, Gordon. *Losing Joe's Place.* Scholastic 1990. (Grades 7-12; 3P, 4Q)

——. *Macdonald Hall Goes Hollywood.* Scholastic 1991. (Grades 5-8; 3P, 3Q)

Kwitz, Mary DeBall. *The Bell Tolls at Mousehaven Manor.* Scholastic 1991. (Grades 3-4; 3P, 3Q)

Lamb, David. *Stolen Season.* Random 1991. (Grades 9-Adult; 1P, 4Q)

Lamb, Wendy, ed. *Hey Little Walter, and Other Prize-Winning Plays.* Delacorte 1991. (Grades 7-12; 3P, 3Q)

Larrick, Nancy, comp. *To the Moon and Back: A Collection of Poems.* Delacorte 1991. (Grades 3-8; 2P, 4Q)

Lawrence, Louise. *Andra.* HarperCollins 1991 (U.S.). (Grades 9-12; 2P, 4Q)

LeShan, Eda. *When Kids Drive Kids Crazy: How to Get Along with Your Friends and Enemies.* Dial 1990. (Grades 5-8; 1P, 3Q)

Levin, Betty. *Brother Moose.* Greenwillow 1990. (Grades 5-6; 4P, 3Q)

Lewis, Claudia. *Up in the Mountains and Other Poems of Long Ago.* HarperCollins 1991. (Grade 5-Adult; 2P, 4Q)

Lindwer, Willy. *The Last Seven Months of Anne Frank.* Random 1991. (Grade 9-Adult; 2P, 3Q)

Lingard, Joan. *Tug of War.* Lodestar 1990. (Grades 5-8; 3P, 3Q)

Lisson, Deborah. *The Devil's Own.* Holiday 1990. (Grades 9-12; 2P, 3Q)

Lopez, Barry. *Crow and Weasel.* North Point 1990. (Grade 3-Adult; 3P, 4Q)

Lowry, Lois. *Anastasia at This Address.* Houghton 1991. (Grades 5-6; 3P, 3Q)

Macauley, David. *Black and White.* Houghton 1990. (Grade 3-Adult; 3P, 4Q)

Macdonald, Maryann. *Fatso Jean, the Ice Cream Queen.* Bantam 1990. (Grades 3-4; 2P, 3Q)

MacLachlan, Patricia. *Journey.* Delacorte 1991. (Grades 3-6; 3P, 4Q)

Mahy, Margaret. *The Door in the Air and Other Stories.* Delacorte 1991. (Grades 3-6; 3P, 4Q)

Manes, Stephen. *Make Four Million Dollars by Next Thursday.* Bantam 1991. (Grades 3-6; 4P, 4Q)

Marino, Jan. *The Day That Elvis Came to Town*. Little 1991. (Grades 7-12; 3P, 3Q)

Marsh, James. *Bizarre Birds and Beasts: Animal Verses*. Dial 1991. (Grades 3-6; 2P, 3Q)

Masters, Susan Rowan. *The Secret Life of Hubie Hartzel*. Lippincott 1990. (Grades 3-6; 3P, 4Q)

Mazer, Harry. *Someone's Mother Is Missing*. Delacorte 1990. (Grades 7-12; 2P, 3Q)

Mazer, Norma Fox. *Babyface*. Greenwillow 1990. (Grades 7-8; 3P, 3Q)

_____. *D, My Name Is Danita*. Scholastic 1991. (Grades 7-12; 4P, 3Q)

McCaffrey, Anne. *The Rowan*. Ace/Putnam 1990. (Grade 9-Adult; 4P, 4Q)

McCuaig, Sandra. *Blindfold*. Holiday 1989. (Grades 7-12; 3P, 3Q)

McVey, Vicki. *The Sierra Club Book of Weatherwisdom*. Sierra Club 1991. (Grades 5-8; 1P, 3Q)

Meyer, Carolyn. *The Two Faces of Adam*. Bantam 1991. (Grades 9-12; 3P, 4Q)

Morpurgo, Michael. *Why the Whales Came*. Scholastic 1990. (Grades 5-8; 2P, 3Q)

Morrison, Lillian, comp. *Yours Till Niagara Falls: A Book of Autograph Verses*. T. Y. Crowell 1990. (Grades 3-8; 3P, 4Q)

Moyers, Bill. *A World of Ideas II*. Doubleday 1990. (Grade 9-Adult; 2P, 3Q)

Munro, Alice. *Friend of My Youth*. Knopf 1990.(Adult; 2P, 4Q)

Murphy, Claire Rudolf. *Friendship Across the Arctic Waters: Alaskan Cub Scouts Visit Their Soviet Neighbors*. Lodestar 1991. (Grades 3-8; 3P, 4Q)

Murrow, Liza Ketchum and Ronald Himler. *Dancing on the Table*. Holiday 1990. (Grades 3-4; 2P, 3Q)

Naylor, Phyllis Reynolds. *Bernie and the Bessledorf Ghost*. Atheneum 1990. (Grades 3-6)

_____. *Reluctantly Alice*. Atheneum 1991. (Grades 5-8; 3P, 4Q)

_____. *Witch Weed*. Delacorte 1991. (Grades 3-6; 4P, 4Q)

Nixon, Joan Lowery. *A Candidate for Murder*. Delacorte 1991. (Grades 7-12; 3P, 4Q)

_____. *High Trail to Danger*. Bantam 1991. (Grades 5-12; 3P, 3Q)

O'Neill, Joseph. *This Is the Life*. Farrar 1991. (Grade 9-Adult; 2P, 3Q)

O'Shaughnessy McKenna, Colleen. *Eenie, Meanie, Murphy, No!*. Scholastic 1990. (Grades 3-6; 4P, 4Q)

Odgers, Sally Farrell. *Drummond: The Search for Sarah*. Holiday 1990. (Grades 3-4; 3P, 3Q)

Okimoto, Jean Davies. *Molly by Any Other Name*. Scholastic 1990. (Grade 7-Adult; 3P, 3Q)

_____. *Take a Chance, Gramps!*. Little 1990. (Grades 5-8; 4P, 3Q)

Orlev, Uri (translated from the Hebrew by Hillel Halkin). *The Man from the Other Side*. Houghton 1991 (U.S.). (Grades 7-12; 3P, 4Q)

Park, Barbara. *Maxie, Rosie and Earl—Partners in Grime*. Knopf 1990. (Grades 3-6; 4P, 4Q)

Paterson, Katherine. *Lyddie*. Lodestar 1991. (Grades 5-8; 4P, 4Q)

Paulsen, Gary. *Canyons*. Delacorte 1990. (Grade 7-Adult; 3P, 4Q)

_____. *The River*. Delacorte 1991. (Grades 5-12; 3P, 4Q)

Pershall, Mary K. *You Take the High Road*. Dial 1990. (Grades 7-12; 3P, 3Q)

Petersen, P. J. *I Hate Camping!*. Dutton 1991. (Grades 3-4; 3P, 3Q)

Peyton, K. M. *Darkling*. Delacorte 1990. (Grades 9-12; 3P, 3Q)

Pfeffer, Susan Beth. *April Upstairs*. Holt 1990. (Grades 5-8; 3P, 3Q)

_____. *Darcy Downstairs*. Holt 1990. (Grades 5-8; 3P, 3Q)

_____. *Most Precious Blood*. Bantam 1991. (Grades 5-12; 3P, 3Q)

Prelutsky, Jack. *For Laughing Out Loud: Poems to Tickle Your Funnybone*. Knopf 1991. (Grades 3-8; 3P, 4Q)

Pullman, Phillip. *The Tiger in the Well*. Knopf 1990. (Grade 7-Adult; 4P, 3Q)

Quindlen, Anna. *Object Lessons*. Random 1991. (Grade 9-Adult; 2P, 3Q)

Rappaport, Doreen. *Escape from Slavery: Five Journeys to Freedom*. HarperCollins 1991. (Grades 3-6; 3P, 4Q)

Regan, Dian Curtis. *Jilly's Ghost*. Avon 1990. (Grades 7–12; 3P, 3Q)

Rice, Anne. *The Witching Hour*. Knopf 1990. (Adults; 4P, 4Q)

Ridley, Philip. *Dakota of the White Flats*. Knopf 1991. (Grades 3–6; 2P, 3Q)

Rinaldi, Ann. *Wolf by the Ears*. Scholastic 1991. (Grade 9–Adult; 2P, 4Q)

Robinson, Nancy K. *Angela and the Broken Heart*. Scholastic 1991. (Grades 5–8; 3P, 3Q)

Roos, Stephen. *Twelve-Year-Old Vows Revenge! After Being Dumped by Extraterrestrial on First Date*. Delacorte 1990. (Grades 5–8; 2P, 4Q)

Roper, Robert. *In Caverns of Blue Ice*. Little 1991. (Grades 7–12; 2P, 3Q)

Rosofsky, Iris. *My Aunt Ruth*. HarperCollins 1991. (Grades 7–12; 3P, 4Q)

Ruch, Sandi Barrett. *Junkyard Dog*. Orchard 1990. (Grades 3–6; 3P, 4Q)

Ryan, Mary E. *My Sister Is Driving Me Crazy*. S&S 1991. (Grades 5–8; 3P, 3Q)

Sachs, Marilyn. *Circles*. Dutton 1991. (Grades 5–8; 4P, 3Q)

San Souci, Robert D. *Larger Than Life: The Adventures of American Legendary Heroes*. Doubleday 1991. (Grades 3–4; 4P, 4Q)

San Souci, Robert D. *The Christmas Ark*. Doubleday 1991. (Grades 3–4; 3P, 4Q)

Sauer, Jim. *Hank*. Delacorte 1990. (Grades 7–12; 4P, 3Q)

Saul, John. *Darkness*. Bantam 1991. (Grade 9–Adult; 4P, 4Q)

Savage, Candace. *Wolves*. Sierra Club 1990. (Grade 9–Adult; 1P, 4Q)

Scarborough, Chuck. *After-Shock*. Crown 1991. (Grade 9–Adult; 3P, 3Q)

Schami, Rafik, translated by Rika Lesser. *A Hand Full of Stars*. Dutton 1990. (Grades 9–12; 3P, 4Q)

Schurke, Paul. *Bering Bridge: The Soviet-American Expedition from Siberia to Alaska*. Pfeifer-Hamilton 1989. (Grade 7–Adult; 2P, 3Q)

Schwartz, Joel L. *Upchuck Summer's Revenge*. Delacorte 1990. (Grades 5–6; 2P, 3Q)

The Scott Newman Center. *Straight Talk with Kids: Improving Communication, Building Trust, and Keeping Your Children Drug-Free*. Bantam 1991. (Adult; 4P, 4Q)

See, Carolyn. *Making History*. Houghton 1991. (Adult; 1P, 3Q)

Shannon, George, retel. *More Stories to Solve: Fifteen Folktales from Around the World*. Greenwillow 1990. (Grades 3–8; 3P, 4Q)

Shearer, Tony. *The Praying Flute*. Bear 1991. (Grade 7–Adult; 2P, 2Q)

Shriver, Jean Adair. *Mayflower Man*. Delacorte 1991. (Grades 5–8; 3P, 3Q)

Singer, Marilyn. *Twenty Ways to Lose Your Best Friend*. Harper 1990. (Grades 3–4; 2P, 4Q)

Skargon, Yvonne (selected by). *The Importance of Being Oscar Wilde*. Fulcrum 1991. (Grade 3–Adult; 3P, 4Q)

Smith, Marya. *Winter-Broken*. Arcade 1990. (Grades 5–8; 3P, 3Q)

Snyder, Zilpha Keatley. *Libby on Wednesday*. Delacorte 1990. (Grades 5–8; 3P, 3Q)

———. *Song of the Gargoyle*. Delacorte 1991. (Grades 5–8; 3P, 3Q)

Sobol, Donald J. and Rose Sobol. *Encyclopedia Brown's Book of Strange but True Crimes*. Scholastic 1991. (Grades 3–8; 4P, 4Q)

Southall, Ivan. *The Mysterious World of Marcus Leadbeater*. Farrar 1990. (Grades 9–12; 2P, 3Q)

Spector, Ronnie with Vince Waldron. *Be My Baby: How I Survived Mascara, Miniskirts and Madness, or My Life as a Fabulous Ronette*. Harmony 1990. (Grade 9–Adult; 1P, 3Q)

Spencer, Scott. *Secret Anniversaries*. Knopf 1990. (Adult; 3P, 3Q)

Spinelli, Jerry. *Fourth Grade Rats*. Scholastic 1991. (Grades 3–6; 3P, 3Q)

Spinka, Penina Keen. *White Hare's Horses*. Atheneum 1991. (Grades 5–12; 3P, 3Q)

Stannard, Russell. *The Time and Space of Uncle Albert*. Holt 1989. (Grades 3–6; 1P, 3Q)

Stern, Jane and Michael. *Sixties People*. Knopf 1990. (Grade 9–Adult; 3P, 3Q)

Stern, Steve. *Harry Kaplan's Adventures Underground*. Houghton 1991. (Grade 9–Adult; 2P, 3Q)

Stowe, Cynthia. *Home Sweet Home, Good-bye*. Scholastic 1990. (Grades 3–6; 3P, 3Q)

Straight Talk with Kids: Improving Communication, Building Trust, and Keeping Your Children Drug-Free. The Scott Newman Center. Bantam 1991. (Adult; 4P, 4Q)

Streiber, Whitley. *Billy.* Putnam 1990. (Grade 9-Adult; 3P, 4Q)

Sweeney, Joyce. *Face the Dragon.* Delacorte 1990. (Grades 7-12; 3P, 3Q)

Tamar, Erika. *High Cheekbones.* Viking 1990. (Grade 7-Adult; 4P, 4Q)

Taylor, Mildred D. *Mississippi Bridge.* Dial 1990. (Grades 5-12; 3P, 4Q)

Tepper, Sheri S. *Beauty.* Doubleday 1991. (Grade 9-Adult; 4P, 4Q)

Thesman, Jean. *Rachel Chance.* Houghton 1990. (Grades 5-8; 3P, 3Q)

Thiele, Colin. *Rotten Egg Paterson to the Rescue.* HarperCollins 1991 (US edition). (Grades 3-6; 3P, 3Q)

Thomas, Joyce Carol. *A Gathering of Flowers.* Harper 1990. (Grades 7-12; 1P, 3Q)

Thomson, David. *Silver Light.* Knopf 1990. (Grade 9-Adult; 3P, 4Q)

Turner, Ana. *Rosemary's Witch.* HarperCollins 1991. (Grades 5-6; 3P, 3Q)

Van Allsburg, Chris. *Just a Dream.* Houghton 1990. (Grades 3-Adult; 2P, 4Q)

Vecchione, Joseph J., ed. *The New York Times Book of Sports Legends.* Times 1991. (Adult; 4P, 4Q)

Verdy, Violette. *Of Swans, Sugarplums, and Satin Slippers: Ballet Stories for Children.* Scholastic 1991. (Grades 3-8; 2P, 3Q)

Wersba, Barbara. *The Farewell Kid.* Harper 1990. (Grades 7-12; 3P, 3Q)

Westall, Robert. *Echoes of War.* Farrar 1991. (Grade 7-Adult; 1P, 3Q)

Westlake, Donald E. *Tomorrow's Crimes.* Mysterious 1990. (Adult; 4P, 3Q)

Westwood, Chris. *He Came from the Shadows.* HarperCollins 1991. (Grades 7-12; 3P, 3Q)

Whelan, Gloria. *Hannah.* Knopf 1991. (Grades 3-6; 3P, 4Q)

———. *The Secret Keeper.* Random 1990. (Grades 7-12; 3P, 4Q)

White, Alana. *Come Next Spring.* Houghton 1990. (Grades 5-8; 3P, 4Q)

Whitmore, Arvella. *The Bread Winner.* Houghton 1990. (Grades 5-8; 2P, 3Q)

Whitney, Phyllis A. *Woman Without a Past.* Doubleday 1991. (Grade 9-Adult; 1P, 3Q)

Wieler, Diana. *Last Chance Summer.* Delacorte 1991. (Grades 7-12; 3P, 4Q)

Wilde, Nicholas. *Into the Dark.* Scholastic 1990. (Grades 5-8; 3P, 3Q)

Willey, Margaret. *Saving Lenny.* Bantam 1990. (Grades 9-12; 3P, 3Q)

Williams-Garcia, Rita. *Fast Talk on a Slow Track.* Lodestar 1991. (Grades 7-12; 2P, 3Q)

Willis, Patricia. *A Place to Claim as Home.* Clarion 1991. (Grades 5-8; 3P, 3Q)

Wilson, Barbara Ker. *Acacia Terrace.* Scholastic 1990. (Grade 3-Adult; 1P, 4Q)

Wilson, Johnniece Marshall. *Robin on His Own.* Scholastic 1990. (Grades 3-6; 3P, 3Q)

Wisler, G. Clifton. *Piper's Ferry.* Lodestar 1990. (Grades 5-8; 2P, 3Q)

Wodruff, Elvira. *George Washington's Socks.* Scholastic 1991. (Grades 3-6; 3P, 4Q)

Wolff, Virginia Euwer. *The Mozart Season.* Holt 1991. (Grades 7-12; 2P, 3Q)

Woodson, Jacqueline. *Last Summer with Maizon.* Delacorte 1990. (Grades 5-6; 3P, 4Q)

Wulffson, Don L. *Amazing True Stories.* Cobblehill 1991. (Grade 5-Adult; 3P, 4Q)

Yep, Laurence. *Dragon Cauldron.* HarperCollins 1991. (Grades 5-8; 2P, 3Q)

Yolen, Jane. *Wizard's Hall.* Harcourt 1991. (Grades 3-6; 4P, 4Q)

———. and Martin H. Greenberg. *Vampires.* HarperCollins 1991. (Grades 7-8; 3P, 4Q)

Zach, Cheryl. *Benny and the Crazy Contest.* Bradbury 1991. (Grades 3-4; 3P, 3Q).

BIBLIOGRAPHY BY AGE LEVEL

Elementary (Grades 3–4)

Acacia Terrace (Wilson)
Balloons and Other Poems (Chandra)
The Bell Tolls at Mousehaven Manor (Kwitz)
Bernie and the Bessledorf Ghost (Naylor)
The Big Book for Peace (Durrell and Sachs)
Bizarre Birds and Beasts: Animal Verses (Marsh)
Black Black and White (Macauley)
Boonsville Bombers (Herzig)
Brother Eagle, Sister Sky (Jeffers)
Bugs Bunny: Fifty Years and Only One Grey Hare (Adamson)
The Chickenhouse House (Howard)
The The Christmas Ark (San Souci)
Coping with Death and Grief (Heegaard)
Cricket and the Cracker Box Kid (Ferguson)
Crow and Weasel (Lopez)
Dakota of the White Flats (Ridley)
Dancing on the Table (Murrow and Himler)
The Door in the Air and Other Stories (Mahy)
Drummond: The Search for Sarah (Ogders)
Eenie, Meanie, Murphy, No! (O'Shaughnessy Mc Kenna)
Encyclopedia Brown's Book of Strange but True Crimes (Sobol and Sobol)
Escape from Slavery: Five Journeys to Freedom (Rappaport)
Fatso Jean, the Ice Cream Queen (Macdonald)
For Laughing Out Loud: Poems to Tickle Your Funnybone (Prelutsky)
Fourth Grade Rats (Spinelli)
Friendship Across the Arctic Waters: Alaskan Cub Scouts Visit Their Soviet Neighbors (Murphy)
Full Moon Soup, or The Fall of the Hotel Splendide (Graham)
George Washington's Socks (Wodruff)
The Greatest Idea Ever (Carris)
Hannah (Whelan)

Harvey's Wacky Parrot Adventure (Clifford)
Home Sweet Home, Good-bye (Stowe)
I Am Leaper (Johnson)
I Bet You Didn't Know That Fish Sleep with Their Eyes Open and Other Facts and Curiosities (Iverson)
I Bet You Didn't Know That Hummingbirds Can Fly Backwards and Other Facts and Curiosities (Iverson)
I Bet You Didn't Know That There Are Golf Balls on the Moon and Other Facts and Curiosities (Iverson)
I Bet You Didn't Know That You Can't Sink in the Dead Sea and Other Facts and Curiosities (Iverson)
I Hate Camping! (Peterson)
The Importance of Being Oscar Wilde (Skargon)
Jeremy Thatcher, Dragon Hatcher (Coville)
Journey (MacLachlan)
Journey Home (Holland)
Junkyard Dog (Ruch)
Just a Dream (Van Allsburg)
Larger Than Life: The Adventures of American Legendary Heroes (San Souci)
The Leaves in October (Ackerman)
Looking Inside: Machines and Constructions (Fleisher and Keeler)
Make Four Million Dollars by Next Thursday (Manes)
Matthew Jackson Meets the Wall (Giff)
Maxie, Rosie and Earl—Partners in Grime (Park)
The Moon Clock (Faulkner)
More Stories to Solve: Fifteen Folktales from Around the World (Shannon)
A Mouse in My Roof (Edwards)
A Newbery Christmas (Greenberg and Waugh)
Of Swans, Sugarplums, and Satin Slippers: Ballet Stories for Children (Verdy)
The Old Coot (Christian)
On the Far Side of the Mountain (George)

Our Sixth-Grade Sugar Baby Blues (Bunting)
The Place My Words Are Looking For: What Poets Say About and Through Their Work (Janeczko)
The Practical Joke War (Ferguson)
Professor Popkin's Prodigious Polish (Brittain)
R-T, Margaret and the Rats of NIMH (Conly)
Robin on His Own (Wilson)
Rotten Egg Paterson to the Rescue (Thiele)
School's Out (Hurwitz)
The Secret Life of Hubie Hartzel (Masters)
Seymour, the Formerly Fearful (Feldman)
Shadows (Haseley)
A Tale of Antarctica (Glimmerveen)
Tales of the Early World (Hughes)
A Telling of Tales (Brooke)
Thin Air (Getz)
The Time and Space of Uncle Albert (Stannard)
To the Moon and Back: A Collection of Poems (Larrick)
Twenty Ways to Lose Your Best Friend (Singer)
Voices on the Wind (Booth)
Wanted . . . Mud Blossom (Byars)
A Wave in Her Pocket: Stories from Trinidad (Joseph)
When Grandfather's Parrot Inherited Kennington Court (Allen)
Window (Baker)
Wings (Brittain)
Witch Weed (Naylor)
Wizard's Hall (Yolen)
You Don't Need Words! (Gross)
Yours Till Niagara Falls: A Book of Autograph Verses (Morrison)

Middle School (Grades 5-6)

Acacia Terrace (Wilson)
The Adventures of Boone Barnaby (Cottonwood)
Agnes Cecilia (Gripe)
Amazing True Stories (Wulffson)
Anastasia at This Address (Lowry)
Angela and the Broken Heart (Robinson)
Animal Amazing (Herbst)
An Owl in the House (Heinrich)
April Upstairs (Pfeffer)
Author! Author! (Ferris)

Bernie and the Bessledorf Ghost (Naylor)
The Big Book for Peace (Durrell and Sachs)
Bizarre Birds and Beasts: Animal Verses (Marsh)
Black and White (Macauley)
Bloodroot (Hobbie)
The Bread Winner (Whitmore)
Breaking Out (DeClements)
Brother Eagle, Sister Sky (Jeffers)
Brother Moose (Levin)
Bugs Bunny: Fifty Years and Only One Grey Hare (Adamson)
Circle of Light (Roe)
Circles (Sachs)
Coaching Evelyn: Fast, Faster, Fastest Woman In The World (Connolly)
Come Next Spring (White)
Contary Imaginations (Callen)
Coping with Death and Grief (Heegaard)
Cricket and the Cracker Box Kid (Ferguson)
Crow and Weasel (Lopez)
Crying for a Dream (Erdoes)
Dagmar Schultz and the Green-Eyed Monster (Hall)
Dakota of the White Flats (Ridley)
Darcy Downstairs (Pfeffer)
Dew Drop Dead (Howe)
Don't Rent My Room! (Angell)
Dragon Cauldron (Yep)
Dream Teams: Best Teams of All Time (Benson)
Eben Tyne, Powdermonkey (Beatty and Robbins)
Eenie, Meanie, Murphy, No! (O'Shaughnessy Mc Kenna)
Encyclopedia Brown's Book of Strange but True Crimes (Sobol and Sobol)
Escape from Slavery: Five Journeys to Freedom (Rappaport)
Everywhere (Brooks)
Fire Mask (Grant)
First Wedding, Once Removed (Deaver)
For Laughing Out Loud: Poems to Tickle Your Funnybone (Prelutsky)
Fourth Grade Rats (Spinelli)
Fresh Brats (Kennedy)
The Door in the Air and Other Stories (Mahy)
Friendship Across the Arctic Waters: Alaskan Cub Scouts Visit Their Soviet Neighbors (Murphy)
Full Moon Soup, or The Fall of the Hotel Splendide (Graham)
Germy Blew the Bugle (Jones)

A Telling of Tales (Brooke)
Thin Air (Getz)
The Time and Space of Uncle Albert (Stannard)
Time Is the Longest Distance: An Anthology of Poems (Gordon)
To the Moon and Back: A Collection of Poems (Larrick)
A Tribe for Lexi (Adler)
Tug of War (Lingard)
Twelve-Year-Old Vows Revenge! After Being Dumped by Extraterrestrial on First Date (Roos)
Twenty Pageants Later (Cooney)
Upchuck Summer's Revenge (Schwartz)
Up in the Mountains and Other Poems of Long Ago (Lewis)
Voices on the Wind (Booth)
War Boy: A Country Childhood (Foreman)
The Warnings (Bufie)
A Wave in Her Pocket: Stories from Trinidad (Joseph)
Weasel (DeFelice)
Whatever Became of Aunt Margaret? (DeWeese)
When I Dance (Berry)
When Kids Drive Kids Crazy: How to Get Along with Your Friends and Enemies (LeShan)
White Hare's Horses (Spinka)
Why the Whales Came (Morpurgo)
Windcatcher (Avi)
Window (Baker)
Wings (Brittain)
Winning Scheherazade (Gorog)
Winter-Broken (Smith)
Wish on a Unicorn (Hesse)
The Witch House (Johnson)
Witch Weed (Naylor)
Wizard's Hall (Yolen)
Wolf by the Ears (Rinaldi)
Wolves (Savage)
Woman Without a Past (Whitney)
A World of Ideas II (Moyers)
You Don't Need Words! (Gross)
Yours Till Niagara Falls: A Book of Autograph Verses (Morrison)

Junior High (Grades 7–8)

Acacia Terrace (Wilson)
The Adventures of Boone Barnaby (Cottonwood)
After-Shock (Scarborough)
Against the Grain (Ferris)

Agnes Cecilia (Gripe)
Amazing Gracie (Cannon)
Amazing True Stories (Wulffson)
Among the Volcanoes (Castaneda)
Andra (Lawrence)
Angela and the Broken Heart (Robinson)
Animal Amazing (Herbst)
An Owl in the House (Heinrich)
April Upstairs (Pfeffer)
Babyface (Mazer)
Beast (Benchley)
Beauty (Tepper)
Be My Baby: How I Survived Mascara, Miniskirts and Madness, or My Life as a Fabulous Ronette (Spector and Waldron)
Bering Bridge: The Soviet-American Expedition from Siberia to Alaska (Schurke)
Beyond the Door (Blackwood)
The Big Book for Peace (Durrell and Sachs)
The Big Book of Hell (Groening)
Billy (Streiber)
Black and White (Macauley)
Black Ice (Cary)
Blindfold (McCuaig)
Bloodroot (Hobbie)
Borderlands (Carter) *The Boy in the Moon* (Koertge)
The Bread Winner (Whitmore)
Brother Eagle, Sister Sky (Jeffers)
Bugs Bunny: Fifty Years and Only One Grey Hare (Adamson)
A Candidate for Murder (Nixon)
Canyons (Paulsen)
Castle in the Air (Jones)
Celebrate You! (Johnson)
Circle of Light (Roe)
Circles (Sachs)
Coaching Evelyn: Fast, Faster, Fastest Woman In The World (Connolly)
Come Next Spring (White)
Contrary Imaginations (Callen)
Crying for a Dream (Erdoes)
D, My Name Is Danita (Mazer)
Dagmar Schultz and the Green-Eyed Monster (Hall)
Darcy Downstairs (Pfeffer)
Darkling (Peyton)
Darkness (Saul)
The Day That Elvis Came to Town (Marino)
The Devil's Own (Lisson)
Dew Drop Dead (Howe)
Distant Fires (Anderson and Kouba)

Don't Rent My Room! (Angell)
Downriver (Hobbs)
Dragon Cauldron (Yep)
Dream Teams: Best Teams of All Time (Benson)
Eben Tyne, Powdermonkey (Beatty and Robbins)
Echoes of War (Westall)
Encyclopedia Brown's Book of Strange but True Crimes (Sobol and Sobol)
Everywhere (Brooks)
Expedition: Being an Account in Words and Artwork of the 2358 A D Voyage to Darwin IV (Barlowe)
Face the Dragon (Sweeney)
The Faces of Ceti (Caraker)
The Farewell Kid (Wersba)
Fast Talk on a Slow Track (Williams-Garcia)
Fiends (Farris)
First Wedding, Once Removed (Deaver)
For Laughing Out Loud: Poems to Tickle Your Funnybone (Prelutsky)
Fresh Brats (Kennedy)
Friendship Across the Arctic Waters: Alaskan Cub Scouts Visit Their Soviet Neighbors (Murphy)
Full Moon Soup, or The Fall of the Hotel Splendide (Graham)
A Gathering of Flowers (Thomas)
The Ghost in the Attic (Cates)
The Girl with the White Flag (Higa)
A Graveyard for Lunatics (Bradbury)
Gruel and Unusual Punishment (Arter)
The Half Child (Hersom)
A Hand Full of Stars (Schami and Lesser)
Hank (Sauer)
Happy Endings (Geras)
Harry Kaplan's Adventures Underground (Stern)
He Came from the Shadows (Westwood)
Hey Little Walter, and Other Prize-Winning Plays (Lamb)
The Hideout (Bunting)
High Cheekbones (Tamar)
High Trail to Danger (Nixon)
The House in the Woods (Holland)
In Caverns of Blue Ice (Roper)
Into the Dark (Wilde)
I Can Hear the Mourning Dove (Bennett)
The Jewel of Life (Kirwan-Vogel)
Jilly's Ghost (Regan)
Journey from the Dawn: Life with the World's First Family (Johanson and O'Farrell)

Jurassic Park (Crichton)
Just a Dream (Van Allsburg)
Kidnapping Kevin Kowalski (Auch)
Kisses (Caseley)
The Kite That Braved Old Orchard Beach: Year-Round Poems for Young People (Kennedy)
Lark in the Morning (Garden)
Last Chance Summer (Wieler)
The Last Seven Months of Anne Frank (Lindwer)
Libby on Wednesday (Snyder)
Long Time Passing (Jones)
Losing Joe's Place (Korman)
Loving Someone Else (Conford)
Lyddie (Paterson)
Macdonald Hall Goes Hollywood (Korman)
Make Like a Tree and Leave (Danziger)
The Man from the Other Side (Orlev)
Mayflower Man (Shriver)
Mississippi Bridge (Taylor)
Molly by Any Other Name (Okimoto)
Monster of the Year (Coville)
More Stories to Solve: Fifteen Folktales from Around the World (Shannon)
Most Precious Blood (Pfeffer)
A Mouse in My Roof (Edwards)
The Mozart Season (Wolff)
Mummy Took Cooking Lessons and Other Poems (Ciardi)
My Aunt Ruth (Rosofsky)
My Crooked Family (Collier)
My Sister Is Driving Me Crazy (Ryan)
The Mysterious World of Marcus Leadbeater (Southall)
Naked in Winter (Brooks)
A Newbery Christmas (Greenberg and Waugh)
Nightfall (Asimov and SIlverberg)
Object Lessons (Quindlen)
Of Swans, Sugarplums, and Satin Slippers: Ballet Stories for Children (Verdy)
On the Far Side of the Mountain (George)
On the Third Ward (Degens)
The Other Victims: First-Person Stories of Non-Jews Persecuted by the Nazis (Friedman)
Otto from Otherwhere (Griffin)
Out of the Ordinary (Dalton)
Paradise Cafe and Other Stories (Brooks)
Piper's Ferry (Wisler)
A Place to Claim as Home (Willis)
The Place My Words Are Looking For:

What Poets Say About and Through Their Work (Janeczko)
Poems for Grandmothers (Cohn)
The Praying Flute (Shearer)
R-T, Margaret and the Rats of NIMH (Conly)
Rachel Chance (Thesman)
Reluctantly Alice (Naylor)
The River (Paulsen)
Round the Bend (Dale)
The Rowan (McCaffrey)
Saturnalia (Fleischman)
Saving Lenny (Willey)
Scotch on the Rocks (Browne)
The Secret Keeper (Whelan)
The Shadow Brothers (Cannon)
Shelter for a Seabird (Farish)
Shiva Accused: An Adventure of the Ice Age (Brennan)
The Sierra Club Book of Weatherwisdom (McVey)
Silver Light (Thomson)
Sisters Long Ago (Kehret)
Sixties People (Stern)
Sleepers, Awake (Jacobs)
Smart Rats (Baird)
Someday I'll Laugh About This (Crew)
Someone's Mother Is Missing (Mazer)
Song of the Gargoyle (Snyder)
Stay Tuned (Corcoran)
Stolen Away (Collins)
Take a Chance, Gramps! (Okimoto)
Tales of the Early World (Hughes)
Teenage Wasteland: Suburbia's Dead End Kids (Gaines)
A Telling of Tales (Brooke)
This Is the Life (O'Neill)
Thunderwith (Hathorn)
The Tiger in the Well (Pullman) *Time Is the Longest Distance: An Anthology of Poems* (Gordon)
Tom Loves Anna Loves Tom (Clements)
The Torment of Mr Gully: Stories of the Supernatural (Clarke)
To the Moon and Back: A Collection of Poems (Larrick)
A Tribe for Lexi (Adler)
Truce: Ending the Sibling War (Bode)
Tug of War (Lingard)
Twelve-Year-Old Vows Revenge! After Being Dumped by Extraterrestrial on First Date (Roos)
Twenty Pageants Later (Cooney)
The Two Faces of Adam (Meyer)
Up in the Mountains and Other Poems of Long Ago (Lewis)

Vampires (Yolen and Greenberg)
Walker of Worlds (DeHaven)
War Boy: A Country Childhood (Foreman)
The Warnings (Bufie)
Weasel (DeFelice)
Whatever Became of Aunt Margaret? (DeWeese)
When Kids Drive Kids Crazy: How to Get Along with Your Friends and Enemies (LeShan)
Where'd You Get the Gun, Billy? (Arrick)
White Hare's Horses (Spinka)
Why the Whales Came (Morpurgo)
Windcatcher (Avi)
Winning Scheherazade (Gorog)
Winter-Broken (Smith)
Witch Baby (Block)
The Witch House (Johnson)
Wolf (Cross)
Wolves (Savage)
Woman Without a Past (Whitney)
Yours Till Niagara Falls: A Book of Autograph Verses (Morrison)
You Take the High Road (Pershall)

High School (Grades 9–12)

After-Shock (Scarborough)
Against the Grain (Ferris)
Amazing Gracie (Cannon)
Amazing True Stories (Wulffson)
Among the Volcanoes (Castaneda)
Andra (Lawrence)
Animal Amazing (Herbst)
An Owl in the House (Heinrich)
Beast (Benchley)
Beauty (Tepper)
Be My Baby: How I Survived Mascara, Miniskirts and Madness, or My Life as a Fabulous Ronette (Spector and Waldron)
Bering Bridge: The Soviet-American Expedition from Siberia to Alaska (Schurke)
The Big Book of Hell (Groening)
Billy (Streiber)
Black Ice (Cary)
Blindfold (McCuaig)
Borderlands (Carter) *The Boy in the Moon* (Koertge)
Brother Eagle, Sister Sky (Jeffers)
Bugs Bunny: Fifty Years and Only One Grey Hare (Adamson)
A Candidate for Murder (Nixon)
Canyons (Paulsen)

The Tiger in the Well (Pullman)
Time Is the Longest Distance: An Anthology of Poems (Gordon)
Tom Loves Anna Loves Tom (Clements)
The Torment of Mr Gully: Stories of the Supernatural (Clarke)
Truce: Ending the Sibling War (Bode)
The Two Faces of Adam (Meyer)
Up in the Mountains and Other Poems of Long Ago (Lewis)
Walker of Worlds (DeHaven)
War Boy: A Country Childhood (Foreman)
Where'd You Get the Gun, Billy? (Arrick)
White Hare's Horses (Spinka)
Window (Baker)
Witch Baby (Block)
When I Dance (Berry)
Where Rag Dolls Hide Their Faces (Koplow)
Wolf (Cross)
Wolf by the Ears (Rinaldi)
Wolves (Savage)
Woman Hollering Creek (Cisneros)
Woman Without a Past (Whitney)
A World of Ideas II (Moyers)
You Take the High Road (Pershall)

Adult

Acacia Terrace (Wilson)
After-Shock (Scarborough)
Almighty Me (Bausch)
Amazing True Stories (Wulffson)
Animal Amazing (Herbst)
An Owl in the House (Heinrich)
Beast (Benchley)
Beauty (Tepper)
Bedrock (Alther)
Be My Baby: How I Survived Mascara, Miniskirts and Madness, or My Life as a Fabulous Ronette (Spector and Waldron)
Bering Bridge: The Soviet-American Expedition from Siberia to Alaska (Schurke)
The Big Book for Peace (Durrell and Sachs)
The Big Book of Hell (Groening)
Billy (Streiber)
Black and White (Macauley)
Black Ice (Cary)
Borderlands (Carter) *The Boss Dog* (Fisher)
Bugs Bunny: Fifty Years and Only One Grey Hare (Adamson)

Cabin Fever (Jolley)
Canyons (Paulsen)
The Colors of Snow (Fenton)
Crow and Weasel (Lopez)
Crying for a Dream (Erdoes)
Dark Horse: The Private Life of George Harrison (Giuliano)
Darkness (Saul)
Dear God: What Religion Were the Dinosaurs? (Heller)
Distant Fires (Anderson and Kouba)
Dream Teams: Best Teams of All Time (Benson)
Echoes of War (Westall)
Expedition: Being an Account in Words and Artwork of the 2358 A D Voyage to Darwin IV (Barlowe)
Fiends (Farris)
Finding Signs (Baker)
Fling (Hersey)
Forever's Team (Feinstein)
The Foxes of FirstDark (Kilworth)
Friend of My Youth (Munro)
A Graveyard for Lunatics (Bradbury)
Growing Up Isn't Hard To Do if You Start Out as a Kid (Heller)
Harry and Catherine (Busch)
Harry Kaplan's Adventures Underground (Stern)
High Cheekbones (Tamar)
I Have Words to Spend: Reflections of a Small-Town Editor (Cormier)
The Importance of Being Oscar Wilde (Skargon)
Journey from the Dawn: Life with the World's First Family (Johanson and O'Farrell)
Jurassic Park (Crichton)
Just a Dream (Van Allsburg)
Last Chance to See (Adams and Carwardine)
The Last Defector (Cape)
The Last Seven Months of Anne Frank (Lindwer)
Leap Year (Cameron)
Line of Duty (Grant)
Long Time Passing (Jones)
Making History (See)
Masquerade (Dailey)
The Matter Is Life (Cooper)
Molly by Any Other Name (Okimoto)
The New York Times Book of Sports Legends (Vecchione)
Nightfall (Asimov and SIlverberg)
Object Lessons (Quindlen)
Phantom (Kay)

Poems for Grandmothers (Cohn)
The Praying Flute (Shearer)
Remember Who You Are: Stories About Being Jewish (Hautzig)
Ride a Cockhorse (Kennedy)
Roger Caras' Treasury of Great Horse Stories (Caras)
The Rowan (McCaffrey)
Scotch on the Rocks (Browne)
Secret Anniversaries (Spencer)
Silver Light (Thomson)
Sixties People (Stern)
Stolen Away (Collins)
Stolen Season (Lamb)
Straight Talk with Kids: Improving Communication, Building Trust, and Keeping Your Children Drug-Free (The Scott Newman Center)
Summer (Gordon and Virga)
A Tale of Antarctica (Glimmerveen)
Teenage Wasteland: Suburbia's Dead End Kids (Gaines)

This Is the Life (O'Neill)
The Tiger in the Well (Pullman) *Time Is the Longest Distance: An Anthology of Poems* (Gordon)
Tomorrow's Crimes (Westlake)
Up in the Mountains and Other Poems of Long Ago (Lewis)
Walker of Worlds (DeHaven)
War Boy: A Country Childhood (Foreman)
When I Dance (Berry)
Where Rag Dolls Hide Their Faces (Koplow)
Window (Baker)
The Witching Hour (Rice)
Wolf by the Ears (Rinaldi)
Wolves (Savage)
Woman Hollering Creek (Cisneros)
Woman Without a Past (Whitney)
A World of Ideas II (Moyers)

SELECTIVE BIBLIOGRAPHY BY THEME AND GENRE

Adventure

After-Shock (Cottonwood) HS-A
Andra (Lawrence) HS
Bartholomew Fair (Stolz) MS-JH
Beast (Benchley) HS-A
Bering Bridge (Schurke) JH-A
Beyond the Door (Blackwood) JH
Billy (Streiber) HS-A
Borderlands (Carter) JH-A
Brother Moose (Levin) MS
Canyons (Paulsen) JH-A
Castle in the Air (Jones) JH-HS
Colors of Snow (Fenton) A
Dakota of the White Flats (Ridley) EL-MS
The Devil's Own (Lisson) HS
Distant Fires (Anderson & Kouba) HS-A
Downriver (Hobbs) JH-HS)
Dragon Cauldron (Yep) MS-JH
Eben Tyne, Powdermonkey (Beatty & Robinson) MS-JH
Escape from Slavery (Rappaport) EL-MS
Faces of Ceti (Caraker) JH-HS
Fire Mask (Grant) MS-JH
The Foxes of FirstDark (Kilworth) HS-A
George Washington's Socks (Woodruff) EL-MS
A Hand Full of Stars (Schami) HS
The Hideout (Bunting) MS-JH
High Trail to Danger (Nixon) MS-HS
I Hate Camping! (Petersen) EL
In Caverns of Blue Ice (Roper) JH-HS
Jeremy Thatcher, Dragon Hatcher (Coville) EL-MS
The Jewel of Life (Kirwan-Vogel) JH
Kidnapping Kevin Kowalski (Auch) MS-JH
Larger Than Life (San Souci) EL-MS
Last Chance to See (Wieler) HS-A
The Last Defector (Cape) A
The Man from the Other Side (Orlev) JH-HS
Masquerade (Dailey) HS-A
The Moon Clock (Faulkner) EL-MS; A
Nightfall (Asimov & Silverberg) HS-A

On the Far Side of the Mountain (George) EL-JH
Piper's Ferry (Wisler) MS-JH
Professor Popkin's Prodigious Polish (Brittain) EL-MS
R-T, Margaret and the Rats of NIMH (Conly) EL-JH
The River (Paulsen) MS-HS
The Rowan (McCaffrey) HS-A
Silver Light (Thomson) HS-A
Smart Rats (Baird) JH-HS
Song of the Gargoyle (Snyder) MS-JH
The Tiger in the Well (Pullman) A
A Tribe for Lexi (Adler) MS-JH
Tug of War (Lingard) MS-JH
Walker of Worlds (DeHaven) HS-A
Weasel (DeFelice) MS-JH
Whatever Became of Aunt Margaret? (DeWeese) MS-JH
White Hair's Horses (Spinka) MS-HS
Why the Whales Came (Morpurgo) MS-JH
Windcatcher (Avi) MS-JH
Winning Scheherazade (Gorog) MS-JH

Aging

Bloodroot (Hobbie) MS-JH
Dancing on the Table (Murrow & Himler) EL
Darkling (Peyton) HS
Everywhere (Brooks) MS-JH
Journey (Maclachlan) EL-MS)
Loving Someone Else (Conford) JH-HS
Make Like a Tree and Leave (Danziger) MS-JH
The Mysterious World of Marcus Leadbeater (Southall) HS
Our Sixth-Grade Sugar Baby Blues (Bunting) EL-MS
Poems for Grandmothers (Livingston) MS-A
Shadows (Haseley) EL
Take a Chance, Gramps (Okimoto) MS-JH
The Warnings (Buffie) MS-JH
Why the Whales Came (Morpurgo) MS-JH

Animals

Animal Amazing (Herbst) MS-A
Beast (Benchley) HS-A
Bizarre Birds and Beasts (Marsh) EL-MS
Boss Dog (Fisher) A
Cricket and the Crackerbox Kid (Ferguson) EL-MS
Darkling (Peyton) HS
Expedition (Barlowe) HS-A
The Farewell Kid (Wersba) JH-HS
The Foxes of FirstDark (Kilworth) A
Halsey's Pride (Hall) MS
Harvey's Wacky Parrot Adventure (Clifford) EL
I Am Leaper (Johnson) EL-MS
The Importance of Being Oscar (Wilde) HS-A
Junkyard Dog (Ruch) EL-MS
Last Chance to See (Adams & Carwardine) HS-A
A Mouse in My Roof (Edwards) EL-JH
On the Far Side of the Mountain (George) EL-JH
R-T, Margaret and the Rats of NIMH (Conly) EL-JH
Roger Caras' Treasury of Great Horse Stories (Caras) JH-A
Rotten Egg Paterson to the Rescue (Thiele) EL-MS
A Tale of Antarctica (Glimmerveen) EL-A
Thunderwith (Hathorn) JH-HS
Wanted . . . Mud Blosson (Byars)
When Grandfather's Parrot Inherited Kennington Court (Allen) EL
White Hare's Horses (Spinka) MS-HS)
Why the Whales Came (Morpurgo) MS-JH
Winter-Broken (Smith) MS-JH
Wolves (Savage) HS-A
Zoobabies (O'Neill & Fireside) EL-A

Art

Against the Grain (Ferris) JH-HS
Black and White (Macauley) EL-A
Bugs Bunny (Adamson) EL-A
My Name Is Sus5an Smith . . . (Plummer) JH-HS
Silver Light (Thomson) HS-A

Biography

Be My Baby (Spector) HS-A
Black Ice (Cary) HS-A
The Bookmaker's Daughter (Abbott) A
Coaching Evelyn (Connolly) MS-HS
Dark Horse (Giuliano) HS-A
Forever's Team (Feinstein) HS-A
Girl with the White Flag (Higa) MS-JH
War Boy (Foreman) MS-A

Child Abuse

Babyface (Mazer) JH
Billy (Streiber) HS-A
The Jewel of Life (Kirwan-Vogel) JH
Lark in the Morning (Garden) HS
Randall's Wall (Fenner) MS
The Secret Keeper (Whelan) JH-HS
Tom Loves Anna Loves Tom (Clements) JH-HS
Where Rag Dolls Hide Their Faces (Koplow) HS-A
Winter-Broken (Smith) MS-JH

Crime and Deliquency

The Adventures of Boone Barnaby (Cottonwood) MS-JH
Billy (Streiber) HS-A
Blindfold (McCuaig) JH-HS
The Bookmaker's Daughter (Abbott) A
Breaking Out (DeClements) MS
Encyclopedia Brown's Book of Strange but True Crimes (Sobol) EL-JH
Gruel and Unusual Punishment (Arter) MS-JH
Harry Kaplan's Adventures Underground (Stern) HS-A
Last Chance Summer (Wieber) JH-HS
Line of Duty (Grant) A
Most Precious Blood (Pfeffer) MS-HS
My Crooked Family (Collier) JH-HS
My Name Is Sus5an Smith . . . (Plummer) JH-HS
The Night the Bells Rang (Kinsey-Warnock) MS
Rachel Chance (Thesman) MS-JH
Ride a Cockhorse (Kennedy) A
Round the Bend (Dale) JH
Saturnalia (Fleischman) JH-HS
Scotch on the Rocks (Browne) HS-A
Shiva Accused (Brennan) MS-JH
Stolen Away (Collins) HS-A
Straight Talk with Kids (The Scott Newman Center) A

Teenage Wasteland (Gaines) HS-A
The Tiger in the Well (Pullman) JH-A
The Two Faces of Adam (Meyer) HS
Weasel (DeFelice) MS-JH
Where'd You Get the Gun, Billy? (Arrick)
    JH-HS

Death and Mourning

Blindfold (McCuaig) JH-HS
Contrary Imaginations (Callen) MS-JH
Coping with Death and Grief (Heegaard)
    EL-MS
Everywhere (Brooks) MS-JH
Hank (Sauer) JH-HS
The House in the Woods (Holland) MS-
    JH
I Can Hear the Mourning Dove (Bennett)
    JH-HS
Journey Home (Holland) EL-MS
Last Summer with Maizon (Woodson)
    MS
Long Time Passing (Jones) HS-A
*The Mysterious World of Marcus
    Leadbeater* (Southall) HS
Object Lessons (Quindlen) HS-A
On the Third Ward (Degens) JH-HS
Robin on His Own (Wilson) EL-MS
Sisters Long Ago (Kehret) MS-JH
Someone's Mother Is Missing (Mazer)
    JH-HS
Take a Chance, Gramps (Okimoto) MS-
    JH
Teenage Wasteland (Gaines) HS-A
Tom Loves Anna Loves Tom (Clements)
    JH-HS
Where'd You Get the Gun, Billy? (Arrick)
    JH-HS
You Take the High Road (Pershall) JH-
    HS

Environmental Issues

Andra (Lawrence) HS
Bloodroot (Hobbie) MS-JH
Brother Eagle, Sister Sky (Jeffers) EL-HS
Crying for a Dream (Erdoes) HS-A
Faces of Ceti (Caraker) JH-HS
I Am Leaper (Johnson) EL-MS
Just a Dream (Allsburg) EL-A
Last Chance to See (Adams & Carwar-
    dine) HS-A
Make Like a Tree and Leave (Danziger)
    MS-JH
Tale of Antarctica (Glimmerveen) EL-A

Why the Whales Came (Morpurgo) MS-
    JH
Window (Baker) EL-A

Family Relationships

Acacia Terrace (Wilson) MS-A
Against the Grain (Ferris) JH-HS
Amazing Gracie (Cannon) JH-HS
Among the Volcanoes (Castaneda) JH-HS
Anastasia at This Address (Lowry) MS
Angela and the Broken Heart (Robinson)
    MS-JH
April Upstairs (Pfeffer) MS-JH
Author! Author! (Ferris) MS
Babyface (Mazer) JH
Beauty (Tepper) HS-A
Bedrock (Alther) A
The Big Book of Hell (Groening) HS-A
Bloodroot (Hobbie) MS-JH
The Bookmaker's Daughter (Abbott) A
The Boonsville Bombers (Herzig) EL
Borderlands (Carter) JH-A
The Bread Winner (Whitmore) MS-JH
Breaking Out (DeClements) MS
Brother Moose (Levin) MS
Cabin Fever (Jolley) A
Candidate for Murder (Nixon) JH-HS
The Chickenhouse House (Howard) EL
The Christmas Ark (San Souci) EL
Circles (Sachs) MS-JH
Contrary Imaginations (Callen) MS-JH
D, My Name Is Danita (Mazer) JH-HS
Dancing on the Table (Murrow & Him-
    ler) EL
Darcy Downstairs (Pfeffer) MS-JH
Darkling (Peyton) HS
The Day That Elvis Came to Town (Ma-
    rino) JH-HS
Don't Rent My Room! (Angell) MS-JH
Downriver (Hobbs) JH-HS
Echoes of War (Westall) JH-A
The Farewell Kid (Wersba) JH-HS
First Wedding, Once Removed (Deaver)
    MS-JH
Friend of My Youth (Munro) A
Growing Up Isn't Hard to Do . . . (Hel-
    ler) A
Gruel and Unusual Punishment (Arter)
    MS-JH
The Half Child (Hersom) JH-HS
Hank (Sauer) JH-HS
Hannah (Whelan) EL-MS
Harry and Catherine (Busch) A
Harry Kaplan's Adventures Underground
    (Stern) HS-A

High Cheekbones (Tamar) JH-HS
High Trail to Danger (Nixon) MS-HS
Home Sweet Home, Goodbye (Stowe) EL-MS
The House in the Woods (Holland) MS-JH
I Hate Camping (Petersen) EL
In Caverns of Blue Ice (Roper) JH-HS
Jilly's Ghost (Regan) JH-HS
Journey(MacLachlan) EL-MS
Junkyard Dog (Ruch) EL-MS
Kidnapping Kevin Kowalski (Auch) MS-JH
Lark in the Morning (Garden) HS
Leap Year (Cameron) A
Leaves in October (Ackerman) EL-MS
Libby on Wednesday (Snyder) MS-JH
Long Time Passing (Jones) HS-A
Losing Joe's Place (Korman) JH-HS
Lyddie (Paterson) MS-JH
Make Like a Tree and Leave (Danziger) MS-JH
Making History (See) A
Masquerade (Dailey) HS-A
Matthew Jackson Meets the Wall (Giff) EL-MS
Mayflower Man (Shriver) MS-JH
Mississippi Bridge (Taylor) MS-HS
Molly by Any Other Name (Okimoto) JH-A
Most Precious Blood (Pfeffer) MS-HS
The Mozart Season (Wolff) JH-HS
My Crooked Family (Collier) JH-HS
My Aunt Ruth (Rosofsky) JH-HS
My Name Is Sus5an Smith . . . (Plummer) JH-HS
My Sister Is Driving Me Crazy (Ryan) MS-JH
The Mysterious World of Marcus Leadbeater (Southall) HS
Naked in Winter (Brooks) JH
A Newbery Christmas (Greenberg & Waugh) EL-JH
Object Lessons (Quindlen) HS-A
The Ogre Downstairs (Jones) EL-JH
Out of the Ordinary (Dalton) JH-HS
Piper's Ferry (Wisler) MS-JH
Poems for Grandmothers (Livingston) MS-A
The Practical Joke War (Ferguson) EL
R-T, Margaret and the Rats of NIMH (Conly) EL-JH
Rachel Chance (Thesman) MS-JH
Randall's Wall (Fenner) MS
Robin on His Own (Wilson) EL-MS
Rosemary's Witch (Turner) MS

Round the Bend (Dale) JH
Saturnalia (Fleischman) JH-HS
Saving Lenny (Willey) HS
School's Out (Hurwitz) EL
The Secret Keeper (Whelan) JH-HS
Seymour, the Formerly Fearful (Feldman) EL-MS
Shadow Brothers (Cannon) JH-HS
Shadows (Haseley) EL
Shelter for a Seabird (Farish) HS
Sisters Long Ago (Kehret) MS-JH
Sleepers, Awake (Farish) MS-JH
Someday I'll Laugh About This (Crew) MS-JH
Someone's Mother Is Missing (Mazer) JH-HS
Take a Chance, Gramps (Okimoto) MS-JH
Thunderwith (Hathorn) JH-HS
Tom Loves Anna Loves Tom (Clements) JH-HS
Truce (Bode) HS
Twenty Pageants Later (Cooney) MS-JH
The Two Faces of Adam (Meyer) HS
The Warnings (Buffie) MS-JH
Weasel (De Felice) MS-JH
Whatever Became of Aunt Margaret? (De Weese) MS-JH
Wings (Brittain) EL-MS
Winter-Broken (Smith) MS-JH
Wish on a Unicorn (Hesse) MS
Witch Baby (Block) JH-HS
Witch House (Johnson) MS-JH
Witch Weed (Naylor) EL-MS
Wolf (Cross) JH-HS
Wolf by the Ears (Rinaldi) HS-A
Woman Without a Past (Whitney) HS-A
You Take the High Road (Pershall) JH-HS

Fantasy (See also Science Fiction; Time Travel)

Almighty Me (Bausch) A
Beauty (Tepper) HS-A
Beyond the Door (Blackwood) JH
Castle in the Air (Jones) JH-HS
Door in the Air (Mahy) EL-MS
Dragon Cauldron (Yep) MS-JH
Drummond (Odgers) EL
The Foxes of FirstDark (Kilworth) A
Jeremy Thatcher, Dragon Hatcher (Coville) EL-MS
The Jewel of Life (Kirwan-Vogel) JH
Out of the Ordinary (Dalton) JH-HS
Phantom (Kay) A

R-T, Margaret and the Rats of NIMH (Conly) EL-JH
The Song of the Gargoyle (Snyder) MS-JH
Tales of the Early World (Hughes) EL-JH
Walker of Worlds (DeHaven) HS-A
Whatever Became of Aunt Margaret? (DeWeese) MS-JH
Wings (Brittain) EL-MS
The Witching Hour (Rice) A
Wizard's Hall (Yolen) EL-MS

Folklore and Folktales

Larger Than Life (San Souci) EL-MS
More Stories to Solve (Shannon) EL-JH
The Old Coot (Christian) EL-MS
Vampires (Yolen & Greenberg) JH
A Wave in Her Pocket (Joseph) EL-MS
Wolves (Savage) HS-A

Friendship

The Adventures of Boone Barnaby (Cottonwood) MS-JH
Against the Grain (Ferris) JH-HS
Anastasia at This Address (Lowry) MS
April Upstairs (Pfeffer) MS-JH
Babyface (Mazer) JH
Bernie and the Bessledorf Ghost (Naylor) EL-MS
Black Ice (Cary) HS-A
Blindfold (McCuaig) JH-HS
The Boy in the Moon (Koertge) JH-HS
Breaking Out (DeClements) MS
Come Next Spring (White) MS-JH
Cricket and the Crackerbox Kid (Ferguson) EL-MS
Crow and Weasel (Lopez) EL-A
Darcy Downstairs (Pfeffer) MS-JH
The Day That Elvis Came to Town (Marino) JH-HS
Dew Drop Dead (Howe) MS-HS
Distant Fires (Anderson & Kouba) HS-A
Downriver (Hobbs) JH-HS
Dragon Cauldron (Yep) MS-JH
Drummond (Odgers) EL
Eben Tyne, Powdermonkey (Beatty & Robinson) MS-JH
Eenie, Meanie, Murphy, No! (McKenna) EL-MS
Face the Dragon (Sweeney) MS-JH
Fast Talk on a Slow Track (Williams-Garcia) JH-HS
Fatso Jean, the Ice Cream Queen (Macdonald) EL
Finding Signs (Baker) A
Forever's Team (Feinstein) HS-A
Friend of My Youth (Munro) A
Friendship Across Arctic Waters (Murphy) EL-JH
George Washington's Socks (Woodruff) EL-MS
Germy Blew the Bugle (Jones) MS
The Ghost in the Attic (Cates) MS-JH
The Greatest Idea Ever (Carris) EL-MS
Gruel and Unusual Punishment (Arter) MS-JH
A Hand Full of Stars (Schami) HS
Happy Endings (Geras) JH-HS
Harry Kaplan's Adventures Underground (Stern) HS-A
Harvey's Wacky Parrot Adventure (Clifford) EL
The Hideout (Bunting) MS-JH
High Cheekbones (Tamar) JH-HS
Into the Dark (Wilde) MS-JH
Jilly's Ghost (Regan) JH-HS
Junkyard Dog Ruch) EL-MS
Just Friends (Allsburg) JH-HS
Kidnapping Kevin Kowalski (Auch) MS-JH
Lark in the Morning (Garden) HS
Last Summer with Maizon (Woodson) MS
Libby on Wednesday (Snyder) MS-JH
Losing Joe's Place (Korman) JH-HS
MacDonald Hall Goes Hollywood (Korman) MS-JH
Make Like a Tree and Leave (Danziger) MS-JH
Matthew Jackson Meets the Wall (Giff) EL-MS
Maxie, Rosie and Earl—Partners in Grime (Park) EL-MS
Mayflower Man (Shriver) MS-JH
Mississippi Bridge (Taylor) MS-JH
Naked in Winter (Brooks) JH
On the Third Ward (Degens) JH-HS
Otto from Otherwhere (Griffin) MS-JH
Our Sixth-Grade Sugar Baby Blues (Bunting) EL-MS
R-T, Margaret and the Rats of NIMH (Conly) EL-JH
Randall's Wall (Fenner) MS
Saving Lenny (Willey) HS
The Secret Life of Hubie Hartzel (Masters) EL-MS
Seymour, the Formerly Fearful (Feldman) EL-MS
Silver Light (Thomson) HS-A

Smart Rats (Baird) JH-HS
Someday I'll Laugh about This (Crew) MS-JH
Stay Tuned (Corcoran) JH
Stonewords (Conrad) MS-JH
The Strange Case of the Reluctant Partners (Geller) MS
Take a Chance, Gramps (Okimoto) MS-JH
Teenage Wasteland (Gaines) HS-A
Thin Air (Getz) EL-MS
A Tribe for Lexi (Adler) MS-JH
Twenty Pageants Later (Cooney) MS-JH
Twenty Ways to Lose Your Best Friend (Singer) EL
Upchuck Summer's Revenge (Schwartz) MS
Whatever Became of Aunt Margaret? (DeWeese) MS-JH
When Kids Drive Kids Crazy (LeShan) MS-JH
Where'd You Get the Gun, Billy? (Arrick) JH-HS
Why the Whales Came (Morpurgo) MS-JH
Wings (Brittain) EL-MS
Winter-Broken (Smith) MS-JH
Witch Baby (Block) JH-HS

Handicaps

B-Ball (Jones) MS-HS
Fatso Jean, the Ice Cream Queen (Macdonald) EL
Half Child (Hersom) JH-HS
Halsey's Pride (Hall) MS
Hannah (Whelan) EL-MS
The House in the Woods (Holland) MS-JH
Into the Dark (Wilde) MS-JH
Kidnapping Kevin Kowalski (Auch) MS-JH
Phantom (Kay) A
Rachel Chance (Thesman) MS-JH
Thin Air (Getz) EL-MS
Where Rag Dolls Hide Their Faces (Koplow) HS-A
Why the Whales Came (Morpurgo) MS-JH
Wish on a Unicorn (Hesse) MS

Health and illness (See also Handicaps; Psychology)

Among the Volcanoes (Castaneda) JH-HS
Everywhere (Brooks) MS-JH
Halsey's Pride (Hall) MS
My Aunt Ruth (Rosofsky) JH-HS
On the Third Ward (Degens) JH-HS
Sisters Long Ago (Kehret) MS-JH
Straight Talk with Kids (The Scott Newman Center) A
Thin Air (Getz) EL-MS

Historical Fiction

Acacia Terrace (Wilson) MS-A
Bartholomew Fair (Stolz) MS-JH
Borderlands (Carter) JH-A
The Bread Winner (Whitmore) MS-JH
Brother Moose (Levin) MS
Cabin Fever (Jolley) A
Come Next Spring (White) MS-JH
Crow and Weasel (Lopez) EL-A
The Chickenhouse House (Howard) EL
The Christmas Ark (San Souci) EL
The Day That Elvis Came to Town (Marino) JH-HS
Eben Tyne, Powdermonkey (Beatty & Robinson) MS-JH
Echoes of War (Westall) JH-A
Friend of My Youth (Munro) A
George Washington's Socks (Woodruff) EL-MS
Journey Home (Holland) EL-MS
Half Child (Hersom) JH-HS
Hannah (Whelan) EL-MS
High Trail to Danger (Nixon) MS-HS
Journey from the Dawn (Johanson & Farrell) HS-A
Long Time Passing (Jones) HS-A
Lyddie (Paterson) MS-JH
The Man from the Other Side (Orlev) JH-HS
Mississippi Bridge (Taylor) MS-HS
My Crooked Family (Collier) JH-HS
The Night the Bells Rang (Kinsey-Warnock) MS
Phantom (Kay) A
Piper's Ferry (Wisler) MS-JH
Professor Popkin's Prodigious Polish (Brittain) EL-MS
Rachel Chance (Thesman) MS-JH
Roger Caras' Treasury of Great Horse Stories (Caras) JH-A
Saturnalia (Fleischman) JH-HS
Scotch on the Rocks (Browne) HS-A
Secret Anniversaries (Spencer) A

Shiva Accused (Brennan) MS-JH
Silver Light (Thomson) HS-A
Stolen Away (Collins) HS-A
The Tiger in the Well (Pullman) JH-A
Tug of War (Lingard) MS-JH
Weasel (DeFelice) MS-JH
White Hare's Horses (Spinka) MS-HS
Why the Whales Came (Morpurgo) MS-JH
The Witching Hour (Rice) HS-A
Wolf by the Ears (Rinaldi) HS-A

History

Brother Eagle, Sister Sky (Jeffers) EL-A
Escape from Slavery (Rappaport) EL-MS
The Girl with the White Flag (Higa) MS-JH
The Last Seven Months of Anne Frank (Lindwer) HS-A
The Other Victims (Friedman) MS-HS
Remember Who You Are (Hautzig) HS-A
Summer (Gordon & Virga) A

Homeless

Last Chance Summer (Wieler) JH-HS
The Leaves in October (Ackerman) EL-MS
Stay Tuned (Corcoran) JH
Wanted . . . Mud Blossom (Byars) EL

Homosexuality

Face the Dragon (Sweeney) JH-HS
Lark in the Morning (Garden) HS

Horror

Billy (Streiber) HS-A
Darkness (Saul) HS-A
Fiends (Farris) HS-A
Fire Mask (Grant) MS-JH
He Came from the Shadows (Westwood) JH-HS
Jurassic Park (Crichton) HS-A
Monster of the Year (Coville) MS-JH
Out of the Ordinary (Dalton) JH-HS
Phantom (Kay) A
The Torment of Mr Gully (Clarke) JH-HS
Vampires (Yolen & Greenberg) JH
The Witching Hour (Rice) HS-A

Humor

Almighty Me (Bausch) A
Anastasia at This Address (Lowry) MS
Angela and the Broken Heart (Robinson) MS-JH
Benny and the Crazy Contest (Zach) EL
The Big Book of Hell (Groening) HS-A
Bizarre Birds and Beasts (Marsh) EL-MS
Black and White (Macauley) EL-A
Boss Dog (Fisher) A
Bugs Bunny (Adamson) EL-A
Dagmar Schultz and the Green-Eyed Monster (Hall) MS-JH
Dakota of the White Flats (Ridley) EL-MS
Dear God: What Religion Were the Dinosaurs? (Heller) A
Don't Rent My Room! (Angell) MS-JH
Eenie, Meanie, Murphy, No! (McKenna) EL-MS
For Laughing Out Loud (Prelutsky) EL-JH
Fourth Grade Rats (Spinelli) EL-MS
Fresh Brats (Kennedy) MS-HS
Full Moon Soup (Graham) EL-JH; A
The Greatest Idea Ever (Carris) EL-MS
Growing Up Isn't Hard to Do (Heller) A
Harry Kaplan's Adventures Underground (Stern) HS-A
Harvey's Wacky Parrot Adventure (Clifford) EL
I Hate Camping! (Petersen) EL
The Importance of Being Oscar (Wilde) EL-A
Kidnapping Kevin Kowalski (Auch) MS-JH
Losing Joe's Place (Korman) EL-MS
MacDonald Hall Goes Hollywood (Korman) MS-JH
Make Four Million Dollars by Next Thursday (Manes) EL-MS
Matthew Jackson Meets the Wall (Giff) EL-MS
Maxie, Rosie and Earl—Partners in Grime (Park) EL—MS
Monster of the Year (Coville) MS-JH
The Moon Clock (Faulkner) EL-MS
A Mouse in My Roof (Edwards) EL-JH
Mummy Took Cooking Lessons (Ciardi) JH-HS
Our Sixth-Grade Sugar Baby Blues (Bunting) EL-MS
The Practical Joke War (Ferguson) EL
Professor Popkin's Prodigious Polish (Brittain) EL-MS

Reluctantly Alice (Naylor) MS-JH
Ride a Cockhorse (Kennedy) A
Rotten Egg Paterson to the Rescue
   (Thiele) EL-MS
School's Out (Hurwitz) EL
Scotch on the Rocks (Browne) A
Sixties People (Stern) HS-A
*The Strange Case of the Reluctant
   Partners* (Geller) MS
Susanna Siegelbaum Gives Up Guys (Fo-
   ley) MS
Tales of the Early World (Hughes) EL-JH
A Telling of Tales (Brooke) EL-JH, A
Twelve-Year-Old Vows Revenge (Roose)
   MS-JH
Upchuck Summer's Revenge (Schwartz)
   MS
Walker of Worlds (DeHaven) HS-A
Yours Till Niagara Falls (Morrison) EL-
   JH

Immigrants

A Gathering of Flowers (Thomas) JH-HS
Journey Home (Holland) EL-MS

Interviews

Growing Up Isn't Hard to Do . . . (Hel-
   ler) A
The Last Seven Months of Anne Frank
   (Lindwer) HS-A
The Other Victims (Friedman) MS-HS
Summer (Gordon & Virga) HS-A
Teenage Wasteland (Gaines) HS-A
Truce (Bode) HS
A World of Ideas II (Moyers) HS-A

Language (See also Poetry)

I Have Words to Spend (Cormier) A
The Old Coot (Christian) EL-MS
You Don't Need Words (Gross) EL-MS

Minorities:
Asian

A Gathering of Flowers (Thomas) JH-HS
The Girl with the White Flag (Higa) MS-
   JH
Molly by Any Other Name (Okimoto)
   JH-A
The Two Faces of Adam (Meyer) HS

Black

Black Ice (Cary) HS-A
Escape from Slavery (Rappaport) EL-MS
A Gathering of Flowers (Thomas) JH-HS
Harry Kaplan's Adventures Underground
   (Stern) HS-A
Last Summer with Maizon (Woodson)
   MS
Mississippi Bridge (Taylor) MS-HS
Robin on His Own (Wilson) EL-MS
When I Dance (Berry) HS-A
Wolf by the Ears (Rinaldi) HS-A

Hispanic

Among the Volcanoes (Castaneda) JH-HS
A Gathering of Flowers (Thomas) JH-HS
Woman Hollering Creek (Cisneros) HS-A

Jewish

A Gathering of Flowers (Thomas) JH-HS
Harry Kaplan's Adventures Underground
   (Stern) HS-A
The Last Seven Months of Anne Frank
   (Lindwer) HS-A
The Man from the Other Side (Orlev)
   JH-HS
The Mozart Season (Wolff) JH-HS
Remember Who You Are (Hautzig) HS-A
Seymour, the Formerly Fearful (Feld-
   man) EL-MS

Native American

Among the Volcanoes (Castaneda) JH-HS
Brother Eagle, Sister Sky (Jeffers) El-HS
Canyons (Paulsen) JH-A
Crow and Weasel (Lopez) EL-A
Crying for a Dream (Erdoes) HS-A
A Gathering of Flowers (Thomas) JH-HS
The Praying Flute (Shearer) JH-A
Saturnalia (Fleischman) JH-HS
The Shadow Brothers Cannon) JH-HS
White Hare's Horses (Spinka) MS-HS

Music

Be My Baby (Spector) HS-A
Dark Horse (Giuliano) HS-A
Kisses (Caseley) JH-HS
The Mozart Season (Wolff) JH-HS
*Of Swans, Sugarplums, and Satin
   Slippers* (Verdy) EL-JH
Phantom (Kay) A

Mystery / Suspense

Agnes Cecilia (Gripe) MS-JH
The Bell Tolls at Mousehaven Manor
    (Kwitz) EL
Billy (Streiber) HS-A
Blindfold (McCuaig) JH-HS
A Candidate for Murder (Nixon) JH-HS
Colors of Snow (Fenton) A
Dakota of the White Flats (Ridley) EL-
    MS
Dew Drop Dead (Howe) MS-HS
*Encyclopedia Brown's Book of Strange
    but True Crimes* (Sobol) EL-JH
George Washington's Socks (Woodruff)
    EL-MS
The Ghost in the Attic (Cates) MS-JH
A Graveyard for Lunatics (Bradbury)
    HS-A
Gruel and Unusual Punishment (Arter)
    MS-JH
Halsey's Pride (Hall) MS
Harvey's Wacky Parrot Adventure (Clif-
    ford) EL
High Trail to Danger (Nixon) MS-HS
The House in the Woods (Holland) MS-
    JH
Into the Dark (Wilde) MS-JH
The Last Defector (Cape) HS-A
Line of Duty (Grant) HS-A
Masquerade (Dailey) HS-A
More Stories to Solve (Shannon) EL-JH
*The Mysterious World of Marcus
    Leadbeater* (Southall) HS
A Place to Claim as Home (Willis) MS-
    JH
The Secret Keeper (Whelan) JH-HS
Shadows (Haseley) EL
Shiva Accused (Brennan) MS-JH
Stolen Away (Collins) HS-A
The Tiger in the Well (Pullman) JH-A
Tomorrow's Crimes (Westlake) A
Wanted . . . Mud Blossom (Byars) EL
*When Grandfather's Parrot Inherited
    Kennington Court* (Allen) EL
Where'd You Get the Gun, Billy? (Arrick)
    JH-HS
Why the Whales Came (Morpurgo) MS-
    JH
Windcatcher (Avi) MS-JH
Winning Scheherazade (Gorog) MS-JH
Witch Weed (Naylor) EL-MS
Wolf (Cross) JH-HS
Woman Without a Past (Whitney) HS-A

Nature

Bizarre Birds and Beasts (Marsh) EL-MS
Brother Eagle, Sister Sky (Jeffers) EL-HS
Last Chance to See (Adams & Carwar-
    dine) HS-A
On the Far Side of the Mountain
    (George) EL-JH
An Owl in the House (Heinrich) MS-A
A Tale of Antarctica (Glimmerveen)
    EL-A
Voices on the Wind (Booth) EL-MS
Wolves (Savage) HS-A

Nonfiction (See also Biography; Poetry)

Amazing True Stories (Wulffson) MS-A
Animal Amazing (Herbst) MS-A
B-Ball (Jones) MS-HS
Bering Bridge (Schurke) JH-A
Brother Eagle, Sister Sky (Jeffers) EL-HS
Bugs Bunny (Adamson) EL-A
Celebrate You (Johnson) JH-HS
Coping with Death and Grief (Heegaard)
    EL-MS
Crying for a Dream (Erdoes) HS-A
*Dear God: What Religion Were the
    Dinoaurs?* (Heller) A
Distant Fires (Anderson & Kouba) HS-A
Dream Teams (Benson) MS-A
*Encyclopedia Brown's Book of Strange
    but True Crimes* (Sobol) EL-JH
Escape from Slavery (Rappaport) EL-MS
Friendship Across Arctic Waters (Mur-
    phy) EL-JH
Growing Up Isn't Hard To Do . . .
    (Heller) A
I Bet You Didn't Know That . . . (series)
    (Iverson) EL-MS
I Have Words to Spend (Cormier) A
Journey from the Dawn (Johanson &
    Farrell) HS-A
Last Chance to See (Adams & Carwar-
    dine) HS-A
The Last Seven Months of Anne Frank
    (Lindwer) HS-A
Looking Inside (Fleisher & Keeler) EL
More Stories to Solve (Shannon) EL-JH
*The New York Times Book of Sports
    Legends* (Vecchione) A
*Of Swans, Sugarplums, and Satin
    Slippers* (Verdy) EL-JH
The Other Victims (Friedman) MS-HS
An Owl in the House (Heinrich) MS-A
Remember Who You Are (Hautzig) HS-A
The Sierra Club Book of Weatherwisdom

(McVey) MS-JH
Sixties People (Stern) HS-A
Stolen Season (Lamb) HS-A
Straight Talk with Kids (Scott Newman Center) A
Summer (Gordon & Virga) HS-A
Teenage Wasteland (Gaines) HS-A
Truce (Bode) HS
When Kids Drive Kids Crazy (LeShan) MS-JH
Where Rag Dolls Hide Their Faces (Koplow) HS-A
Wolves (Savage) HS-A
A World of Ideas II (Moyers) HS-A
You Don't Need Words (Gross) EL-MS
Zoobabies (O'Neill & Fireside) EL-MS

Occult / Supernatural

Amazing True Stories (Wulffson) MS-A
Andra (Lawrence) HS
The Bell Tolls at Mousehaven Manor (Kwitz) EL
Bernie and the Bessledorf Ghost (Naylor) EL-MS
Canyons (Paulsen) JH-A
Darkness (Saul) HS-A
Everywhere (Brooks) MS-JH
Fiends (Farris) HS-A
Fire Mask (Grant) MS-JH
Full Moon Soup (Graham) EL-A
George Washington's Socks (Woodruff) EL-MS
Ghost in the Attic (Cates) MS-JH
Graveyard for Lunatics (Bradbury) HS-A
He Came from the Shadows (Westwood) JH-HS
Into the Dark (Wilde) MS-JH
The Jewel of Life (Kirwan-Vogel) JH
Jilly's Ghost (Regan) JH-HS
The Ogre Downstairs (Jones) EL-MS
Out of the Ordinary (Dalton) JH-HS
Professor Popkin's Prodigious Polish (Brittain) EL-MS
Rosemary's Witch (Turner) MS
The Rowan (McCaffrey) HS-A
Sisters Long Ago (Kehret) MS-JH
Stonewords (Conrad) MS-JH
Vampires (Yolen & Greenberg) JH
The Warnings (Buffie) MS-JH
A Wave in Her Pocket (Joseph) EL-MS
Why the Whales Came (Morpurgo) MS-JH
Witch House (Johnson) MS-JH
The Witching Hour (Rice) HS-A
Witch Weed (Naylor) EL-MS

Other Countries / Other Cultures

Acacia Terrace (Wilson) MS-A
Agnes Cecelia (Gripe) MS-JH
Among the Volcanoes (Castaneda) JH-HS
Bartholomew Fair (Stolz) MS-JH
Bering Bridge (Schurke) JH-A
Boss Dog (Fisher) A
Cabin Fever (Jolley) A
Distant Fires (Anderson & Kouba) HS-A
Friend of My Youth (Munro) A
Friendship Across Arctic Waters (Murphy) EL-MS
The Girl with the White Flag (Higa) MS-JH
Half Child (Hersom) JH-HS
A Hand Full of Stars (Schami) HS
Into the Dark (Wilde) MS-JH
The Last Seven Months of Anne Frank (Lindwer) HS-A
The Man from the Other Side (Orlev) JH-HS
The Mysterious World of Marcus Leadbeater (Southall) HS
Out of the Ordinary (Dalton) JH-HS
Phantom (Kay) A
Remember Who You Are (Hautzig) HS-A
Rotten Egg Paterson to the Rescue (Thiele) EL-MS
A Tale of Antarctica (Glimmerveen) EL-A
Thunderwith (Hathorn) JH-HS
Tiger in the Well (Pullman) JH-A
War Boy (Foreman) MS-A
A Wave in Her Pocket (Joseph) EL-MS
When I Dance (Berry) HS-A
Why the Whales Came (Morpurgo) MS-JH
Winning Scheherazade (Gorog) MS-JH
The Witching Hour (Rice) HS-A
Wolf (Cross) JH-HS

Peer Pressure

Breaking Out (DeClements) EL-MS
Face the Dragon (Sweeney) JH-HS
Fast Talk on a Slow Track (Williams-Garcia) JH-HS
Fatso Jean, the Ice Cream Queen (Macdonald) EL
Fourth Grade Rats (Spinelli) EL-MS
Germy Blew the Bugle (Jones) MS
Molly by Any Other Name (Okimoto) JH-A
Teenage Wasteland (Gaines) HS-A
Twelve-Year-Old Vows Revenge (Roos) MS-JH

Poetry

Balloons and Other Poems (Chandra) EL
Bizarre Birds and Beasts (Marsh) EL-MS
For Laughing Out Loud (Prelutsky) EL-JH
Fresh Brats (Kennedy) MS-HS
The Kite That Braved Old Orchard Beach (Kennedy) MS-HS
A Mouse in My Roof (Edwards) EL-JH
Mummy Took Cooking Lessons (Ciardi) JH-HS
The Place My Words Are Looking For (Janeczko) EL-JH
Poems for Grandmothers (Livingston) MS-A
Time Is the Longest Distance (Gordon) MS-A
To the Moon and Back (Larrick) EL-JH
Up in the Mountains (Lewis) MS-A
Voices on the Wind (Booth) EL-MS
When I Dance (Berry) HS-A
Yours Till Niagara Falls (Morrison) EL-JH

Psychology and Mental Illness

Amazing Gracie (Cannon) JH-HS
Be My Baby (Spector) HS-A
Celebrate You (Johnson) JH-HS
Coping with Death and Grief (Heegaard) EL-MS
Gruel and Unusual Punishment (Arter) MS-JH
I Can Hear the Mourning Dove (Bennett) JH-HS
Lark in the Morning (Garden) HS
Randall's Wall (Fenner) MS
Round the Bend (Dale) JH
Saving Lenny (Willey) HS
Someone's Mother Is Missing (Mazer) JH-HS
Sixties People (Stern) HS-A
Straight Talk with Kids (The Scott Newman Center) A
Teenage Wasteland (Gaines) HS-A
A Tribe for Lexi (Adler) MS-JH
Truce (Bode) HS
When Kids Drive Kids Crazy (LeShan) MS-JH
Where Rag Dolls Hide Their Faces (Koplow) HS-A

Religion

Almighty Me (Bausch) A
Dear God: What Religion Were the Dinosaurs? (Heller) A
Journey Home (Holland) EL-MS
The Man from the Other Side (Orlev) JH-HS
Old Blue Tilley (Branscum) MS

Romance

Against the Grain (Ferris) JH-HS
Anastasia at This Address (Lowry) MS
Angela and the Broken Heart (Robinson) MS-JH
Beauty (Tepper) HS-A
Beyond the Door (Blackwood) JH
The Boy in the Moon (Koertge) JH-HS
Castle in the Air (Jones) JH-HS
Circles (Sachs) MS-JH
Colors of Snow (Fenton) A
D, My Name Is Danita (Mazer) JH-HS
Darkling (Peyton) HS
A Door in the Air (Mahy) EL-MS
Downriver (Hobbs) JH-HS
Eenie, Meanie, Murphy, No! (McKenna) EL-MS
Face the Dragon (Sweeney) JH-HS
The Farewell Kid (Wersba) JH-HS
Finding Signs (Baker) A
First Wedding, Once Removed (Deaver) MS-JH
Fourth Grade Rats (Spinelli) EL-MS
Hank (Sauer) JH-HS
Happy Endings (Geras) JH-HS
Harry and Catherine (Busch) A
Kisses (Caseley) JH-HS
Leap Year (Cameron) A
Long Time Passing (Jones) HS-A
Masquerade (Dailey) HS-A
My Name Is Sus5an Smith . . . (Plummer) JH-HS
Our Sixth-Grade Sugar Baby Blues (Bunting) EL-MS
Paradise Cafe (Brooks) JH-HS
Phantom (Kay) A
Reluctantly Alice (Naylor) MS-JH
The Rowan (McCaffrey) HS-A
Saving Lenny (Willey) HS
Secret Anniversaries (Spencer) A
Shelter for a Seabird (Farish) HS
Susanna Siegelbaum Gives Up Guys (Foley) MS
Take a Chance, Gramps (Okimoto) MS-JH
Tom Loves Anna Loves Tom (Clements)

JH-HS
Tug of War (Lingard) MS-JH
Wanted . . . Mud Blossom (Byars) EL
Witch Baby (Block) JH-HS
The Witching Hour (Rice) HS-A

Runaways

Downriver (Hobbs) JH-HS
The Hideout (Bunting) MS-JH
Lark in the Morning (Garden) HS
Last Chance Summer (Wieler) JH-HS
Stay Tuned (Corcoran) JH
A Tribe for Lexi (Adler) MS-JH

School

Angela and the Broken Heart (Robinson) MS-JH
April Upstairs (Pfeffer) MS-JH
Black Ice (Cary) HS-A
Breaking Out (DeClements) MS
Circles (Sachs) MS-JH
Dagmar Schultz and the Green-Eyed Monster (Hall) MS-JH
Darcy Downstairs (Pfeffer) MS-JH
Face the Dragon (Sweeney) JH-HS
Fast Talk on a Slow Track (Williams-Garcia) JH-HS
Fatso Jean, the Ice Cream Queen (Macdonald) EL
Fourth Grade Rats (Spinelli) EL-MS
Germy Blew the Bugle (Jones) MS
The Greatest Idea Ever (Carris) EL-MS
Gruel and Unusual Punishment (Arter) MS-JH
Hannah (Whelan) EL-MS
Libby on Wednesday (Snyder) MS-JH
Macdonald Hall Goes Hollywood (Korman) MS-JH
Make Like a Tree and Leave (Danziger) MS-JH
Matthew Jackson Meets the Wall (Giff) EL-MS
Maxie, Rosie and Earl—Partners in Grime (Park) EL-MS
My Sister Is Driving Me Crazy (Ryan) MS-JH
Otto from Otherwhere (Griffin) MS-JH
Our Sixth-Grade Sugar Baby Blues (Bunting) EL-MS
Randall's Wall (Fenner) MS
Reluctantly Alice (Naylor) MS-JH
Rotten Egg Paterson to the Rescue (Thiele) EL-MS

Round the Bend (Dale) JH
The Secret Life of Hubie Hartzel (Masters) EL-MS
Seymour, the Formerly Fearful (Feldman) EL-MS
The Strange Case of the Reluctant Partners (Geller) MS
Susanna Siegelbaum Gives Up Guys (Foley) MS
Teenage Wasteland (Gaines) HS-A
Thin Air (Getz) EL-MS
The Torment of Mr Gully (Clarke) JH-HS
Twenty Pageants Later (Cooney) MS-JH
Twenty Ways to Lose Your Best Friend (Singer) EL
The Two Faces of Adam (Meyer) HS
When Kids Drive Kids Crazy (LeShan) MS-JH
Where Rag Dolls Hide Their Faces (Koplow) HS-A
Where'd You Get the Gun, Billy? (Arrick) JH-HS

Science

I Bet You Didn't Know That . . . (series) (Iverson) EL-MS
Journey from the Dawn (Johanson & Farrell) HS-A
Last Chance to See (Adams & Carwardine) HS-A
Looking Inside (Fleisher & Keeler) EL
An Owl in the House (Heinrich) MS-A
The Sierra Club Book of Weatherwisdom (McVey) MS-JH
A Tale of Antarctica (Glimmerveen) EL-A
Wolves (Savage) HS-A

Science Fiction

Andra (Lawrence) HS
Beyond the Door (Blackwood) JH
Expedition (Barlowe) HS-A
Faces of Ceti (Caraker) JH-HS
I Am Leaper (Johnson) EL-MS
Jurassic Park (Crichton) HS-A
Just a Dream (Allsburg) EL-A
Nightfall (Asimov & Silverberg) HS-A
The Ogre Downstairs (Jones) EL-JH
Otto from Otherwhere (Griffin) MS-JH
The Rowan (McCaffrey) HS-A
Sleepers, Awake (Jacobs) MS-JH
Smart Rats (Baird) JH-HS

The Time and Space of Uncle Albert
(Stannard) EL-MS
Tomorrow's Crimes (Westlake) A
Walker of Worlds (DeHaven) HS-A
Whatever Became of Aunt Margaret?
(DeWeese) MS-JH

Self-Help

Celebrate You (Johnson) JH-HS
Coping with Death and Grief (Heegaard)
EL-MS
Straight Talk with Kids (The Scott New-
man Center) A
Truce (Bode) HS
When Kids Drive Kids Crazy (LeShan)
MS-JH

Self-Knowledge

Against the Grain (Ferris) JH-HS
Amazing Gracie (Cannon) JH-HS
Among the Volcanoes (Castaneda) JH-HS
April Upstairs (Pfeffer) MS-JH
Author! Author! (Ferris) MS
Bartholomew Fair (Stolz) MS-JH
Bedrock (Alther) A
Benny and the Crazy Contest (Zach) EL
Black Ice (Cary) HS-A
Bloodroot (Hobbie) MS-JH
Borderlands (Carter) JH-A
Boss Dog (Fisher) A
The Boy in the Moon (Koertge) JH-HS
Breaking Out (DeClements) MS
Cabin Fever (Jolley) A
Canyons (Paulsen) JH-A
Celebrate You (Johnson) JH-HS
Chickenhouse House (Howard) EL
Circles (Sachs) MS-JH
Crow and Weasel (Lopez) EL-A
Dancing on the Table (Murrow & Him-
ler) EL
Darcy Downstairs (Pfeffer) MS-JH
The Day That Elvis Came to Town (Ma-
rino) JH-HS
Don't Rent My Room! (Angell) MS-JH
Downriver (Hobbs) JH-HS
Echoes of War (Westall) JH-A
Eenie, Meanie, Murphy, No! (McKenna)
EL-MS
Face the Dragon (Sweeney) JH-HS
Fast Talk on a Slow Track (Williams-
Garcia) JH-HS
Fatso Jean, the Ice Cream Queen (Mac-
donald) EL

Finding Signs (Baker) A
First Wedding, Once Removed (Deaver)
MS-JH
Haley's Pride (Hall) MS
Happy Endings (Geras) JH-HS
High Cheekbones (Tamar) JH-HS
I Can Hear the Mourning Dove (Bennett)
JH-HS
I Have Words to Spend (Cormier) A
Journey (MacLachlan) EL-MS
Kisses (Caseley) JH-HS
Leap Year (Cameron)
Long Time Passing (Jones) HS-A
Loving Someone Else (Conford) JH-HS
Lyddie (Paterson) MS-JH
The Man from the Other Side (Orlev)
JH-HS
Masquerade (Dailey) HS-A
Matthew Jackson Meets the Wall (Giff)
EL-MS
Molly by Any Other Name (Okimoto)
JH-A
The Moon Clock (Faulkner) EL-MS
Most Precious Blood (Pfeffer) MS-HS
The Mozart Season (Wolff) JH-HS
My Crooked Family (Collier) JH-HS
My Aunt Ruth (Rosofsky) JH-HS
My Sister Is Driving Me Crazy (Ryan)
MS-JH
*The Mysterious World of Marcus
Leadbeater* (Southall) HS
Naked in Winter (Brooks) JH
The Night the Bells Rang (Kinsey-
Warnock) MS
Object Lessons (Quindlen) HS-A
On the Far Side of the Mountain
(George) EL-JH
Our Sixth Grade Sugar Baby Blues (Bun-
ting) EL-MS
The River (Paulsen) MS-HS
Rosemary's Witch (Turner) MS
Round the Bend (Dale) JH
Saving Lenny (Willey) HS
Secret Anniversaries (Spencer) A
The Secret Keeper (Whelan) JH-HS
The Shadow Brothers (Cannon) JH-HS
Shelter for a Seabird (Farish) HS
Sleepers, Awake (Jacobs) MS-JH
This Is the Life (O'Neill) HS-A
A Tribe for Lexi (Adler) MS-JH
Twenty Pageants Later (Cooney) MS-JH
The Two Faces of Adam (Meyer) HS
When Kids Drive Kids Crazy (LeShan)
MS-JH
Winter-Broken (Smith) MS-JH
Witch Baby (Block) JH-HS

Wizard's Hall (Yolen) MS-JH
Wolf by the Ears (Rinaldi) HS-A

Sex and Sexuality

The Boy in the Moon (Koertge) JH-HS
The Day That Elvis Came to Town (Marino) JH-HS
Face the Dragon (Sweeney) JH-HS
Lark in the Morning (Garden) HS
Paradise Cafe (Brooks) JH-HS
Secret Anniversaries (Spencer) A
Shelter for a Seabird (Farish) HS

Short Stories

Amazing True Stories (Wulffson) MS-A
The Big Book for Peace (Durell & Sachs) EL-A
The Door in the Air (Mahy) EL-MS
Echoes of War (Westall) JH-A
Fling (Hersey) A
Friend of My Youth (Munro) A
A Gathering of Flowers (Thomas) JH-HS
Larger Than Life (San Souci) EL
The Matter Is Life (Cooper) A
More Stories to Solve (Shannon) EL-JH
A Newbery Christmas (Greenberg & Waugh) EL-JH
Paradise Cafe (Brooks) JH-HS
Roger Caras' Treasury of Great Horse Stories (Caras) HS-A
A Telling of Tales (Brooke) EL-JH, A
Tomorrow's Crimes (Westlake) A
The Torment of Mr Gully (Clarke) JH-HS
Vampires (Yolen & Greenberg) JH
A Wave in Her Pocket (Joseph) EL-MS
Woman Hollering Creek (Cisneros) HS-A

Sports

The Adventures of Boone Barnaby (Cottonwood) MS-JH
B-Ball (Jones) MS-JH
The Boonsville Bombers (Herzig) EL
Coaching Evelyn (Connolly) MS-HS
Dream Teams (Benson) MS-A
Forever's Team (Feinstein) HS-A
In Caverns of Blue Ice (Roper) JH-HS
The New York Times Book of Sports Legends (Vecchione) HS-A
The Shadow Brothers (Cannon) JH-HS
Stolen Season (Lamb) HS-A

Substance Abuse

Be My Baby (Spector) HS-A
Coaching Evelyn (Connolly) MS-HS
The Day That Elvis Came to Town (Marino) JH-HS
Line of Duty (Grant) A
My Crooked Family (Collier) JH-HS
Straight Talk with Kids (The Scott Newman Center) A
Teenage Wasteland (Gaines) HS-A
The Two Faces of Adam (Meyer) HS
Winter-Broken (Smith) MS-JH

Survival

After-Shock (Scarborough) HS-A
Beast (Benchley) HS-A
Bering Bridge (Schurke) JH-A
Billy (Streiber) HS-A
Brother Moose (Levin) MS
The Devil's Own (Lisson) HS
Distant Fires (Anderson & Kouba) HS-A
Downriver (Hobbs) JH-HS
Escape from Slavery (Rappaport) EL-MS
Faces of Ceti (Caraker) JH-HS
Foxes of FirstDark (Kilworth) A
The Hideout (Bunting) MS-JH
In Caverns of Blue Ice (Roper) JH-HS
The Last Seven Months of Anne Frank (Lindwer) HS-A
Nightfall (Asimov & Silverberg) HS-A
On the Far Side of the Mountain (George) EL-JH
Remember Who You Are (Hautzig) HS-A
The River (Paulsen) MS-HS
The Rowan (McCaffrey) HS-A
Smart Rats (Baird) JH-HS
The Song of the Gargoyle (Snyder) MS-JH
Tug of War (Lingard) MS-JH
White Hare's Horses (Spinka) MS-HS

Theater

Circles (Sachs) MS-JH
Happy Endings (Geras) JH-HS
Hey, Little Walter (Lamb) JH-HS
My Aunt Ruth (Rosofsky) JH-HS
Of Swans, Sugarplums, and Satin Slippers (Verdy) EL-JH

Time Travel

Beauty (Tepper) HS-A
The Devil's Own (Lisson) HS
George Washington's Socks (Woodruff)
   EL-MS
Stonewords (Conrad) MS-JH
The Time and Space of Uncle Albert
   (Stannard) EL-MS
Whatever Became of Aunt Margaret?
   (DeWeese) MS-JH

Trivia

Amazing True Stories (Wulffson) MS-A
*Encyclopedia Brown's Book of Strange
   but True Crimes* (Sobol) EL-JH
I Bet You Didn't Know That . . . (series)
   (Iverson) EL-MS

War

The Big Book for Peace (Durell & Sachs)
   EL-A
Eben Tyne, Powdermonkey (Beatty &
   Robinson) MS-JH
Echoes of War (Westall) A
George Washington's Socks (Woodruff)
   EL-MS
The Girl with the White Flag (Higa) MS-
   JH
The Last Seven Months of Anne Frank
   (Lindwer) HS-A
Long Time Passing (Jones) HS-A
The Other Victims (Friedman) MS-JH
The Man from the Other Side (Orlev)
   JH-HS
Remember Who You Are (Hautzig) HS-A
Tug of War (Lingard) MS-JH
War Boy (Foreman) MS-A

Women's Issues

Black Ice (Cary) HS-A
The Bookmaker's Daughter (Abbott) A
The Boonsville Bombers (Herzig) EL
Cabin Fever (Jolley) A
Coaching Evelyn (Connolly) MS-HS
In Caverns of Blue Ice (Roper) JH-HS
Kisses (Caseley) JH-HS
Ride a Cockhorse (Kennedy) A
The Rowan (McCaffrey) HS-A
Woman Hollering Creek (Cisneros) HS-A

Working

The Adventures of Boone Barnaby (Cot-
   tonwood) MS-JH
Against the Grain (Ferris) JH-HS
Author! Author! (Ferris) MS
Borderlands (Carter) JH-A
The Boy in the Moon (Koertge) JH-HS
The Bread Winner (Whitmore) MS-JH
Coaching Evelyn (Connolly) MS-JH
Don't Rent My Room! (Angell) MS-JH
The Farewell Kid (Wersba) JH-HS
Fast Talk on a Slow Track (Williams-
   Garcia) JH-HS
High Cheekbones (Tamar) JH-HS
In Caverns of Blue Ice (Roper) JH-HS
Losing Joe's Place (Korman) EL-MS
Loving Someone Else (Conford) JH-HS
Lyddie (Paterson) MS-JH
Monster of the Year (Coville) MS-JH
My Name Is Sus5an Smith . . . (Plum-
   mer) JH-HS
Ride a Cockhorse (Kennedy) A
Secret Keeper (Whelan) JH-HS
Stolen Season (Lanb) HS-A
This Is the Life (O'Neill) HS-A
Twelve-Year-Old Vows Revenge (Roos)
   MS-JH
Upchuck Summer's Revenge (Schwartz)
   MS

LIST OF PUBLISHERS

Ace. Ace Books, 200 Madison Avenue, New York, NY 10016

Addison-Wesley. Addison-Wesley Publishing Co. Inc., Jacob Way, Reading, MA 01867

Arcade. Arcade Publishing Inc , 141 Fifth Avenue, New York, NY 10010

Atheneum. Atheneum Publishers, 866 Third Avenue, New York, NY 10022

Avon. Avon Books, 1350 Avenue of the Americas, New York, NY 10019

Bantam. Bantam Books, 666 Fifth Avenue, New York, NY 10103

Bear. Bear & Company, Inc., PO Drawer 2860, Santa Fe, NM 87504- 2860

Bradbury. Bradbury Press, 866 Third Avenue, New York, NY 10022

Clarion. Clarion Books, 215 Park Avenue South, New York, NY 10003

Cobblehill. Cobblehill Books, 375 Hudson Street, New York, NY 10014

Crowell. Thomas Y. Crowell Co. c/o HarperCollins, 10 East 53rd Street, New York, NY 10022

Crown. Crown Publishing Group, 201 East 50th Street, New York, NY 10022

Dark Harvest. Dark Harvest, PO Box 941, Arlington Heights, IL 60006

Delacorte. Delacorte Press, 666 Fifth Avenue, New York, NY 10103

Dial. Dial Books for Young Readers, 375 Hudson Street, New York, NY 10014

Doubleday. Doubleday, 666 Fifth Avenue, New York, NY 10103

Dutton. E P Dutton, 375 Hudson Street, New York, NY 10014

Farrar. Farrar, Straus & Giroux Inc., 19 Union Square West, New York, NY 10003

Fulcrum. Fulcrum Publishers, 350 Indiana Street, Suite 350, Golden, CO 80401

Greenwillow. Greenwillow Books, 1350 Avenue of the Americas, New York, NY 10019

Harcourt. Harcourt Brace Jovanovich, Publishers, 1250 Sixth Avenue, San Diego, CA 92101

Harmony. Harmony Books, 201 East 50th Street, New York, NY 10022

HarperCollins. HarperCollins Publishers, 10 East 53rd Street, New York, NY 10022

Holiday. Holiday House Inc., 425 Madison Avenue, New York, NY 10017

Holt. Henry Holt and Co. Inc., 115 West 18th Street, New York, NY 10011

Houghton. Houghton Mifflin Co., One Beacon Street, Boston, MA 02108

Joy Street. Joy Street Books, 34 Beacon Street, Boston, MA 02108

Kodansha. Kodansha International/USA, 114 Fifth Avenue, New York, NY 10011

Knopf. Alfred A Knopf Inc., 201 East 50th Street, New York, NY 10022

Lerner. Lerner Publications Co., 241 First Avenue North, Minneapolis, MN 55401

Lippincott. J B Lippincott Co., 227 East Washington Square, Philadelphia, PA 19106

Little. Little, Brown & Co. Inc., 34 Beacon Street, Boston, MA 02108

Lodestar. Lodestar Books, 375 Hudson Street, New York, NY 10014

Macmillan. Macmillan Publishing Co., 866 Third Avenue, New York, NY 10022

McElderry. Margaret K McElderry Books, 866 Third Avenue, New York, NY 10022

Morrow. William Morrow & Co. Inc., 1350 Avenue of the Americas, New York, NY 10019

Mysterious. The Mysterious Press, 1271 Avenue of the Americas New York, NY 10021

North Point. North Point Press, 1563 Solano Avenue, Suite 353, Berkeley, CA 94707- 2116

Orchard. Orchard Books, 387 Park Avenue South, New York, NY 10016

Pantheon. Pantheon Books, 201 East 50th Street, New York, NY 10022

Pfeifer-Hamilton. Pfeifer-Hamilton Publishers, 210 West Michigan, Duluth, MN 55802-1908

Pocket. Pocket Books, 1230 Avenue of the Americas, New York, NY 10020

Putnam. G. P. Putnam's Sons, 200 Madison Avenue, New York, NY 10016

Random. Random House Inc., 201 East 50th Street, New York, NY 10022

S&S. Simon & Schuster, Inc., 1230 Avenue of the Americas, New York, NY 10020

Scholastic. Scholastic Inc., 730 Broadway, New York, NY 10003

Scribners. Charles Scribner's Sons, 866 Third Avenue, New York, NY 10022

Sierra Club. Sierra Club Books, 100 Bush Street, San Francisco, CA 94103

Ticknor & Fields. Ticknor & Fields, 215 Park Avenue South, New York, NY 10003

Times. Times Books, 201 East 50th Street, New York, NY 10022

Viking. Viking Penguin, 375 Hudson Street, New York, NY 10014

Villard. Villard Books, 201 East 50th Street, New York, NY 10022

Watts. Franklin Watts Inc., 387 Park Avenue South, New York, NY 10016

Workman. Workman Publishing Co., 708 Broadway, New York, NY 10003

INDEX